WHEN GOD MOVES

John H. Armstrong

HARVEST HOUSE PUBLISHERS
Eugene, Oregon 97402

WHEN GOD MOVES
Copyright © 1998 by John H. Armstrong
Published by Harvest House Publishers
Eugene, Oregon 97402

Library of Congress Cataloging-in-Publication Data

Armstrong, John
    When God moves / John Armstrong.
      p. cm.
    Includes bibliographical references.
    ISBN 1-56507-868-3
    1. Revivals. I. Armstrong, John H. (John Harper) , 1949-
II. Title.
BV3790.A723 1998
269'.24—dc21   98-12644
                                                                                   CIP

98 99 00 01 02 /LP/ 10 9 8 7 6 5 4 3 2 1

For the reformation of the church and the revival of
biblical Christianity in an increasingly dark time in history,
when integrity in both life and doctrine is
the crying need of evangelical Christianity.

And for
Dr. Arthur B. and Helen E. Siml,
my parents-in-law, who gladly gave to me the
greatest gift a family can give, their beautiful
daughter, and who have loved me, supported me,
and faithfully and lovingly shared in my ministry for over 27 years.

CONTENTS

ACKNOWLEDGMENTS

The work involved in this book has been a labor of profound love. More than any writing project I have yet undertaken this book is the result of an entire lifetime of interest. I have been asked to teach more on this subject than any other. I have read more on it than I can remember. I listen to every account of revival with rapt interest, hoping to hear of another true move of God.

The desire to write such a book on revival actually began over 25 years ago. In God's kind providence it was a matter of time until my desire came to this written expression. Being a perfectionist by temperament, I would have enjoyed another ten years to write this book. It is not all that I would have said nor is it said as well as hopefully I might have said it, given further time to reflect. Deadlines and other constraints have made this impossible.

Having now completed the task I am certain of several things. First, I have intentionally aimed at the earnest Christian who wishes to think and pray more seriously about the work of the Holy Spirit in revival. I realize that this actually limits my audience, since so few people today seem interested in the present health of the church. I have also realized in these efforts that even as this book goes to print I am, and always will be, "an unprofitable servant." But being "an unprofitable servant" of the King of the universe is a high privilege joined with great responsibility. To Him I shall give thanks through all eternity!

I trust I have written so as to encourage the church to seek God alone for what He can give—*real revival*. If this book might be used to cause a growing number of Christians to see more clearly how much the church needs Him, then I will be rewarded beyond measure.

In all that I do I am profoundly grateful for the men who work with me on the Board of Directors of Reformation & Revival Ministries—Bruce Bickel, John Sale, Bob Mulder, Tom Shaw, Richard Johnson, Andy Froiland, Art Azurdia, Kent Hughes, Irv Queal, Wendell Hawley, Mark Talbot, and Donald Anderson. These brothers are a wonderful blessing. I could not find better counsel and more godly support.

Thanks also to my staff—Rev. Jules Polachek, Executive Director of Reformation & Revival Ministries, who came at just the right time to hold up my arms in the battle; Micha Babbitt, who is a careful and faithful servant in managing our office; and Dr. Wendell Hawley, who, in retirement from the world of publishing, now lends me his great wisdom and prayerful counsel as a special consultant to this ministry.

Thanks are also in order for Harvest House Publishers. Bob Hawkins, Jr., has demonstrated to me how much a publisher can really care about an author. He has shown grace, warmth, and real friendship in how he has built a valuable relationship with me. I believe the trust that we have established was worth the effort. Steve Miller is everything an author would desire in an editor—fair, honest, and very encouraging.

The most profound gratitude of all goes to my dear wife Anita. She has once again joyfully put up with long days of work while I was away from her, immersed in another writing project. There must be a special reward for spouses of authors who support their mates with such encouragement. Anita kept other projects afloat while I devoted my undivided efforts to this one.

It is my earnest prayer that God will bless this book for the purpose of reformation and revival in our time. In the course of writing what follows, I have often thought of the prophet's prayer: "Who knows? He may turn and have pity and leave behind a blessing" (Joel 2:14).

Foreword

This is a book that needed to be written.

Here, at last, you are holding in your hands a book that separates the chaff from the wheat, the good from the best. No one who reads these pages will ever think of revival in the say way again. In this volume the careless use of the word *revival* is exposed historically and biblically. And in the process God and His Word are exalted.

For quite some time I have believed that the word *revival* is abused in our day. It is time that someone stepped forward to help us clarify what a revival is and what it is not. It is time that someone was willing to call us back to a rigorous biblical examination of what a revival really is.

This is not a book that any historian or theologian could have written. John Armstrong is a rare man with a broad knowledge of theology and history, but he also has a personal passion for revival. And yet his love of revival did not keep him from giving a critique of many of the present-day movements that we glibly call *revival*. John loves revival so much that he is distressed when the whole concept of revival is trivialized. Worse, the concept is often based on a faulty theological premise.

Not everyone will like what John has written. He does mention names, places, and movements, critiquing them in light of the Scriptures. He gives a critical assessment of the kind of revivalism that many of us understand so well. He weighs these movements in the balances of Scripture and they come up wanting.

I found this to be a book of hope, for if God is God, He might be pleased to send us a revival and nothing can thwart His plans. Even if we do not see a revival in our day, we can personally rejoice in God's gracious plans for His people. Individually, we can be revived whenever we are willing to walk in obedience to God's truth.

John does not believe that we simply sit by and wait for revival to come much like anticipating a thunderbolt from heaven. No, there is work to be done. And if we are faithful in preaching and praying, God, though He does not owe us a revival, might be pleased to refresh our churches and our land.

Join me in desiring nothing less than a movement of God and let us be ready should it come. And if it doesn't, we can rejoice that God is always faithful toward His people. Just ask Isaiah, who ministered to the hardened Israel, or the apostle Paul, who was not spared a martyr's death in Rome.

Do yourself a favor. Read this book and then pass it along to a friend. It will create within you a desire to see God "rend the heavens and come down." And it will remind you that we all must stand in awe of God.

—Dr. Erwin W. Lutzer
Author and Senior Pastor of
Moody Church, Chicago

IN SEARCH OF TRUE REVIVAL

EVER SINCE I can remember I have heard about revival. My first recollection is still quite clear—it was a sign in front of my home church which read simply, "Fall Revival." I can also remember the time I drove through a town in Alabama and observed a curious sign which said, "Revival Here: Monday through Wednesday, and Sunday." I wondered to myself, *Why not on Thursday, Friday, and Saturday if we are having real revival?* My limited understanding in those years eventually gave way to some mild skepticism. If revivals were simply annual meetings, planned and scheduled, why the big deal anyway? All that was needed was to secure the right evangelist, pray a good bit more than usual, invite your friends to some special meetings at the church or the tent, and then watch as "real" revival happened.

Then, in 1970, while I was a college student in Illinois, I came face to face with a week "when God moved." For some months I had agonized over the downgrade of love for Christ, the Word of God, and prayer that I witnessed at my evangelical college. The sixties had truly left their mark across the nation. Christian colleges were often places where vital piety was at a very low point. Without any outside prompting I had asked several students to join me in regular prayer. (At the time, I didn't know what I know today about prayer's role in preceding a revival; I just knew we needed to pray.) We invited the president of the college, Dr. Hudson T. Armerding, to join with us because he eagerly shared our hopes and concerns. We eventually enlisted 96 people to pray in 15-minute time slots around the clock for one week. All of this was done preceding the arrival of Dr. Raymond Ortlund, Sr., the speaker for our annual "Spiritual Emphasis Week." The morning daily chapel meetings were mandatory but the evening services were not. The evening attendance was quite sparse early in the week, so there was no reason to think anything out of the ordinary was about to happen. (Indeed, the previous September we had heard wonderfully clear sermons from Dr. David Burnham and the response had ranged from hostility to boredom.) Quite simply, cynicism ran very high on our campus. There was more interest in protesting the war in Vietnam than in prayer and confession of sin.

On Thursday evening of that week in 1970, hundreds of us experienced what was later termed a campus revival. I am much more sanguine, nearly 30 years later, about using such language to describe what actually transpired (I would prefer to call it a visitation). In retrospect I have no doubt of this fact: God moved and thus manifested to us something of His presence. Students lined up for hours to confess their sin and to seek God. Some even called upon Christ to save them. By 10 P.M. the building was nearly full and a radio broadcast of the events brought in people from all over the suburban Chicago area. Through the night and early morning hours we remained. It was all rather quiet. There were no outbursts. There were none of the emotional elements we hear about so frequently today. Just heartfelt confession, a few rich hymns, simple prayers, and reminders from the Word of God.

Ever since that snowy February in 1970 I have followed a definite course with regard to the subject of revival. After that week I resolved to learn all that I could about surprising, providential interruptions of God, often called revivals, or spiritual awakenings. This path has led me to purchase and read hundreds of books and articles about revival. It has prompted me to discuss this subject with scores of Christian leaders from around the world, some favorable to the subject and some not so favorable. I have even visited the historical sites of several past revivals, both in North America and Great Britain. Ten years ago I preached in villages in south India where I witnessed something like an ongoing authentic revival movement right before my eyes. Eventually my path providentially took me, after 21 years of local church pastoral ministry, into an itinerant preaching and writing ministry devoted to the themes and concerns associated with this very subject.

This personal interest in revival will undoubtedly go on for me. An expression of it is this present book, which is my earnest attempt to give the church a readable, clear, and biblical resource which takes theology seriously. We are clearly living in a time when interest in revival seems to be running high. It appears that many are talking about it, but not everyone is talking about the same thing. The word *revival* is being used freely, yet few bother to communicate even a clear definition of what they are talking about. Fewer still attempt to develop a serious theological context for understanding what is true and false in revival. I am convinced that the level of misunderstanding regarding this subject is now serious. I am also convinced that we still need careful reflection upon this wonderful topic. My prayer is that *When God Moves* will prove to be both a corrective of false hopes as well as a positive contribution to the growing body of material that currently exists on this subject.

Recently, there has been a good deal made of counterfeit revival movements. I believe that much of what is being called revival today is, even with its positive contributions, more counterfeit than authentic. I am also persuaded that where the counterfeit is witnessed it stands to reason that the real thing still exists, even if not in the same place. Because of this belief I have chosen, in this book, to emphasize the *positive* side of revival. In later chapters I will interact with some of the individuals of our time who claim they see revival taking place somewhere, or at least speak boldly of it coming soon. My primary purpose, beginning with this introduction, will be to establish the great truths of real revival for a confused generation.

In addition, we will survey how real revival has impacted church history, and thus see what practical concerns we ought to address regarding revival in our own time. Even here my purpose remains positive, wherever possible. My evaluations of historical events are my own; some will disagree with me. I hope I have written with charity and in a measured and careful way. I can only urge serious readers to go further and discover for themselves if I am correct in these basic evaluations. While I believe that I am, I wish to always remain teachable. I surely have much more to learn about God, His truth, and the subject of revival; in the writing of this book I feel as if I have only just begun to scratch the surface of all that there is to discover.

My prayerful goal in this book is to introduce you, by way of a serious but readable treatment, to what actually happens *when God moves*. If we settle for anything less than a real, Christ-glorifying, doctrinally informed, movement of the Holy Spirit we may get another cotton-candy meal of neo-experientialism on the pretense that this is really a full-blown, five-course meal. The church needs much more, and the time is genuinely ripe for true revival.

Soli Deo Gloria!

Part One

WHAT MIGHT REVIVAL LOOK LIKE?

One

A Day in the Life of Pastor Ray

"Revival cannot be planned. It is a divine interruption."
—John Blanchard

"Sunday-morning Christianity is the greatest hindrance to true revival."
—Vance Havner

"Revival makes the ideal real within the church of God."
—Arthur Skevington Wood

THE LORD'S DAY began as it almost always did, with Pastor Ray rising early to pray and prepare his heart and mind. The family slept soundly as Ray crept quietly into his study at 5:00 A.M. Coffee in hand, he knelt to ask God's blessing upon his ministry. He had been here before—many times, in fact. Almost every time he wondered, with a measure of faith mixed with honest doubt, *What would happen if God were pleased to visit my church with revival?* He knew he didn't much care for the idea of people falling down and making strange noises. He had already made a journey, at the urging of several fellow pastors, to the scene of one of these so-called revival blessings. At this moment he knew one thing about revival—the subject had no great appeal to him. His confidence was never going to be placed in the emotional manipulation he had seen in well-advertised spiritual sideshows.

On this particular day Ray felt nothing unusual. He had no specific feelings or impressions. He knew, as he always knew in the wee hours of a Sunday morning, that this business of handling the Word of God was serious. He also knew that this was his distinct calling—he was a minister of the gospel who had been called by God to "preach the Word." He had been here before, and by God's grace he would be here again—seeking to be faithful to His divine calling.

For over two decades Ray had faithfully cared for the church of God. This was his second pastoral ministry, and recently he had mused aloud to his wife if it might not be time to think of moving again. He knew he loved the ministry, even though the hard times caused him to consider quitting. He also knew quitting was not a serious option since his call was something that had been settled years ago, long before seminary.

Ray further realized what it was like to preach till he had nothing left, both emotionally and physically. Sometimes—very rarely, it seemed to him—there was a special sense of enablement in his preaching. What this actually was he didn't know for sure. He read somewhere that preachers in another era called this "the unction of the Spirit." However, he was so tired of the many claims to "anointing" and "unction" that were proclaimed on religious television he chose not to think this way.

While getting dressed on this very cold winter morning, Ray sensed that he should be more earnest in his efforts. He knew his heart was not stone cold, but neither was it fervent for the glory of Christ. He also realized that too frequently he fell into the trap of professionalization. He confessed this sin to God, as he had on previous Sundays, and pled for forgiveness and fresh help.

The normal schedule at First Church called for two morning worship services to take place, with Sunday school positioned between the worship services. The first service was generally smaller in number and the people were often less responsive. The second service, by contrast, was often full and generally more alive. (The one exception to this was during football season, when many in Ray's congregation, like so many in similar urban churches, came to the early service in order to get home in time for the kickoff of the football game!)

Prior to the first service, Ray prayed with several of his elders and associate pastors. As on most Sunday mornings, the prayers were not all that remarkable—just heartfelt and short. A last-minute microphone check was made. (*I wonder how Paul could have preached without a wireless,* Ray occasionally thought to himself.) The bulletin, that perennial "special aid" for so-called nonliturgical worship, was also well marked and neatly tucked into Ray's Bible. The choir entered the sanctuary on cue. The service began.

But something seemed different this morning. As the choir sang, "Holy, Holy, Holy" Ray felt a melting within his own heart. He didn't quite know what to call this but he felt as if something had opened his heart to the words of this grand hymn as never before.

> Holy, holy, holy, Lord God Almighty!
> Early in the morning our song shall rise to thee.
> Holy, holy, holy! Merciful and mighty!
> God in three persons, blessed Trinity!

Ray's heart reflected upon these words as if he had never sung them before. *Merciful and mighty,* Ray thought, . . . *if God is almighty, and not merciful as well, then I am in trouble. But if He is merciful without being almighty, then there is no hope for me either.* This thought sobered Ray in an unusual manner. It was as if God were bearing down upon Ray's mind directly through the rich words of this nineteenth-century hymn. When it came time to sing the third stanza Ray sang more passionately:

> Holy, holy, holy! Though the darkness hide Thee,
> Though the eye of sinful man Thy glory may not see,
> Only Thou art holy; there is none beside Thee
> Perfect in power, in love and purity.

Ray was again gripped profoundly. He pondered pensively, *God alone is holy! He alone is "perfect in power, in love and purity." Who is like unto the Lord? There is none!* Ray was deeply moved. He never realized how much truth there was in this hymn.

The service progressed, and Ray felt even more drawn out of himself and into the truth of what was being sung when the congregation sang "Immortal, Invisible, God Only Wise" and "Great Is Thy Faithfulness." When it came time to offer the pastoral prayer Ray was almost overcome with an incredible sense of the nearness of God. His mind was not so focused on what he was to say or do, but rather upon the world to come. He found himself praying with profound affection. His voice broke once or twice and tears filled his eyes. Gathering himself, because this was not the way things were generally done at First Church, Ray pressed on, lifting his heart up to God as honestly as he could. For a few moments he felt as if no one else were in the sanctuary. The congregation seemed almost nonexistent; it seemed as if there was an audience of only One.

By the time Ray was ready to read the Scripture text for that morning his mind was flooded with biblical truth. For many years now he had preached expositionally—that is, he preached verse by verse through a book of the Bible. He had been taught this approach in seminary. He generally spent 20-25 hours during the week studying his text, reading his sources, and getting background information established in his mind. Then he worked hard at the meaning of the text, getting what he saw to be the truth of the Word of God. This is what he sought to firmly plant in his own thinking. Only after all this hard work did he actually begin to outline and write his sermon. He also learned long ago that the less written material he took into the pulpit with him the better he seemed to communicate with his people. On this day his mind was lifted to the very glories of the age to come. He wasn't even sure how he could preach the sermon he had prepared. He began to read his text with unusual care and reverence:

> Since, then, you have been raised with Christ, set your hearts on
> things above, where Christ is seated at the right hand of God. Set

your minds on things above, not on earthly things. For you died, and your life is now hidden with Christ in God. When Christ, who is your life, appears, then you also will appear with him in glory (Colossians 3:1-4).

As Ray began to explain this text in his usual manner, he was overwhelmingly impressed with the thought that he could not speak to the people as he had in the past. He felt as if the force of God's truth had to be pressed upon his people as never before. For a moment he wondered if this might be his last sermon and thus he wanted it to be a word he could leave with them and go in peace, whether into God's presence or into a different ministry.

What filled Ray's mind was not so much the sensation of something happening to him as much as the wonder and glory of the subject of his sermon—the Lord Jesus Christ. Jesus was everything! Ray was filled with thoughts of Christ, of His life and death, of His resurrection and ascension. He wanted to plead with his people to set their hearts on things above, where his heart seemed so amazingly set at this moment.

Time seemed irrelevant; eternity seemed to be all that mattered. As Ray continued he saw that it was not just him who was experiencing this incredible sense of God's presence. His people were not only alert, they couldn't even take notes as many of them had done for years. An occasional sob was heard, but above all else, an eerie stillness and silence pervaded the group. Not even coughing was heard. The children were very quiet—no fidgeting, no rustling of candy wrappers. *What is this?* Ray wondered.

As the time drew near for the early service to end, no one closed their Bibles, put on their coats, or went through the other rituals of getting ready to depart. The people seemed unable to get ready to leave. Something about the service made this seem impossible. When the benediction was pronounced people did not rush off to their classes and other routines. It was as if God had said, "Stay here, I am not done yet!" Ray could only watch and wonder, but he knew this was not coming from his will. So Ray invited those who sensed their need for more a personal time with God to remain and pray. Hundreds stayed, and what amazed Ray was that he wasn't really surprised. This service *was* different.

Then Ray wondered if he should give a kind of altar call, but he felt this was too sacred a moment to ask people to move. This was too holy to interrupt with human appeals that would prompt people to do almost anything Ray asked them to do. He decided it was better to leave the people to seek after God.

The people who were now arriving for the Sunday School hour could tell by the empty classrooms and hallways that those who attended the first service were still in the sanctuary. One by one these people quietly entered the sanctuary, and before long it was packed. Prayers filled the building. Junior and senior high school students cried out to God in ways that had never been heard before. Those who couldn't enter the crowded sanctuary found other rooms and formed groups for confession and prayer. Some simply knelt in private to seek God. Within the next few hours, hundreds of people would confess sin that had been pocketed years before. Others would come to realize that they had never been truly born of God's Spirit. Ray didn't even have to explain this, they just knew it. People who carried bitterness toward others went to them to confess their sins. The whole place seemed to be alive with God's presence.

By 2:00 in the afternoon Ray felt it was time to encourage people to go home. He knew that the sheer physical weariness of such a meeting could wear out people, possibly causing them to lose their ability to be discerning and careful about what they said and did. He also knew that if this was a move of God, ending this one public service would most definitely not end God's gracious work.

As Ray prayed he pled with God to come upon the church with ever-increasing power. He also prayed for other churches in their city. He longed for others to experience this same "visitation." This much he knew—he would never be the same after this Lord's Day. That evening the church continued in prayer. Ray wanted the people to hear from God so he preached the Scriptures faithfully, with more power than he had ever known. People listened with uncommon eagerness and hunger. The meeting lasted long into the evening with Ray again exercising wise leadership in sending people home after a three-hour service.

Over the next few weeks Ray saw ongoing evidence that God had indeed poured out His Spirit upon First Church. His counseling turned from helping people who came complaining about a lack of happiness in their marriage or job to helping people with deep concerns about the state of their eternal soul. He found that he could read a passage of the Bible to a person and they would often melt before his eyes. He didn't have to plead or cajole. Conversions were happening day by day. People would phone Ray during the night, even coming by his home at all hours. Some, who had resisted the gospel for years, were broken in a matter of moments. Others, who had seemed so spiritually minded before these unusual occurrences began, opposed all of this as an emotional extravaganza. "The whole thing is weird," they argued. "We want church the way we used to have it, beginning on time and ending on time. After all, we have a family meal planned and there is a game this Sunday." This serious prayer and confession was a bit too much for them. "Why," they argued, "are all these new converts getting so much attention?" Some of these church pillars even tried to critically associate the events at First Church with stories they had read about "revivals" elsewhere. By this means the enemy gained a foothold in some lives.

After a few months, the services at First Church seemed to return to normal. Yet things would never be quite "normal" for years to come. The Holy Spirit had added so many young converts to the church that Ray's whole life would be absorbed in their growth over the upcoming months. Further, several elders had been converted and many church workers had stepped back from ministry because of sin they had to deal with during the recent showers of blessing.

First Church would still have regular services for worship. The music would not change much, though the great hymns of the faith now had a new meaning for many. The preaching of the Word took on new interest for multitudes, young and old alike. Teens crowded the church and wanted the Word of God, not entertainment. The lives of many had changed dramatically and with proper biblical sustenance there would be no apparent reason for them to fall back into their old paths. Remembering the Lord Jesus at the communion table now took on greater significance as people took more seriously this holy time of reflection. People who often missed the monthly communion services would not miss it now for any reason. Fresh enablement for joyful service equipped many individuals to pursue new avenues of witness in their community.

Ray wasn't sure what to call all that had happened to his church on that one special Lord's Day and in the months that followed. He knew a commencement of something fresh and vital had begun. He was sure the Holy Spirit had done it because the fruit bore clear testimony to what God's Word said about the ministry of the Spirit. As Ray pondered these events more, he began to study, pray, and read even more. In time he began to tell people, "God moved across my flock!" After more time he became aware that what he had witnessed at First Church was what used to be called revival. He also knew he might never see a shower like this again, even if he remained faithful to his work day in and day out.

Ray gave thanks to God that this blessing had interrupted his life and ministry with fresh, holy power from on high. And he committed the following years of his ministry to working for biblical reformation in a host of areas that needed specific change. He now understood how vital such change really was, and as a result longed to bring both his life and the ministry of this church into closer harmony with the Scriptures.

Part Two

BIBLICAL AND
THEOLOGICAL ISSUES

Two

THE PLACE TO BEGIN

A revival of religion...consists in new spiritual life imparted to the dead and in new spiritual health imparted to the living.
—James Buchanan

A revival is from God or it is no revival at all.
—Wilbur M. Smith

Revival is God rending the heavens and coming down upon His people.
—Vance Havner

SOME WORDS ARE seriously overworked and misused. They are useful words, to be sure, but they have lost their meaning through careless usage. One such word is *revival*.

It seems as if everyone is using the word *revival* these days. Yet few bother to define it biblically or theologically. Many people aren't sure exactly what it means, and thus end up using the word to desribe things that aren't really revival at all. The result is great confusion in the modern church—a confusion that does more to hinder revival than encourage it.

In the last few decades, it's been common for evangelistic campaigns or city-wide crusades to be called a revival. A concerted effort for prayer is even termed a revival. Groups of ministers meeting together to confess sin and enjoy sweet fellowship are widely reported as revivals, or at least the first stages of great awakenings about to burst upon the church scene. Large crowds fill halls and athletic stadiums, and regardless of what eventually happens, these are labeled revivals. The Christian media reports that revival is breaking out on every hand. The word *revival*, then, is used by a variety of people in a variety of ways. But what *is* revival, really?

DEFINING REVIVAL

Understanding true revival clearly begins with having a proper definition of what it is. But where do we turn for a clear definition? Biblically rooted evangelicals must always turn to the Word of God first, believing that Scripture is the sole religious authority for the church. But there is a slight problem when we turn to the Bible to see how it uses the word *revival*—strictly speaking, the word is never found in the sacred Scriptures.

Initially, this absence would appear to create an insurmountable problem, but such is not actually the case. The verb "to revive" *is* used frequently in Scripture. Furthermore, the concept of what has been known as revival, historically at least, can be found in a number of contexts in Scripture.

The word *revive*, in several instances, means "to come back to life from the dead." It is used quite literally (1 Kings 17:22) to describe how the prayer of Elijah was the means of giving life back to the deceased son of Zarephath's widow. In reference to Christ's living again after His resurrection, the word is used (in the Greek text) in Romans 14:9. Regarding the word *revival*, one writer said that in Hebrew and Greek, "even when this is not the meaning, the word carries greater force than it bears to us today, for we have confused revivalism with evangelism."[1] He is correct—and this is why we continue to have difficulty with the modern use of the word *revival*.

What Revival Is Not

Both biblically and historically, revival is not a series of *special* meetings. Meetings for special prayer, crusades for evangelism, conferences for Bible teaching and exposition, and even designated calls to repentance (whether national, corporate, or personal) are *not* revival. As long as these types of things are confused with revival, the word *revival* will continue to be drained of its vital significance. Furthermore, the church will never long for God's manifest presence as she ought if she persists in believing that she can create revival through special plans and meetings.

This means that no plan or program can bring, prompt, or create revival. What we need is no less than "resurrection from the dead" in terms of both the power needed and the life granted. If this is true, then revival cannot be engineered by human strategy. We cannot bring together a committee of some kind and plan on beginning a revival at noon on the fifth day of the next month. As preposterous as such thinking is, it is still quite common in our time. We must understand that it is not within our ability to "create" revival.

Even more important for clear understanding is this: We cannot cause God to send revival. Special pleading, signed agreements, corporate assemblies for confession, denominational (or interdenominational) repentance—none of these can cause revival. These might well precede authentic revival but they cannot guarantee it—nor do they bring it, at least in the sense that *we cause God to take action*. This point, which I will stress again and again throughout this book, must not be missed. As long as we think we can contribute something to revival we will not remain dependent upon the sovereign God of the Scriptures. This is the mistake most careless sinners make when they think they can cause God to save them. It is always better when lost souls are pierced with the realization that their cry ought to be, "Nothing in my hands I bring, simply to Thy cross I cling."

True revival is not fleeting, a will-o'-the-wisp something that is here one day and gone the next. Many people have become skeptical of the very concept of revival because they associate the word with some kind of emotional disturbance that will have little lasting spiritual and doctrinal benefit. Sometimes the results that follow modern "revivals" actually create conditions worse than what existed before the "revival" began. Church history actually demonstrates that

true revival mercies may fall as a downpour, with few or no precursors
at all. Sometimes these mercies may fall after extended seasons of
prayer and confession. (D. Martyn Lloyd-Jones used to say that if you
want living proof of the sovereignty of God, study revivals!) Either
way, when revival does come, a blessing occurs which is both sub-
stantial and lasting. The work of advancing God's kingdom will be
stronger and more biblically rooted as a result of authentic revival.

Put another way, true revival does not support or baptize popular culture, whether in the church or in society at large. Kenneth
Myers, writing about popular culture in general and popular music
in particular, said, "Pop culture gives us what we already know and
leaves us where it found us." Authentic revival, by contrast, does not
provide what we already have and it most definitely does not leave us
where it found us.

In addition, true revival is not miracles, unusual phenomena, or
even "signs and wonders." We will take up these matters in chapter
twelve, but for now suffice it to say that authentic revivals have been
attended by unusual providences. Some of these providences have
included elements that are both strange and wonderful. The point I
wish to make here is vital: North American Christians, in the twentieth century, have probably seen more emphasis upon phenomena
than those who lived through any other century in church history.
At the same time we have seen a continued decline in fidelity to the
basic truths of the gospel. Recent Gallup Surveys and Barna
Research have plainly revealed that we have multitudes of so-called
"born again" Christians who know virtually nothing of the gospel.
Modern "revival movements" have actually helped to produce this
massive confusion, as we shall see more clearly later on.

We must also conclude that revival is not national moral recovery or renewed political involvement by evangelical Christians.
While it's true that there are great ills in Western society, correcting
these problems is not the same thing as revival. Evangelicals who are
supportive of the idea of moral re-armament often associate biblical
revival with their efforts to renew the national spirit. When we hold
this mindset, we shift from a legitimate love of country to a kind of

patriotic nationalism which eventually associates the love of God with the love of country. This dual emphasis is often popularly associated with revival in today's Christian mind. We seem to believe that our moral efforts to recover decency in society, restore stability in the home, and elect conservative legislators are all precursors to God-given revival. In reality the greater evidences of true revival are never to be found in these causes, as good and right as the causes might be. Gerald R. McDermott, a historian who has done a careful study of these things, has provided a brief history lesson that we ought to ponder. McDermott writes:

> American evangelicals are frustrated because their attempts to transform American culture seem to have failed. After electing three presidents and sending hundreds of legislators to Washington, and despite influencing public policy with blizzards of mail and armies of lobbyists, evangelicals cannot point to a transformed America. As Charles Colson recently wrote in *Christianity Today*, "Belief in the Bible has declined and religious influence has been so thoroughly scrubbed from public life that any honest observer would have to regard this as a post-Christian culture. Gallup reports the most bewildering paradox: religion up, morality down. . . . We've protected our enterprises but in the process lost the culture."
>
> A history lesson might provide perspective. Evangelicals in America and England felt a similar frustration in 1730. They, too, had failed to reform their societies after decades of political and social effort. Preaching endlessly for moral reformation elicited boredom and contempt; reducing standards for church membership brought in more people but few conversions; and political leaders paid lip service to evangelical religion while furthering the secularization of society.[2]

McDermott goes on to say that within the decade following the 1730s the greatest evangelical revival since the Protestant Reformation broke across America and Great Britain. The results of this widespread revival were amazing—culture was changed, many political problems were solved, and morality actually improved.

Finally, we need to understand that revival is not evangelism. Evangelism and the harvest of new converts will inevitably follow authentic revival. (Such a harvest generally begins within the visible church itself.) Also, evangelism is an ongoing work in the church regardless of whether we see authentic revival in our time. A fresh obedience to the work of evangelism may well precede revival, but evangelism and evangelistic efforts do not equal revival. If we persist in calling outreach crusades "revivals," we will also persist in thinking that what is needed is to be found in outreach efforts. Revival, by deduction, is always the return of fresh life to the people of God. It is the awakening of the Christian community, the church.

What Revival Is

Dictionaries offer a number of definitions for the noun *revival* or for the verb *revive* when used in a strictly religious context. Revival is said to be "the return of life" or "the act of restoring life to the church after decline." One entry states that revival is "recovery from *apparent* death." This last statement may well be the best since true Christians never decline into a state of complete spiritual death. The church may languish, and even appear to be completely lifeless, but she will never die. God has a people who belong to Him and they have His life, even when that life is in a weakened and exhausted state.

But how are we to understand revival biblically? This is an important question for those who are truly evangelical.

To the surprise of many, as previously noted, the word *revival* (strictly speaking) is not actually found in the Bible. (This is really not a problem so long as the idea is genuinely biblical.) Various forms of the verb "to revive" are frequently used in Scripture. Words such as "to restore" or "to awaken" or "refresh" are all used. A representative text that deals with corporate revival is Psalm 85:6, which asks of God, "Will you not revive us again, that your people may rejoice in you?" On a more personal level we read of God reviving the individual person in Isaiah 57:15:

> This is what the high and lofty One says—
>> he who lives forever, whose name is holy:
> "I live in a high and holy place,
>> but also with him who is contrite and lowly in spirit,
> to revive the spirit of the lowly
>> and to revive the heart of the contrite."

A number of Old Testament terms describe what is meant by revival. It is "an outpouring of the Spirit" (viewed as falling rain or fire, or a mighty blowing wind) It is also God renewing His mighty deeds, where "in wrath [He] remember(s) mercy" (Habakkuk 3:2). The prophet Isaiah speaks of revival as a time when God powerfully manifests His presence among His people.

> Oh, that you would rend the heavens and come down,
>> that the mountains would tremble before you!
> As when fire sets twigs ablaze
>> and causes water to boil,
> come down to make your name known to your enemies
>> and cause the nations to quake before you! (Isaiah 64:1,2).

Please notice that the prophet speaks of God making His name known even to His enemies. It is God who comes and causes the nations to tremble before His presence.

The Hebrew word for *revive* literally means, "to live again" (see 1 Kings 17:22; 2 Kings 13:21). The root idea of the Hebrew word refers to "breathing." A range of words are used to translate this term, including "restore, preserve, heal, prosper, and flourish." Simply put, to experience the imparting of fresh divine life is to be revived by God.

Other uses of the word occur in texts such as 1 Chronicles 11:8, where the word used is translated "restored." In Judges 15:19 the word is used in a literal way to describe a recovery from sheer physical exhaustion, while in Numbers 21:9 it describes a similar recovery from physical sickness. In the book of Psalms, our word takes on an obviously *spiritual* meaning (see Psalm 80:18,19; 119:25,37,40,149,154,156; and so on) In Psalm 119, for example, revival refers more precisely to God's powerful and sovereign activity in renewing His own people, both personally and collectively. Here the word clearly takes on the meaning most closely associated with its historic Christian use.

Revival, in the corporate sense, should then be understood as a powerful work of God's Spirit coming upon large numbers of people at the same time. By this visitation of God spiritual concerns become the absorbing passion of a multitude. In this sense revival is the living God mightily visiting a locality, a nation, even a continent. The effects of this moving of God the Spirit will be the renewing of Christians "in spirit and in truth" (John 4:24), as well as the conversion of unbelievers. Such genuine revival is always a possibility with God regardless of how dark the times might be. The New Testament church experienced this on a local level in both Acts 2 and 4. Since the days of the apostles, the church has experienced similar movements in many places and at many times throughout history.

One of the reasons revivals have often been termed "awakenings" should also be noted here. In revivals, dead sinners, often with no previous interest in the things of God, come to life in a widespread *spiritual awakening*. Surrounding communities are greatly influenced by revival, though this response takes a number of forms.

Both terms, *revival* and *spiritual awakening*, have been used so interchangeably as to become virtually synonymous. And both are so often misused and overused as to be virtually irrelevant in our day. Personally, I believe that it would be better if we withheld using such terms in assessing modern movements until we have a longer and larger perspective on what is really happening. (I have in mind here the growing number of books that claim we are presently seeing revival all across North America.) We know from history that real revivals resulted in people becoming joyfully responsive to the Word of God preached. We also know from history that real revivals resulted in an increase of passionate prayer, which in turn resulted in an outward movement toward a lost world. This renewed preaching and effectual prayer brought intense and renewed efforts to reach the lost and the weak in society at large. This often resulted in a massive response. For such reasons we should not be too quick to apply the term *revival* to every new movement of our time.

Recent writers on the subject of revival candidly admit the difficulty in providing a single, simple definition that is agreeable to all. This should be enough to let us know there is need to exercise caution when using the term. At the same time, given the sheer importance of revival, as well as the present growing interest in it among so many Christians, I am convinced we should not abandon the pursuit of a richer, deeper, and fuller understanding of both the word *revival* and all that it stands for.

One modern writer who has labored extensively to clearly define this term concludes: "In using the term revival, I am speaking of an extraordinary movement of the Holy Spirit producing extraordinary results."[3] The same writer adds:

> If we persist in describing human efforts as revival and continue to think in terms of "annual revival meetings," believing that the work we are doing for God is revival, then we must content ourselves with far less than God is willing and able to give. If, on the other hand, we can realize that revival is truly God at work in a most unusual fashion, then our entire being can be stirred with longings and supplications to see such an outpouring of God's mighty power in our day.[4]

After nearly 30 years of reading and considering the subject of revival I have come to the conclusion that true revival is this: *A sovereign intervention of the Holy Spirit of God, the Spirit of Pentecost, powerfully sweeping across the visible church in blessing the normal ministry of the Word of God, and prayer, in the lives of both believers and new converts. It is best understood as an extraordinarily intense season of blessing upon that which is normal New Testament Christianity.*

In revival we do not enter into a new kind of Christianity. We experience a divine empowering that makes it *appear* we have entered into something quite new. In reality what was there all along is still there, in both the Word and the sacraments. What is new is the fresh empowering of God's sovereign presence, which makes it seem as if previously used means of grace are now new. In such holy seasons of blessing God is pleased to allow us to know His presence in ways that will surprise us. He is in full control. We are the beneficiaries of His presence and blessing. The glory belongs entirely to God!

WHY PRESERVE THE WORD *REVIVAL*?

With all the confusion in our time, why not just drop the word *revival* altogether? Why not find a new word to describe extraordinary movements of God? This might end much of the confusion among Christians today. This may appear to be a reasonable suggestion, and is one that I have actually heard proposed for several decades. I hope to show why this is not the best course to follow. Let me explain further.

What is really important is the *reality* of revival, not the use of a word. That God does impart new life to the church, and that He has done this often in remarkable ways, is beyond doubt. Such extraordinary visitations, or renewals, are accompanied by outreach which results in lasting fruit that far exceeds anything known in the normal course of things.

But why should we retain this word, especially since it has so much baggage? One reason is this word has a long and significant history. In America the word has been used almost from the time of the earliest settlements. Cotton Mather (1663-1728) spoke of the great works of Christ in the early colonies in terms of revivals.

In the book of Job, Elihu correctly concludes: "How great is God—beyond our understanding!" (Job 36:26). The simple fact is this: We do not know *how* the Spirit of God dwells in us nor can we understand *how* the Holy Spirit caused the Scriptures to be "God-breathed" (2 Timothy 3:16), thus making the Bible the very word of God. We *do know* that God made these things happen and that the mystery of godliness is great. We recognize the mystery of these things, yet we speak of them with words that communicate the realities. Similarly, though revival may be hard for us to fully understand, the realities of revival are undeniable and we can communicate them through words.

Further, the Bible clearly contains a theology of revival, as we will see in our next chapter. The fact that we use and sadly misuse the term revival indicates that there is actually something in the word itself which desperately needs fresh understanding. This is especially true, it seems to me, in a generation where this word is being widely used without careful biblical thought.

The word *Trinity* has suffered much the same fate. The doctrine of the Trinity is revealed in Scripture, even though the word itself never appears. Much like the word *revival*, *Trinity* has been variously misused, misunderstood, and debated. Yet we continue to use the word. Why? Because it arose in a definite historical and biblical context. It became the term which was most useful for the church when people were talking about God the Father, God the Son, and God the Holy Spirit as one. We use other terms, such as tri-unity, or three persons in one divine being, to further explain the Trinity, but the word *Trinity* still serves the church well. Just because a multitude of people have misunderstood the doctrine of the Trinity and have thus misused the term does not mean we should give up the word. I believe the same argument can be used, though in a lesser sense, in defense of the word *revival*.

Clearly there is much misunderstanding associated with the word *revival* in our time. But this should not discourage us from wanting to have anything to do with revival. Revival can increase our longing for God to do in us, and in the church, a deeper and more extraordinary work—a work that will bring glory to the enthroned Christ. Until this century, at least, the evangelical church in America, and in other Western nations, relied almost exclusively upon God's visitations in revivals to mightily advance the cause of Christ. But that has changed. Now we have come to rely heavily upon the plans and programs of men and movements. We organize religiously, but infrequently do we agonize. If revival is anything it is an unplanned visitation of God. Revival is not something we can organize. It is God, and not man, doing the work. While He uses men and women as instruments, it is God who works and will get the glory in true revival. If we persist in producing results by our own power, then we will never truly desire for God to manifest His awakening power.

The Bible does contain a theology of revival. An understanding of this theology is desperately needed today. If we persist in calling various contemporary movements revival we will likely miss the true longings we ought to have for God to exalt His name in an extraordinary season of divine awakening. To call something revival when it is not revival is to sadly misuse the truth of God. It also abuses this rich word and creates confusion among God's people. The end result may well be even an deeper despair in the church.

The answer to these problems can be discovered by returning to the Word of God. This alone brings true reformation. We must engage in every effort to pursue such reformation, and this effort begins with a careful search of the Holy Scriptures. I believe the effect of such search will be renewed prayerful interest in this great subject of revival. The church in our time desperately needs for God to move across her ministries with true revival; no one who cares for the true prosperity of Christ's church should seriously doubt this.

Three

IS REVIVAL BIBLICAL?

Christian men should never speak of "getting up a revival."
Where are you going to get it up from?
— Charles H. Spurgeon

Revival is not some emotion or worked-up excitement; it is
an invasion from heaven that brings a conscious awareness
of God.
— Stephen F. Olford

AS WE HAVE already seen, revival describes the condition in which churches and Christians are sovereignly empowered by God in ways that bring about an unusual intensity of spiritual activity and profound spiritual blessing. Two results are essential to genuine revival—the Holy Spirit enlivening and empowering believers, and the Holy Spirit regenerating sinners. Revival is always to be understood as a quickening, or a divine visitation. One nineteenth-century writer who understood this idea concluded that "the power of the work of grace may be estimated by the degree with which the Divine Spirit produces these blessed results."[1]

The great Welsh preacher, D. Martyn Lloyd-Jones, also understood this point when he said:

Everything that God does is marvelous and wonderful and transcends our highest imagination and yet we find these contrasts in the Scriptures between God doing what he normally does, and God doing the unusual, God coming down.... It is a consciousness of God the Holy Spirit literally in the midst of the people. Probably most of us who are here have never known that, but that is exactly what is meant by a visitation of God's Spirit. It is all above and beyond the highest experiences in the normal life and working of the Church. Suddenly those present in the meeting become aware that someone has come amongst them, they are aware of a glory, they are aware of a presence. They cannot define it, they cannot describe it, they cannot put it into words, they just know that they have never known anything like this before.[2]

Wesley Duewel, a missionary to India for over 25 years, understands also when he concludes:

Revival days are not normal days in the life of the church. They are supernormal, supernatural. They are the great days of the church when God manifests His presence in overwhelming reality. They leave you with a profound realization of God's greatness and transcendence and of your own unworthiness and dependence on Him.

God's presence and power are so mightily and extensively at work during revival that God accomplishes more in hours or days than usually results from years of faithful nonrevival ministry.[3]

Among those who take the Bible seriously and work within the parameters of orthodox Christianity there have generally been three prevailing views with regard to the subject of revival. In order to develop an adequate understanding of revival it will be helpful for us to survey these three views. In this chapter we will consider the first of these views and in the next we will consider the other two.

I will attempt, as fairly as I can, to explain why earnest believers have held differing views on revival. Often we can learn the most from those who disagree with our own view if we will take the time to listen to them more calmly and carefully.

One of the most critical needs in our day is to develop a fresh and accurate theology of revival. This needs to be a theology deeply rooted in the text of the Bible. It also needs to be a theology that corresponds to confessional orthodox Christianity. This has never been more true than today, when subjectivism and antibiblical notions run rampant. To develop a proper theology of revival is not, however, as easy a task as some may be inclined to think.

THE "NO REVIVAL" VIEW

Examining the Perspective

Some Christians evidently believe that the idea of occasional and periodic revivals is not biblical. Those who think this way generally do not hold to this view because they reject the supernatural; such a conclusion would be grossly unfair. Rather, these individuals generally hold this view because they believe it to be the closest to the evidence of the New Testament itself.

During the last two centuries, there have been some Christians who do not believe revival, as I have defined it, is desirable or biblical. Historically there have been times when you could divide Christians into two rather simple positions on this matter—those who believed in revival and those who did not. This division was profoundly changed in the nineteenth century. Early in the century, when Princeton Theological Seminary was founded (1812), the General Assembly of the Presbyterian Church felt it was important to state the new institution's position with regard to revivals. The church stated that the seminary existed in order "to train up persons for the ministry, who shall be . . . friends of revivals of religion." Even today, many who are concerned for serious biblical theology and the recovery of confessional orthodoxy do not think of themselves as "the friends of revival."

The fact is this: Not everyone who believes in the present ministry of the Holy Spirit is in agreement on the details of the nature of the Spirit's work in the present age. Some individuals have reasoned that if the Holy Spirit was poured out upon the church definitively at Pentecost, in a mighty historical and prophetical event, then that which was promised by God for the church in this age has been given once and for all. Everything regarding the work of the Holy Spirit in the New Testament must relate, in some manner, to Pentecost. This relationship can be seen either in looking back to the historic event itself, or in looking forward to the implications of this event for the present life of the church.

A vexing question for those who interpret Scripture has always been this: What actually happened at Pentecost, and what is the significance of this event for us now? Answers to this question should not be hastily given until a historical/redemptive theology has been developed from New Testament texts. The concern of those who do not see revival in the New Testament is often established by the belief that we are not warranted by the New Testament to expect "new" Pentecosts, or "showers of blessing" that flow out of the original Pentecost since this was clearly a "once-for-all" event.

Simply stated, Pentecost must always be interpreted by the work of Christ. The outpouring of the Holy Spirit should be seen as the fulfillment of God's promises centered in Christ alone. New Testament scholar Richard Gaffin is correct when he says:

> Peter's sermon on the day of Pentecost (Acts 2:14-39) is basically Christ-centered. Peter explains the coming of the Spirit by preaching Christ. . . . The outpouring of the Spirit as the promise of the Father (cf. 1:4; Luke 24:49), and so the essence of the entire fulfillment awaited under the old covenant (Acts 2:39; cf. Galatians 3:14; Ephesians 1:13), is here seen to be closely connected with the epochal, climactic events of Christ's work, especially His resurrection and ascension. Together with these other events Pentecost is part of a single, unified complex

of events and is epochal on the order that they are. In their mutual once-for-all significance the one event could not have occurred without the others.[4]

In an era like the present, when many Christians are so greatly confused about the nature of Pentecost, a serious theology of revival must be especially careful to protect the relationship between the Holy Spirit and the person and work of Christ. Too much emphasis on distinction here has already caused significant harm to the church. When I speak of revival I am not personally advocating something *new* that the Christian and the church do not presently possess in the very gift of salvation itself. The fullness of the Spirit, granted in wide measure during revival, is ultimately the working of God to bring about a deeper love for Christ and greater appreciation for what He has already done for those who believe upon Him. Gaffin is again helpful as a theological guide when he writes:

> Emerging . . . then, is one of the most basic, controlling princi-
> ples of both the christology and pneumatology of the New
> Testament, namely, the absolute coalescence, the total congru-
> ence in the church between the work of the exalted Christ and
> the work of the Holy Spirit. The work of the Spirit is not some
> addendum to the work of Christ. It is not some more or less
> independent sphere of activity that goes beyond or supple-
> ments what Christ has done. The Spirit's work is not a
> "bonus" added to the basic salvation secured by Christ. Rather
> the coming of the Spirit brings to light not only that Christ
> has lived and has done certain things but that he, as the source
> of eschatological life, now lives and is at work in the church.
> By and in the Spirit Christ reveals himself as present. The
> Spirit is the powerfully open secret, the revealed mystery, of
> Christ's abiding presence in the church.[5]

Pentecost uniquely establishes the church as the new covenant people of God. This makes the body of Christ the dwelling place of God in and by the Holy Spirit (Ephesians 2:22). Paul refers to the church congregation as "God's temple" (1 Corinthians 3:16). All who are brought into the body of Christ are incorporated into the church by Spirit baptism and thus have a share in the gift of the Holy Spirit, which is given freely to all who truly trust in Christ as the Redeemer (1 Corinthians 12:13).

This is the point Paul makes in Romans 8:9-10, where he shows that there are really only two kinds of people—those controlled by the sinful flesh and those controlled by the Holy Spirit. Christ will give life to our mortal bodies because the Spirit of Christ lives in those who believe. This is why we must live by the Spirit and not according to the sinful flesh. We do this by putting "to death the misdeeds of the body" by the Spirit (Romans 8:12-13).

Pentecost should be understood then as a "once-for-all accomplishment of redemption (*historia salutis*) rather than as a part of its ongoing, continual application (*ordo salutis*). Obviously the two are intimately related and inseparable, but they must not be confused. To do so jeopardizes the absolute sufficiency and finality of Christ's work."[6]

Furthermore, if we read John 14 carefully, we see that the promises our Lord makes in that chapter must have been fulfilled at Pentecost. Here's what our Lord taught His disciples regarding the promise of the Holy Spirit for *all* who believe:

> *If you love me, you will obey what I command. And I will ask the Father, and he will give you another Counselor to be with you forever—the Spirit of truth. The world cannot accept him, because it neither sees him nor knows him. But you know him, for he lives with you and will be in you. I will not leave you as orphans; I will come to you. Before long, the world will not see me anymore, but you will see me. Because I live, you also will live. On that day you will realize that I am in my Father, and you are in me,*

and I am in you. Whoever has my commands and obeys them, he is the one who loves me. He who loves me will be loved by my Father, and I too will love him and show myself to him (John 14:15-21).

Later our Lord adds:

All this I have spoken while still with you. But the Counselor, the Holy Spirit, whom the Father will send in my name, will teach you all things and will remind you of everything I have said to you (14:25-26).

The apostle John makes it plain that we cannot know God apart from the historical revelation of Jesus Christ. His life, His death, His resurrection, and His ascension are all part and parcel of true saving faith. But there is much more here. These statements clearly contain a momentous promise of experiential fellowship with God through the ministry of the Holy Spirit, or the Counselor (Gk.-*parakletos*). The intimacy of this relationship is clearly in view.

The word "Counselor" in the English text is not an easy word to translate. Donald A. Carson notes, "Etymologically the word seems to refer to 'one who is called alongside'; but etymology by itself rarely determines the meaning of a word. It is related to a verb which means 'to encourage' or 'to exhort'; so it is possible that a Paraclete is one who encourages or exhorts."[7]

Now Scripture makes it clear that the Counselor comes in the place of Jesus, i.e. as "another" (John 14:16). His coming is clearly to be identified with the historical event of Pentecost, as noted above. When the Spirit comes He never leaves the child of God. This gift of the Spirit is connected, as we see further in John 16, to the departure of Jesus from this world. His "going away" *must* precede the Spirit's coming (see John 7:39):

*Now I am going to him who sent me, yet none of you asks me,
"Where are you going?" Because I have said these things, you are
filled with grief. But I tell you the truth: It is for your good that
I am going away. Unless I go away, the Counselor will not come
to you; but if I go, I will send him to you. When he comes, he
will convict the world of guilt in regard to sin and righteousness
and judgment: in regard to sin, because men do not believe in me;
in regard to righteousness, because I am going to the Father,
where you can see me no longer; and in regard to judgment,
because the prince of this world now stands condemned.*

*I have much more to say to you, more than you can now bear.
But when he, the Spirit of truth, comes, he will guide you into all
truth. He will not speak on his own; he will speak only what he
hears, and he will tell you what is yet to come. He will bring glory
to me by taking from what is mine and making it known to you.
All that belongs to the Father is mine. That is why I said the
Spirit will take from what is mine and make it known to you
(16:5-15).*

Considering the Questions and Conclusions

Those who are not disposed to revival in our time often remind
us that the frequently used phrase "the baptism [in] with the Holy
Spirit" (often associated with the concept of revival) is grossly misused. The simple facts are these: 1) This phrase occurs seven times
in the New Testament; 2) six of the seven uses plainly refer to
Pentecost, or as Gaffin notes, "more accurately, to the once-for-all
Pentecost event-complex" (e.g. Matthew 3:11; Mark 1:8; Luke 3:16;
John 1:33; Acts 1:5; 11:16); 3) the seventh use of this controverted
and misused term is to be found in 1 Corinthians 12:13, where as
Gaffin notes "[it is] addressed to the situation of believers (like the
church today) who were not present at Pentecost or the associated
epochal events recorded in Acts."[8]

For this reason, some people have come to believe that Scripture opposes the whole idea of revival under the new covenant. If the Spirit has come and remains with us and in us, then how can there be "fuller" or "greater" outpourings of the Spirit *subsequent* to Pentecost? If the historical/redemptive meaning of these texts has been fulfilled in the epochal events of Pentecost, as we have seen, what else can there be to look for in the future? These questions are indeed significant; we cannot simply ignore them.

Those who hold this view reason that we should not be looking for an extraordinary event (such as a fresh outpouring, revival, or awakening) if the promise of the Father and the Son has already been given. They point out that revival, as we have defined it, is an *extraordinary* event. Where are we justified in expecting future *extraordinary* visitations of the Spirit upon the church? Moreover, do we have *biblical* warrant to pray and talk about such visitations of the Spirit or seasons of unusual blessing? Rather, in the light of the aforementioned epochal events, we are told that our concern should be obedience (see John 14:21).

This kind of thinking, or something like it, has been held by some very great theologians in the history of the church. Distinguished individuals such as Abraham Kuyper and Charles Hodge can be numbered among those who held this view of revival. Martyn Lloyd-Jones once stated why men like Charles Hodge were not interested in revival:

> A man like Charles Hodge becomes a theologian and he tends therefore not to think as he should in terms of the church in its local concrete situation, but in terms of great abstract systems of truth. He lives in the realm of comparisons and arguments and contrasts, of systems and especially of philosophy, and almost inevitably he ceases to think as he should about revival and the immediate rations of the Spirit.[9]

Lewis Sperry Chafer, the well-known dispensational theologian of an earlier era, devoted an entire volume to the doctrine of the Holy Spirit, yet not once did he ever mention the subject of revival. Many other dispensational commentators have not looked with a great deal of favor upon revival(s) either. My observation is that such writers have not reached these conclusions without some warrant. This is especially true, as we shall see, in the face of modern revivalism and its often blatant misuse of Old Testament texts. These texts have often been forced in a way that makes them artificially applicable to the church under the new covenant. Some people have even endeavored to apply these texts to the modern nation of America. One common example is 2 Chronicles 7:14, which says, "If my people, who are called by my name, will humble themselves and seek my face and turn from their wicked ways, then will I hear from heaven and will forgive their sin and will heal their land." Such usage of Old Testament scriptures, however, is without exegetical warrant.

An illustration of how this school of thought understands a frequently referenced text regarding revival can be seen in an oft-quoted text in Acts 3. Here we read the words of Peter, who is clearly preaching to a Jewish audience. He commands his hearers:

> Repent, then, and turn to God, so that your sins may be wiped out, that times of refreshing may come from the Lord, and that he may send the Christ, who has been appointed for you—even Jesus. He must remain in heaven until the time comes for God to restore everything, as he promised long ago through his holy prophets (Acts 3:19-21)

A dispensational commentator of apparently similar persuasion concludes:

> Although Peter seems to allow some excuse for ignorance, yet only sincere repentance could blot out the crime of rejecting the Messiah, and make possible His return in blessing. The phrases

in 19-21 must be interpreted in the light of the many prophecies of blessings on Israel and the nations in the coming kingdom. It would be absurdly anachronistic to suppose that Peter was applying them to the church by a spiritualizing method![10]

Another dispensational writer, when referring to the phrase "times of refreshing" in Acts 3:19, reasons that the phrase "refers to the millenial kingdom." The same commentator concludes that the oft-quoted reference to revival in Ezekiel 34 should be understood in a similar manner when he says, "The kingdom [i.e., millenium] will be a time of much-needed refreshing for Israel. Ezekiel said it would be a time of 'showers of blessing' (34:26)."[11]

A contemporary theologian who appears to hold similar views, from a nondispensational framework, is Frederick Dale Bruner. His book *The Theology of the Holy Spirit* is a marvelous and measured treatment. Bruner notes that "faith is not a heroic work. Faith is letting God alone be heroic; it is letting God be God. Simple faith in Christ receives *everything* God has to give."[12] Because of Pentecostalism's continued stress upon "something more," Bruner, like so many, has little or nothing to say about revival. (He does reveal some of the profound errors present in modern revivalism, many of which we will observe in chapter twelve.)

In summary, the *no revival position*—regardless of how it is expressed or upon what basis it is argued—follows this line of thinking: The whole Christian era is to be understood as an age of revival (in some sense). Revival, when defined properly, is *not* an extraordinary event but rather the permanent essence of the whole New Testament era. The no-revival proponents look to Scripture and argue that the Old Testament church prayed for revival, God promised to revive His people by the outpouring of His Holy Spirit, and these promises were ultimately fulfilled on the day of Pentecost, exactly as prophesied. The Comforter has already been given to the church. What Christians need to do now, in the age following Pentecost, is realize what their possession is and obey the Spirit's leading given through the Word of God. Iain H. Murray concludes:

Thus, according to this view, revival will not be a periodic occurrence, or something to be prayed for and awaited, rather it belongs to the church as part of her present inheritance in Christ. Or to put it in another form, they argue that the blessing of Pentecost belongs to all Christians—not to Christians of 1740 only, nor to those of 1904, but to all believers, for does not the Scripture say, "If any man have not the Spirit of Christ, he is none of his" (Romans 8:9)?[13]

But does this framework adequately explain the periodic seasons of extraordinary spiritual blessing witnessed throughout church history? How do we understand these times of "refreshing sent from the Lord" if we do not think of them as revivals given by God under the new covenant? We seek to answer this vital question next.

Four

THEOLOGY STILL MATTERS

Though there be a more constant influence of the Spirit attending his ordinances, yet the way in which the greatest things have been done has been by remarkable effusions, at special seasons of mercy.

Jonathan Edwards

In one sense, Pentecost can never happen again. In another sense, it may always be happening, since we live in the age of the Spirit.

—Arthur Skevington Wood

AS WE OBSERVED in the previous chapter, some individuals do not expect revivals in this present age and, as a result, do not encourage prayer for revival. Such a view, however, is hard-pressed to explain certain happenings in church history, much less several important New Testament texts. While those who hold to the *no revival position* have legitimate concerns, we must consider additional evidence before we settle for a specific viewpoint.

THE "REVIVAL IS POSSIBLE" VIEWS

Among those who believe that revival is still a gift of God for this present age, there are essentially two historic views.

Revival Comes When Conditions Are Met

The first view states that revivals are always desirable, generally necessary, and consistently possible if we meet the *specific conditions*

37

given to us in Scripture. These individuals say that revival is dependent, in some manner, upon the behavior of Christians. In this understanding, the *means* of revival, such as prayer and evangelism, are often associated with the *presence* of revival, namely the Spirit's great blessing and extraordinary work. To a large extent the father of this view is nineteenth-century New York evangelist Charles G. Finney. Finney, who was an ardent postmillennialist, actually believed that "the millenium could come in three years if only Christians would do their duty." (We will consider Finney more extensively in chapter twelve.)

A major pre-condition for revival, according to this view, is believed to be holiness (i.e. clean hands and a pure heart). Duncan Campbell, a widely traveled revival minister in Scotland between 1949-53, claimed that the blessings of the Lewis Revival were given because "a local postman truly fulfilled the conditions of 2 Chronicles 7:14" (Note: *conditions* here is the key word).

This view believes that revival can take place upon meeting one or more of the conditions given in texts such as the familiar 2 Chronicles 7:14. Sometimes whole movements of people, believing this text to be the divine prerequisite for revival, seek to covenant together in order to meet these conditions, hoping thereby to prompt God to grant the desired revival. Later we will come to see how this perspective influences a great deal of what is going on today in specific prayer movements for revival.

While serious efforts at evangelism will bring a measure of blessing, and attempts to make holiness central are always desirable, neither of them guarantees revival. Neither Scripture nor history bears out the conclusion that an increase in either evangelism or holiness—or both—will bring revival.

The question we ask here is simple: Where is the *promise* that God will bring about revival if we do the right thing? Where do we find guarantees that earnest, Spirit-anointed preaching will bring remarkable results in terms of large numbers of converts in spiritual awakening? Nowhere does the Word of God teach that God's work done properly, in faith and obedience, will always bring *proportionate* fruit. Consider these facts: Peter preached at Pentecost and 3,000 were converted immediately. Paul, preaching in Philippi, saw one woman converted. And further, what about Paul's mission in Athens? Here, only a few responded to a strongly given apostolic witness. The point is this: Where Christ is preached there will be fruit, but not always in the measure and proportion that we expect or even desire.

The evidence of church history, which has been variously interpreted, is unambiguously clear at this point. We must labor, we must plant, and we must water, but God alone gives the increase (see 1 Corinthians 3:5-8). We must never "dictate the results" by how we speak, how we pray, and especially how we plan. The harvest truly belongs to the Lord. We must bow before this reality. It is ours to be faithful to the task and it is also ours to wait upon the Lord to grant what He ordains. His ways are not our ways.

This can be illustrated by several accounts. When the great evangelist George Whitefield came to the American colonies in 1740 he itinerated for several years traveling up and down the eastern seaboard. Whitefield saw the most amazing harvest as revival mercies attended his labors everywhere he preached. Whitefield made return trips to America over the several decades that followed and he once again preached with what others felt was the same power and clarity as during the 1740-42 revival season, yet Whitefield never again saw the increase and bountiful harvest that resulted during his first visit to America.

The famous Charles H. Spurgeon took a prominent London pastorate at the ripe age of 19. Just a few short years later he saw an increase of over 1,000 converts in one year. Over the next 30 years Spurgeon enjoyed a steady and consistent ministry of fruitful evangelism, but he never again saw anything like what he witnessed in his early years. (Strangely, this is true with many other figures—revival mercies attended their ministry while they were still young and they never saw the same effects in the years that followed.)

Furthermore, the theory that serious efforts at evangelism will assure true revival is plainly contradicted by the facts. William Chalmers Burns, a Scottish minister, witnessed marvelous fruit in his ministry in Scotland between 1839-42. After 1846 he went to China as a missionary. He spent his remaining 21 years in China where he witnessed effectively. Burns never again saw revival, and everywhere he went in China the number of converts were few. The truth to be concluded from such accounts is that God has His own time, His own ways, and His own purposes!

But what about repentance? And holiness? Will not a true repenting of all known sin and a turning to God for practical and personal holiness result in true revival, especially if many people do this simultaneously? Again, the facts simply do not support such a sweeping conclusion.

Let's consider once again 2 Chronicles 7:14, a text frequently used to conclude that if we meet the right conditions God will grant revival. Let's read the verse in its context:

> When Solomon had finished the temple of the LORD and the royal palace, and had succeeded in carrying out all he had in mind to do in the temple of the LORD and in his own palace, the Lord appeared to him at night and said: "I have heard your prayer and have chosen this place for myself as a temple for sacrifices. When I shut up the heavens so that there is no rain, or command locusts to devour the land or send a plague among my people, if my people, who are called by my name, will humble themselves and pray and seek my face and turn from their wicked ways, then will I hear from heaven and will forgive their sin and heal their land. Now my eyes will be open and my ears attentive to the prayers offered in this place. I have chosen and consecrated this temple so that my Name may be there forever. My eyes and my heart will always be there" (2 Chronicles. 7:11-16).

Observe carefully: This revelation was given to Solomon in a context that related specifically to the Solomonic temple as God's unique earthly dwelling place. It was also given to a particular people in a definite time. The "land" that would be healed is not America but the land of Israel, a land given by the promise of God under a much earlier covenant. If this text is saying anything to us who live under the new covenant it must be this: God requires obedience and holiness from His people. When God's people repent, they will receive help from Him. But there is no promise here of widespread revival upon our land if we meet the conditions stated in this passage. The nation that is explicitly promised blessing under the new covenant is called "a holy nation." This nation consists of those people who are "chosen" and who belong to God (1 Peter 2:9). This "holy nation" is the church of Jesus Christ (see also 2:4-8).

"But," some people ask, "Can't the Chronicles text can be used to show what happens when the 'holy nation' (i.e., the church) repents and seeks God? Perhaps the verse has nothing to do with America, as has been widely taught, but doesn't the text apply to *the church in general?*"

My answer is that the promises of the old covenant regarding restoration and revival are inextricably linked to the whole idea of the theocracy that exsited in ancient Israel. These promises were part of the covenant that was then in place. The theocracy consisted of several things, two of which are important to our understanding at this point: 1) a system of clear regulations designed for a unique people and given directly from heaven; 2) a covenantal arrangement including the exercise of a peculiar providence in the support of this nation through the conferring of both abundant mercies and national judgments. These were generally immediate, and sometimes came in a most extraordinary manner. The blessings and cursings were of a very direct kind, included much physical evidence, and were tied to the national entity itself. Though we may be warranted to draw modest conclusions based upon a more general providence regarding the nations, we are certainly *not* warranted to conclude that the old covenant is in force in the same manner in this present age.

If my conclusion is correct, then we must go somewhere else to find texts that speak directly to the subject of revival during this age of the Spirit. I can see no other sound theological conclusion that can be drawn from Scripture itself if we understand the covenantal arrangements as presented in God's Word. This conclusion takes us to the very heart of the theological issue involved in defining and explaining the phenomenon of revival. We must examine the facts and evidence very carefully if we want to understand the problems and the blessings associated with the modern-day interest in revival.

An important text for us to consider, in light of the transition that comes at the passing away of the old covenant, is found in the Gospel of John:

> On the last and greatest day of the Feast, Jesus stood and said in a loud voice, "If anyone is thirsty, let him come to me and drink. Whoever believes in me, as the Scripture has said, streams of living water will flow from within him." By this he meant the Spirit, whom those who believed in him were later to receive. Up to that time the Spirit had not been given, since Jesus had not yet been glorified (John 7:37-39).

Notice what verse 39 says: Those who believed "were later to receive" the Holy Spirit since "up to that time the Spirit had not been given." We cannot miss the obvious connection to the historic event of Pentecost because the text goes on to say that this gift of the Spirit was clearly linked to Jesus being "glorified." It would be Jesus—crucified, raised, ascended, and now glorified—who would grant the gift of the Spirit to His disciples (John 14:16).

Any conception of a promise regarding revival must be biblically connected to the new covenant promise of the Holy Spirit to all who believe. The old covenant promises associated with the land and its attendant economic, social, and religious prosperity illustrate beneficial principles in several ways, but these simply cannot be promises of new effusions of the Spirit upon the church.

Further, the new covenant promise of the Spirit is dependent upon the inauguration of the new age. This age has come in and through the death, burial, resurrection, and ascension of Jesus Christ. The promise of an abundant measure of the Holy Spirit's power and presence must always be uniquely connected to the person and work of Jesus. To miss this is to severely confuse the theology of revival. The results of this confusion abound; this is the theological point missed in most of the revival literature in our time. This may also be one of the reasons many serious students of the Bible are not interested in revival.

The church of the new covenant is not an earthly entity—at least not in the way Israel was an earthly entity. She is not linked to a geographical place, such as Jerusalem. Her dwelling is said to be above, in the heavenly Jerusalem. She lives on the earth, serving the Lord and ministering, and she will also inherit the earth (Matthew 5:5), but her ultimate glory is to be seen as above. The gospel brings believers into a multiethnic community as well as the mercy of God through the work of the Spirit. But the idea that one person's conversion will revive a whole nation, or even an entire congregation, is not to be found in the new covenant. Yes, God does bring blessing when one person obeys Him. He will even send showers of blessing upon the church through the means of one praying person. (We will see more of this as we go along.) But the measure and nature of God's blessing is not *directly determined* by the measure and nature of the repentance and personal pursuit of holiness.

Did the apostle John fulfill the conditions of revival, so-called, on the Isle of Patmos? I believe he did, in terms of what many people today say those conditions are. Yet John was in a time of tribulation that cannot be seen as revival by modern proponents of the conditional view. Consider a more current example: Did the church in

Uganda, living under the dictator Idi Amin, meet the basic conditions for revival? What about the church in China in the last 40 years or so? In both cases, amazing spiritual fruit has has been witnessed by the church in these lands, but none of it is of the sort that is associated with what is considered "revival" here in America.

Pentecost lifted the church out of its old covenant infancy and into the adult status of the new age. Pentecost, as we've seen, ushered in a new era. Things are radically different now. To talk about revival in an old covenant sense, with constant references to Scripture texts that promise national or corporate blessings upon obedience, is to confuse the subject seriously. The results of this confusion are massive, and the damage done has greatly altered the church and her ministry.

Revival Is God's Prerogative

The second historic view among those who believe revival does still occur states that God alone gets the credit for revival showers.

We need to be perfectly clear: The only person who ever received the Holy Spirit without measure was the Lord Jesus Christ (John 3:34). Christ promised that after He ascended into heaven, He would send us a gift. This gift, given to all who believe, is the anointing Spirit of God. The apostle John wrote:

> You [believers] have an anointing from the Holy One, and all of you know the truth. . . . I am writing these things to you about those who are trying to lead you astray. As for you, the anointing you received from him remains in you, and you do not need anyone to teach you. But as his anointing teaches you about all things and as that anointing is real, not counterfeit—just as it has taught you, remain in him (1 John 2:20,26-27).

What actually happened on the day of Pentecost? First, a promise long made was fulfilled. A new norm was established in the community of God. Things would never be the same. Second, a largesse of the Spirit's work was evident. The degree, or the measure, of the Spirit's work under the new covenant is extraordinary when contrasted with any previous outpouring under the old covenant. Indeed, we could say that this first outpouring at Pentecost resulted in continued blessings that flowed from the throne of Christ all throughout the age that followed. As we see in the New Testament, these effusions were sometimes quite large and remarkable, while at other times they were small. In every case the work was of Christ. It was He who sent the Spirit as He purposed.

Furthermore, Pentecost was not an everyday thing. It was a non-repeatable event in terms of its historical-redemptive purpose and fulfillment. People who underwent this great event did not remain in permanent possession of all the blessings that attended that particular day. We can easily assume that up until Pentecost the disciples were cowards and weaklings, and that after Pentecost they always showed great boldness and strength. But that's not the case. Even after Pentecost, the apostle Peter still showed himself to be a coward and one who frequently lacked power.

In Acts 4 we find evidence of the Spirit's outpouring after the day of Pentecost. Verse 8 tells us that when Peter spoke to the Sanhedrin, or the ruling body comprised of Jewish rulers, elders, and teachers, he was "filled with the Holy Spirit." This account follows Pentecost as surely as revival has followed revival throughout church history. And in verse 13 we are told that the disciples had "courage" (a word used frequently in Acts to describe the result of the Spirit's empowerment of believers, especially in preaching). In this same verse, Luke adds that people were "astonished and . . . took note that these men had been with Jesus." Later in the same chapter when the church lifted its voice to the Lord in collective prayer, they asked Him "[to] . . . enable your servants to speak your word with great boldness" (verse 29). Then we read that "they were all filled with the Holy Spirit and spoke the word of God boldly" (29,31).

What we have here is a *new* effusion given to the people of God. Many Bible scholars have accurately noted that these were days of revival in Jerusalem. The Holy Spirit had been given in abundance. But we should note that the measure of the Spirit's blessing, or the plenitude of the Spirit, was not given in a static way. It seems apparent that during special seasons, larger measures of grace and power were given by Christ to His people.

In Ephesians chapter 1, Paul assures us regarding salvation:

> You also were included in Christ when you heard the word of truth, the gospel of your salvation. Having believed, you were marked in him with a seal, the promised Holy Spirit, who is a deposit guaranteeing our inheritance until the redemption of those who are God's possession—to the praise of his glory (13-14).

The Ephesians were marked with a seal by virtue of their union with Christ. This seal is said to be the person of the Holy Spirit. It is He who guarantees, as our seal, that we are God's possession and that we will receive our inheritance.

Then in Ephesians 3, Paul tells the Ephesian believers he is praying that they will grow more in their experience of the Spirit of God:

> For this reason I kneel before the Father, from whom his whole family in heaven and on earth derives its name. I pray that out of his glorious riches he may strengthen you with power through his Spirit in your inner being, so that Christ may dwell in your hearts through faith. And I pray that you, being rooted and established in love, may have power, together with all the saints, to grasp how wide and long and high and deep is the love of Christ, and to know this love that surpasses knowledge—that you may be filled to the measure of all the fullness of God (14-19).

There is clearly room here for growth in our experience of the Holy Spirit. A genuine theology of revival must be built upon such a recognition. It is right to desire fuller and richer knowledge of the Father by the Spirit. In the experiential theology of Paul, the Spirit is never a static *influence*. The Spirit sometimes provides specific help, often in and through prayer. This help is not something unrelated to Pentecost and the age in which we now live (Philippians 1:19). Pentecost was the beginning; it brought a river of blessing for all the people of God throughout this present age. But it can also be understood as the first in a series of fillings, or effusions. This observation does not deny anything we have previously observed.

When our Lord speaks to the church at Sardis (Revelation 3:1) He proclaims Himself to be the one "who holds the seven spirits of God and the seven stars." The sovereign Christ holds the seven spirits in His hand and He alone can grant new and powerful effusions of the Spirit throughout this present age.

Before this century, orthodox theologians generally understood Pentecost in the manner I have outlined. That is why you often read the older writers speaking of a Pentecostal shower as revival, or vice versa. Upon a more careful reading it becomes apparent that these writers were not speaking of a "second-stage" blessing as evidenced in the gift of tongues or the manifestation of any other spiritual gift. When they wrote of Pentecostal blessings, they were actually speaking of revival as the sovereign gift of grace. (This can be seen in some of our older church hymns.) They expected there to be both ordinary and extraordinary givings of the Spirit throughout this entire age. Revival, for them, was the *descriptive term for extraordinary showers of blessing.* This is exactly how Alexander Moody-Stuart spoke of the Revival of 1859 when he said that they experienced "a larger measure [of the Holy Spirit's presence] than usual."

What we are contending for theologically and practically is this: Christ, as mediator and head of His body, continues to give the "actual influence"[1] of the Spirit as and when He pleases. Iain Murray concludes:

> Thus, although the Spirit was initially bestowed on the church by Christ at Pentecost, His influences are not uniform and

unchanging; there are variations in the measure in which He
continues to be given. In the book of Acts times of quickened
spiritual prosperity and growth in the church are traced to new
and larger measures of the influence of the Holy Spirit (Acts
4:31-33; 11:15-16; 13:52–14:1), and so, through Christian history, the church has been raised to new energy and success by
"remarkable communications of the Spirit of God . . . at special
seasons of mercy."[2]

For those who held this view, terms such as *effusion*, *baptism*, and
the outpouring of the Spirit are all virtually synonymous with the term
revival. Only later did this historical sense of the term shift in meaning to the conditional view now so commonly held by the majority
of American evangelical Christians.

THE THREE VIEWS SUMMARIZED

Iain H. Murray has helpfully noted that each of the three views
we've considered has a strong point.[3] The first view reminds us to
never think of the Holy Spirit as here today and absent tomorrow.
An adequate focus upon John chapters 14 and 16 is needed. This
approach protects us from many of the excesses that we see in modern revivalism. The weakness of this view, however, is that it ends up
expecting nothing new—nothing more than what we already know.
With this view, it is not difficult to reason that all the Spirit's influence
we will ever need is already with us. Why talk about *more*? Why pray
for *more*? This weakness is particularly apparent in churches where
revival is seen as undesirable. Too much is assumed by this understanding, and as a result, experiential Christianity tends to suffer.

The second view, by emphasizing evangelism, repentance, concerts of prayer, and genuine personal holiness, places a *necessary*
emphasis upon human responsibility. (Those who hold to the older
historical view need to be continually reminded that God would
have His people pray, seek Him, and continually repent.) In Martin
Luther's famous Ninety-Five Theses, the first thesis stated what every

Christian needs to understand: "When our Lord and Master Jesus Christ said, 'Repent' [Matthew 4:17], He willed the entire life of believers to be one of repentance." This conditional view fails, it seems to me, in this: It makes revival the norm, not something *extraordinary*. It promotes the notion that there is no revival simply because we have not repented enough, prayed enough, or sought God deeply enough. Charles G. Finney said, "A revival of religion is indispensable to the church." If this is true, then the church that believes and practices this theology will tend to make revival an end in itself. It will also tend to have constant revivals, whether God actually grants them or not. Often people of this persuasion will stress the seeking of revival in ways that eventually bring great harm to the regular work of preaching and disciple-making.

The third view strikes the proper balance. Its strength is that God alone gets the credit for revival showers. It preserves the glory to the giver Himself. Its weakness can be seen in that it engenders, in some who use it wrongly, a false passivity. Practically, this causes some people to never expect or pray for the extraordinary at all. They fall into a fatalism not warranted by an open Bible and a believing heart. Therefore, the historical view can strike a blow at personal responsibility if it is not properly understood and held in careful biblical balance.

Five

GOD AT WORK:
THE MARKS OF TRUE REVIVAL

It is a revival of scriptural knowledge, of vital godliness and of practical obedience.

—William B. Sprague

The characteristic of a revival is that a profound consciousness of sin is produced in many persons at the same time by an awareness of God.

—Iain H. Murray

THE ESSENCE OF true revival is that the Holy Spirit comes down upon a number of people simultaneously. The recipients might be a church congregation, a number of churches together, scores of churches and people in a large geographical area, or even a nation. Revival is, as we have observed, a visitation, an outpouring of the Holy Spirit. It is God moving among His people, renewing and refreshing their lives through the third person of the Trinity. In revival the Holy Spirit seems to take charge in a direct manner, causing people to say, "He is surely here!"

But much of this sounds strange to our generation. Most of us, quite honestly, have never seen God move in this way. We know very little personally about real revival except for what we have read in the historical accounts of the past. Given that many of us have never witnessed revival, how can we really know if revival has come? What are the general characteristics of a genuine movement of God? Are there any general characteristics, or marks, that should be noted in all true revivals? It appears that we have good reason to conclude that there are several essential marks of true revival; historians and theologians alike have reached remarkable agreement among themselves about these particular characteristics.

AN AWARENESS OF GOD'S PRESENCE

The most immediate effect of a genuine move of God upon a people is their acute sense that He is present among them in a mighty way. D. Martyn Lloyd-Jones mentions this characteristic when he writes:

> The immediate effect is that the people present begin to have an awareness of spiritual things and clear views of them such as they have never had before. Now again I am talking about believers, members of the Christian church, when they suddenly become conscious of this presence and of this power, and the first effect is that spiritual things become realities. They have heard all these things before, they may have heard them a thousand times, but what they testify is this: "You know, the whole thing suddenly became clear to me. I was suddenly illuminated, things that I was so familiar with stood out in letters of gold, as it were. I understood. I saw it all in a way that I had never done in the whole of my life." That is what they say. The Holy Spirit enlightens the mind and the understanding. They begin not only to see these things clearly but to feel their power.[1]

What is in view here is simply an awesome (awful, terrible) sense of the presence of God. This characteristic is also evidenced at Pentecost, according to the account recorded in Acts 2. Here God manifested His presence to the disciples first, who were still gathered in the upper room. Then a multitude of people who were gathered outside sensed that something was happening, and thousands fell under the same weight of God's holy presence.

Duncan Campbell, an itinerant evangelist who was a human instrument in the 1949-53 Lewis Awakening, noted this same mark as the chief evidence of God's work among the people on the Isle of Lewis. When he was asked about the most outstanding characteristic of this movement of the Spirit, Campbell answered:

> First the presence of God. To be fully realized, it had to be felt. A Rector of the Church of England, referring to his visit to Lewis, said, "What I felt apart from what I saw, convinced me at once that this was no ordinary movement." I have known men out in the fields, so overcome by this sense of God that they were found prostrate on the ground. Here are the words of one who felt the hand of God upon him: "The grass beneath my feet and rocks around me seem to cry, 'Flee to Christ for refuge.'" This supernatural illumination of the Holy Spirit led many to a saving knowledge of the Lord Jesus Christ before they came near to any meeting connected with the movement. I have no hesitation in saying that this awareness of God is the crying need of the church today.[2]

"The spirit of revival," noted the late Arthur Wallis, is always "the consciousness of God." Both believers and unbelievers become consciously aware that God Himself is present in a powerful way!

When the prophet Habakkuk prayed that God would remember mercy in the display of wrath (Habakkuk 3:2) he asked for the Lord to "make them [i.e., His great deeds of mercy] known." In the next verse the prophet records God's response to his cry with the simple phrase, "God came . . ." (verse 3). What follows is a description of the glory, brightness, and power of the Almighty Himself.

What did Habakkuk mean when he said, "God came"? How are we to reconcile the idea of God coming, or of what I have called "a visitation of God," with the doctrine of God's omnipresence? Our answer must be in harmony with the words of Scripture—words such as these:

Where can I go from your Spirit?
  Where can I flee from your presence?
If I go up to the heavens, you are there;
  if I make my bed in the depths, you are there.
If I rise on the wings of the dawn,
  if I settle on the far side of the sea,
even there your hand will guide me,
  your right hand will hold me fast (Psalm 139:7-10).

God is present everywhere! This is an essential doctrine of the Bible. But it is also true that God is present in some places in a way that He is not in others. He is, for example, in the hearts of those who love Him in a manner in which He is not present in the hearts of those who hate Him. The apostle Paul said God "alone is immortal and . . . lives in unapproachable light, whom no one has seen or can see" (1 Timothy 6:16). No one on earth can see His glory, for such a sight would reduce them to ash!

Yet we can—indeed, I submit that we must—speak of God dwelling in places which differ from His dwelling in all places as an omnipresent God. Consider these words from the prophet Isaiah:

This is what the high and lofty One says—
  he who lives forever, whose name is holy:
"I live in a high and holy place,
  but also with him who is contrite and lowly in spirit,
to revive the spirit of the lowly
  and to revive the heart of the contrite" (Isaiah. 57:15).

God is present in the assembly of a New Testament church in a manner that He is not present in a tavern. God reveals Himself to believers in the preaching of His Word. He may reveal Himself in the reading of a news account, but this is not normally His way. God reveals Himself to us in the Lord's Supper and in baptism. In fact, both preaching and the sacraments are appointed by God as "means of grace." Let me explain.

One of the classic Protestant statements of faith from church history is the *Westminster Confession of Faith*. It has a marvelous statement regarding the sacraments that most evangelicals would have gladly agreed with many years ago. (By the way, a person does not have to agree with the practice of infant baptism, also taught in this same confession, in order to agree with the Confession's statements regarding the grace of God and the use of the sacraments.) This historic creed states:

> The grace which is exhibited in or by the sacraments rightly used, is not conferred by any power in them; neither doth the efficacy of a sacrament depend upon the piety or intention of him that doth administer it: *but upon the work of the Spirit, and the word of institution, which contains, together with a precept authorizing the use thereof, a promise of benefit to worthy receivers* (emphasis added).

So the Lord's Supper is a time in which the Holy Spirit "visits" the believer with the promise and blessing of God. It is not a time so much for what I do or what I offer in dedication as it is a time and occasion when God grants benefits to my soul through His appointed means. This is not magic! I must come with faith, but the point is this: God, not me, has ordained the *means* of this particular blessing.

Now, when we speak of God coming to His people in revival, or of a visitation of the Spirit, we must be careful to not denigrate the regular means of grace. In fact, as we have noted, it is often through these regular means of grace that God "visits" His people with revival. (True believers can and do receive "personal" revival when the Spirit is pleased to use these means for their benefit, whether or not the church or churches experience revival in the broader sense.)

What I am stressing here is what older divines called the "manifest presence of God"—God coming to His people in a manner beyond the normal experience. This coming of God's holiness and power overshadows human personalities and plans. God breaks into the conscious awareness of people with sovereign majesty. This is not a normal thing, yet it employs the normal means God has ordained.

Pentecost models what we are talking about: It was unique, and yet it was also a specimen awakening from which others flow. The uniqueness of Pentecost can be seen in that it was the first such manifestation in the new age following Christ's accomplished work of redemption. Pentecost was a clear and dramatic fulfillment of the prophecy of Joel, who said, "And afterward, I will pour out my Spirit on all people . . ." (Joel 2:28). Yet Peter, quoting from Joel, changes the phrase "And afterward . . ." to read, "In the last days, God says, I will pour out my Spirit on all people" (Acts 2:17). Joel's promise of the outpouring of the Spirit refers to a *period* of time, not a *point* in time, for the phrase "in the last days" cannot be confined to one event or to one point in time. In light of what follows (Acts 2:19-21), it appears that this prophecy must stretch forward, in some sense, till the end of this age.

Indeed, an outpouring of the Spirit took place at Caesarea in Acts 10, where we read, "While Peter was still speaking these words, the Holy Spirit came on all who heard the message" (Acts 10:44). The next verse says that the Jewish believers who came along with Peter "were astonished that the gift of the Holy Spirit had been *poured out* even on the Gentiles" (emphasis added). Even Paul, who was not present either at Pentecost or Caesarea, speaks of the renewing of the Holy Spirit in his salvation as being that which God "*poured out* on us generously through Jesus Christ our Savior" (Titus 3:6, emphasis added).

Every revival since the days of the New Testament has been marked by a similar outpouring of the Spirit which makes those visited by God acutely aware of His presence. Jonathan Edwards put this plainly:

> God hath it much on His heart from all eternity to glorify His
> dear and only begotten Son; and there are some special seasons

that He appoints to that end, wherein He comes forth with
omnipotent power to fulfill His promise and oath to Him.
And these times are times of remarkable pouring out of His
Spirit to advance His kingdom. Such a day is a day of His
power.[4]

Anecdotes demonstrating this characteristic can be seen in all
the histories of revival. David Brainerd, who witnessed a wonderful
movement of the Holy Spirit among the Indians, recorded this:

> The power of God seemed to descend upon the assembly like a
> mighty rushing wind and with an astonishing energy bore
> down all before it. I stood amazed at the influence that seized
> the audience almost universally, and could compare it to noth-
> ing more aptly than the irresistible force of a mighty torrent.[5]

In the 1858 prayer revival in America it was noted that as ships
drew near American ports, sudden conviction of sin and real conversion would become a common sight on board. On one ship the
captain and his crew of 30 men were all strikingly converted.

At the beginning of the 1904 Welsh Revival, a meeting in the
town of Gorseinon was in progress when a notoriously sinful and
careless miner saw the light of the chapel and went to investigate.
When the curious miner opened the door to the chapel he was overcome by the sense of God's presence and cried out, "Oh, God is
here!" He was afraid to move into the building and he was afraid to
leave. As he stood on the doorstep, a great work of conversion began
in his heart.[6]

AN UNCOMMON READINESS TO HEAR GOD

True revivals have always resulted in a deep thirst for the Word
of God, especially when it is preached. One of the surest marks of
spiritual declension in a congregation is when the people lose their
appetite for the preached Word. Preaching which is conscience-
searching, heart-disturbing, and life-transforming seems to be quite

rare in our time. Very few churches today long to hear biblical preaching. In revival, this would be reversed. People become immediately open to the preached Word during times of refreshing sent from the Lord. The most basic truths, presented by the Spirit's power, grip multitudes.

A revival on the Island of Arran in 1812 produced the following account. It bears witness to my observation:

> For some months after the commencement of the awakening, the subjects of it manifested an uncommon thirst after the means of grace. Both old and young flocked in multitudes to hear the Word of God. The house, and the place employed for private meetings, were frequently so crowded that the people, as it were, trod one upon another. To travel ten or fifteen miles to hear a sermon was considered a very small matter.[7]

Revival preachers used mightily by God have never adopted new themes. Their subject matter has always been the same: God, ruin caused by sin, the judgment which is to come, the person and work of Christ, and the freeness of grace for all who believe. In addition, revival preachers have been both fearless and urgent. People are generally unused to this type of ministry, especially in spiritually sleepy times like ours.

A description of Duncan Campbell as a preacher affirms the distinctives I've just described:

> There was nothing complicated about Duncan's preaching. It was fearless and uncompromising. He exposed sin in its ugliness and dwelt at length on the consequences of living and dying without Christ. With a penetrating gaze on the congregation, and perspiration streaming down his face, he set before men and women the way of life and the way of death. It was a solemn thought to him that the eternity of his hearers might turn upon his faithfulness. He was standing before his fellow

men in Christ's stead and could be neither perfunctory nor formal. His words were not just a repetition of accumulated ideas, but the expression of his whole being. He gave the impression of preaching with his entire personality, not merely with his voice.[8]

An interesting exception to this should be noted in the 1904 Welsh Revival. Often Welsh ministers felt unable to speak during those gatherings, and many of the people were often not willing to listen. That is, there was a general hunger for the Word of God but a decided reaction against the clergy. The 1904 revival soon fell into significant error related to mysticism and the giving of far too much attention to the stratagems of Satan. Brian Edwards concludes,

> Though thousands were saved, and the fire of revival in Wales spread all over the world, its failure to survive long, and the disproportionate number of those who fell away, was in large measure due to the fact that in many areas preaching was neglected.[9]

One of the better known texts in Paul's epistle to the Romans states this point plainly: "Faith comes from hearing the message, and the message is heard through the word of Christ" (10:17). Faith comes from "hearing" a message—that is, something is spoken or given out orally. And this message is "heard through the word of Christ." This seems to be a clear reference to preaching. In fact, that is the reason several versions of the Bible translate the latter part of the verse "what is heard comes *by the preaching of Christ*" (emphasis added). God has ordained preaching as the primary means for feeding the church of God, and He has ordained pastors to feed the flock with the Word of God. Authentic revivals have always restored powerful preaching.

A DEEP CONVITION OVER ONE'S SIN

During seasons of revival, people are made deeply conscious of God. Christians not only come to know *about* God's power, His love, His wisdom, His greatness, and His sovereignty, but they *experience* these divine excellencies. This acute awareness of God's presence inevitably brings about deep conviction over one's personal sinfulness. This should be expected. When Isaiah experienced a personal vision of the Lord seated on His throne, he heard the seraphs calling to one another "Holy, holy, holy is the LORD Almighty" (Isaiah 6:3). The prophet was profoundly moved in his inner being. His response was, "Woe to me! . . . I am ruined! For I am a man of unclean lips, and I live among a people of unclean lips, and my eyes have seen the King, the LORD Almighty" (Isaiah 6:5). This kind of experience is a consistent feature of true revival. Both Christians and non-Christians alike are profoundly convicted of their innate sinfulness. Duncan Campbell so often saw such deep conviction of sin during the Lewis Revival that he wrote, "I have known occasions when it was necessary to stop preaching because of the distress manifested by the anxious."[10]

In the face of the intense light shone by the Spirit through the Word of God into human hearts, the terrifying darkness of sin becomes readily apparent. Those convicted see themselves as in a mirror. James Burns notes:

> . . . every fault, every meanness, every deviation from the truth,
> every act of self-interest, of betrayal, of hypocrisy, confronts
> them; their sins drag them to judgment; they cry out in their
> despair; an awful terror seizes them; under the pressure of the
> Spirit they often fall to the ground with loud cries and tears,
> the conviction of sin burns like fire. Yet this "terror of the
> Lord," remarkable though it may seem, is not the terror of
> punishment; it is inspired by a sense of having rebelled against
> the divine love, of having failed to give glory to God, of having

crucified Christ afresh. This is the sin, which above all others, gives the awakened soul at such times its most poignant bitterness.[11]

Under this pressure, attended by the agony of deep conviction, confession is the only avenue open to those who are believers. Deeply stirred by the Spirit of God, multitudes flee to the fountain opened for all in the blood of Christ.

One individual who witnessed intense dealings with God and personal sin in the Manchurian Revival in China (1906-09) wrote, "I cannot describe the scene. It made one think of the Judgment Day. God had come among us." The same observer added, "All knew it, and every heart was open before Him. For myself, I had the most intense realization of the holiness of God, and of my uncleanness in His sight." Even the heathen who had never previously heard the name of Christ were attracted to these meetings. Said one, "Whenever I entered I felt some mysterious power seize me, impelling me to confess my sins, and it was only with the utmost difficulty I could drag myself away." Others would remain in the meetings, and as one missionary put it, "were brought under conviction and converted."[12]

The *reformation* of the church, which is quite obviously needed in our time, must be pursued one person and one church at a time. This will always be so. Such work is generally slow, arduous, and difficult. It involves battles won and battles lost, and often over a period of years. Sometimes pastors have to leave and plant a new church in times of reformation. But reformation joined with *revival* brings dramatic, sudden growth. Large numbers of revived believers, along with masses of new converts—all with sin confessed and hearts right before God—help to bring fresh life into the churches. Such life will undoubtedly transform a church. It will also have a significant impact on the culture surrounding it.

A HEARTFELT REPENTANCE

Another mark of a true movement of God's Spirit in revival is that sin will be forsaken. Repentance will be genuine, deep, and life-changing. Sorrow and shame for previous backsliding will fill the minds of believers with incredible remorse and result in dramatic changes in their lives.

In Zechariah 12:10, God said, "I will pour out on the house of David and the inhabitants of Jerusalem a spirit of grace and supplication." What will be the result of this outpouring? What will be its chief fruit? Profound joy? Or perhaps changes in personal conduct? If the answer is simply joy, then the danger of delusion is real, because true revival is accompanied by transformed lives. If the answer is change in conduct and there's no accompanying joy in Christ, then we've just seen moralism raise its head. (After all, we can all "turn over a new leaf" when we decide to do it!) But Zechariah 12:10 says the outpouring that will come in the age of the new covenant will be one of "a spirit of grace and supplication." This outpouring will result in the reality that "they will look on me, the one they have pierced, and they will mourn for him as one mourns for an only child, and grieve bitterly for him as one mourns for an only child" (verse 10).

One mark of repentance in the age of the Spirit, then, is that people will not simply believe, but they will mourn. Those who have the Spirit of God will mourn over the particular dishonors that they have brought upon His holy name. They will mourn over their wicked unbelief and impenitence. They will mourn over their estrangement from the One who loved them and gave Himself for them.

But what is repentance? Perhaps no better definition has been written in the English language than this:

> Repentance unto life is a saving grace whereby a sinner, out of
> a true sense of his sin, and apprehension of the mercy of God

in Christ, doth, with grief and hatred of his sin, turn from it unto God, with full purpose of, and endeavour after, new obedience.[13]

Repentance is necessary for a person to enter into the salvation offered through Christ. But this initial repentance unto life is not the terminus, it is only the beginning. Those who truly believe will spend the rest of their lives repenting. In times of revival, this gift of repentance will be given to the church with profound power, and it will have a general effect upon many people at the same time.

Brokenhearted, Christ-centered confession and repentance will characterize a true movement of the Spirit. People will sometimes weep under the most profound impressions of sin. But weeping is not an actual evidence of revival. Repentance and the attendant fruit of the Spirit, which cannot be imitated by the enemy, is the real fruit of true revival.

AN EXTRAORDINARY CONCERN FOR OTHERS

True revival never creates an atmosphere of self-centeredness. There is always a definite connection between right doctrine and right practice. When the church begins to act more like what she was designed to be, her life spills over into the world with great force and effect. Even those who despise revivals must admit that authentic awakenings have helped to build hospitals, taught the illiterate to read, clothed the naked, fed the poor, moved entire nations to act more justly, and even caused general reductions in crime and family dissolution.

Simply put, revivals have a clear ethical aspect to them. This aspect may depend upon the circumstances and the times, but the love of Christ always causes revived people to reach out beyond themselves. Revivals that have too great an emphasis on the emotions often miss this element.

It has been said by historians that Chrysostom's preaching denounced sin in high places and thus eventually led to his banishment. Savanarola appealed for moral amendment in corrupt

Florence, with good effect. "Women cast off their jewels and dressed simply, young profligates were transformed into sober religious men, the churches were filled with people of prayer and the Bible was diligently read."[14]

> No student of church history can ignore or minimize the moral betterment that followed the work of Luther in Middle Europe, of Calvin in Geneva, of Knox in Scotland, or of Wesley in England. As a rule, then as now, moral betterment came as a by-product of revival and evangelism—both of them Biblical and doctrinal. . . . Reform ought always to follow conversion. From this ethical point of view, we conservatives appraise or approve revival and evangelism. . . . We who accept the doctrine of Holy writ, must never rest content with revival or evangelism which does not issue in transformed lives and communities. Christian ethics must come through revival and evangelism as in the days of Wesley or of Paul.[15]

Another result of revivals is that God has used them to raise up new generations of ministers, teachers, evangelists, and missionaries. The Lord of the harvest "thrusts workers out into the harvest fields" in answer to the church's cry for the ends of the earth.

I have supplied only a brief synopsis in this chapter of some of the things the Spirit does when He comes upon the church with reviving power. The simple fact is this: When the Spirit comes and renews Christian believers, they cannot help but tell others— husbands, wives, children, parents, fellow workers, neighbors, and so on. An internal compulsion drives them—a compulsion that Thomas Chalmers so powerfully termed "the expulsive power of a new affection."

BRINGING ABOUT TRUE CHANGE

There is a developing awareness among some individuals in our time that the church is tragically unable to cope with the challenges of the postmodern world. We are a people immersed in the mire of pluralism and spiritual apostasy. Talk of revival is in the air, but talk can still be cheap. While the world searches for spiritual answers and turns to the East with unprecedented interest, the church talks openly to the world about "felt needs." The hunger and thirst of spiritually starving people is real, almost palpable. There is ample evidence that the world of our time is becoming increasingly like the world of the Roman Empire. That was the world system, we should remember, that was faced by Peter and Paul just after Pentecost. What their dark world needed was exactly what it received—a flood of new spiritual life and a reawakened love for God. This is what God gave to the church, small and weak as it was in those days. What this demonstrates is simple: When the church is the church, the world will become the beneficiary!

Columnist Cal Thomas recently editorialized about the Christian Coalition and the retirement of its executive director, Ralph Reed, by reminding us of what the church's real purpose is in this present age:

> When Christian activists moved into the political arena, they targeted pornography, offensive television, drugs, the gay-rights movement and crumbling families. Pornography is worse than ever, television continues to stink, drugs remain a problem, the gay-rights agenda advances and the divorce rate remains about the same.

> . . . conservative evangelicals run the risk of depreciating their ultimate value, that of speaking of and building a kingdom "not of this world." There is precedent for what happens to the church's primary witness when it becomes overly entangled in the cares of this world. Look at the liberal churches, which long ago gave up preaching salvation and now mainly focus on political themes.

Christians have strayed too far from their leader's admonition to "love your enemies; pray for those who persecute you; feed the hungry, clothe the naked and visit those in prison." Clearly, the Christian Coalition's attempt to organize a minority constituency to influence a majority who do not share their views is not working (otherwise, our culture would not have declined to the point it has). Suppose the coalition became known for transforming people's lives instead of trying to transform Congress and the White House? Might it be argued that their example would be so compelling that millions of Americans would follow it?

Conservative Christians claim that by force of numbers alone, which they do not have, they can redeem a culture gone sour. It won't happen through the ballot box, no matter who is elected. It can happen only through the heart.

C.S. Lewis put it bluntly: "If you read history, you will find that the Christians who did the most for the present world were just those who thought most of the next. The apostles, themselves, who set on foot the conversion of the Roman Empire, the great men who built up the Middle Ages, the English evangelicals who abolished the slave trade, all left their mark on Earth, precisely because their minds were occupied with heaven. It is since Christians have largely ceased to think of the other world that they have become so ineffective in this one. Aim at heaven and you will get earth 'thrown in.' Aim at earth and you will get neither."

The Christian Coalition won't redeem the culture from the top down. It might succeed if it started at the bottom and worked upward.[16]

Cal Thomas is correct in his assessments. When God floods the church with true revival, Christian faith and practice are radically altered. The church will once again make its mark on the culture, a mark that emphasizes changed lives rather than political agendas.

For the church, revival means humiliation and the bitter acknowledgment of our unworthiness before a holy God. Such an acknowledgment will be followed by contrition and the confession of sin. Then we will be ready to hear God speak through His Word, even through the simplest instrument anointed and raised up by the Holy Spirit. Then the church will have something to give to the world.

Only when we see the marks of an authentic move of God—such as those cited in this chapter— should we begin to speak about revival happening. It seems as if the more we claim revival is already occurring, the further we move away from the true marks of a genuine work of God.

If you love the cause of Christ, then set about encouraging the recovery of the marks of God at work. Pray that you will become more and more aware of God's presence. Prepare yourself to hear God speak to you through preaching, and pray for your pastor, that he will know the Spirit's anointing upon his work. Seek God for deep and powerful conviction in your life and church. Turn from sin wherever you see it. Repent with wholehearted abandon. Cultivate deeper concern for others, and beseech God to move afresh in our time . . . for His own glory!

Six

GREAT TRUTHS:
EXALTED BY REVIVAL

A wave of authentic revival sweeps over the church when three things happen together: teaching the great truths of the gospel with clarity, applying those truths to people's lives with spiritual power, and extending that experience to large numbers of people. We evangelicals urgently need such an awakening today. We need to rediscover the gospel

—Raymond Ortlund, Jr.

THE GREAT TRUTHS of the gospel have been lost to an entire generation of evangelical Christians. I know this is hard to imagine, but data from a recent Barna Research Group national telephone survey shows just how far adrift evangelicals really are in their understanding of essential biblical truths directly related to the gospel of Christ.

Some of the trends cited by George Barna and published in his research organization's newsletter included the following:

- Over 80% of born-again Christians agreed with the statement that "the Bible teaches [in the matter of salvation] that God helps those who help themselves."

- 49% said, "The devil, or Satan, is not a living being, but a symbol of evil."

- Over 30% said, "When He lived on earth, Jesus Christ was human and committed sins, like other people."

- 75% did not believe in absolute truth.

- 40% said that if a person is "good" their works will earn them a place in heaven.

- 30% claim that "Jesus Christ was a great teacher, but did not come back to physical life after He was crucified."

- 19% said hell was merely a symbolic term, not a real place.

George Barna's research further noted that church attendance is at an all-time low in the 15 years of his own recordkeeping.

In 1993 George Gallup's organization did extensive new research among the 32% of the adult population in America that claimed to be evangelical. This new study added several modest tests to determine the level of understanding and commitment among those who claimed the new birth. In addition to asking if respondents were born again they also asked questions such as, Do you go to church with some regularity? Do you pray with some regularity? Do you have some formal minimal confession of Christian faith? When these tests were added, the percentage of born-again adults dropped to only 8% of the population in America. Theologian David Wells notes:

> And if we were to probe just a little bit more, and if we were to ask: first "Are you regenerate?"; second, "Do you have a sufficiently cogent worldview to make a difference in society?"; and third, "Do you have a sufficiently formed Christian character to want to do so?", based on some ongoing research I have seen, my guess is that the figure may be no more than 1% or 2%. What this means, my brothers and sisters, is that we may

have been living in a fool's paradise. When Gallup produced his figures in the 1970s, and has repeated them every year ever since, it seemed like evangelicals were on a roll with such wide popular support and with churches that were growing. It looked as though we were on the verge of sweeping all of our religious and cultural opponents before us. That was why these figures stirred such alarm in the secular media, why they created some heartburn in the mainline Protestant denominations, and why they produced just a little power-mongering amongst evangelicals. But it has turned out to be an optical illusion. The reality that we have to face today is that we have produced a plague of nominal evangelicalism which is as trite and as superficial as we have seen in Catholic Europe.[1]

The primary reason Professor Wells suggests for this "plague of nominal evangelicalism" begins with the "crumbling of our theological character." Wells cogently argued in his seminal book, *No Place for Truth*, that theology has "disappeared" in the evangelical world. He wrote, "It is not that theological beliefs are denied, but that they have little cash value. They don't matter."[2]

A great sense of uneasiness exists in our evangelical institutions and organizations. The percentage of people who believe the Bible is inerrant has risen in the past ten years. (I suspect this is the result of the efforts made in the '70s and '80s to explain and affirm inerrancy.) At the same time, the number of people who know the great truths the Bible teaches is at an all-time low. An unpublished, private survey, this one done with seminary students at several evangelical institutions, reveals the magnitude of our problem. This survey demonstrated the following:

- 41% of evangelical seminary students said, "Realizing my full potential as human being is as important as serving other people in ministry."

- 67% saw new insights into the self-life as a major part of their thought and concern in ministry.

- 52% said they spent a great deal of time thinking about themselves.

- 31% affirmed that God was a small influence in shaping their thoughts about who they really are as people.

- 51% said, "I am the primary shaper of who I am as a human person."

- 42% said, "It is in poor taste to tell a person that they are lost without Christ."

This same survey also revealed that these students were regular Bible readers. Over 60% of those surveyed read the Bible every day for at least 15 minutes or more. When asked to choose one category which best described their primary view of God's relationship to mankind, the numbers are staggering:

- 78% say, "God's love includes all people and all should know Him."

- 18% say, "God is holy and evil will not ultimately triumph."

What has brought about this crisis in the evangelical church? Wells is sobering when he concludes, ". . . the centrality of God is disappearing. God now comes to rest inconsequentially upon the church."[3] If 75% of us do not believe in absolute truth, we are, to put it mildly, in a serious crisis akin to a theological free-fall. (Interestingly, the percentage of those who do not believe in absolute truth in the wider culture is 67%.) God is "weightless" in the evangelical world of North America. We still believe in God, but we have rounded off the rough edges and tamed Him. We think of God in terms of a therapeutic relationship. He is there to bring ultimate happiness to us. God, in this environment, is neither heavy nor morally angular, but rather "lite" and rounded.

REVIVAL AND THE PLACE OF DOCTRINE

When historian Gerald R. McDermott wrote a summary article on the evangelical awakening in America and Britain, he noted that "the 18th-century awakening consisted of three massive revivals divided by an ocean, a sea, and thousands of miles." He also observed that, though divided in this way, these revivals were all united by ten common characteristics. He noted as his third characteristic that "revivals were sparked and sustained by the preaching of Reformation doctrines." His full statement is rich with meaning, especially in light of the statistics I've cited that demonstrate the breakdown of modern evangelicalism. McDermott's comments are worth reading in full:

> Revival preachers in the 18th century explicitly denounced "legalistic" and "rationalist" preaching that taught "mere morality." In contrast, they emphasized justification by faith in the atoning death of Christ. Wesley taught the absolute necessity of the new birth, and George Whitefield borrowed from the Wesley brothers, John and Charles, their emphasis on faith alone as the prerequisite for salvation.
>
> Terror was preached before grace by ministers in the Connecticut Valley. They were sons of thunder as well as sons of consolation. In the 1720s, following the lead of Edwards's grandfather, Solomon Stoddard, revivalists were already preaching the terrors of damnation as a prelude to the glorious offer of free grace. Edwards reported that his sermon, "The Justice of God in the Damnation of Sinners," was his most effective tool in the 1734-35 harvest of souls. The sermon was an exposition

of Romans 3:19—"That every mouth may be stopped"—and explained that "it would be just with God forever to reject and cast off mere natural men." If a sinner received grace, there-fore, it was an unmerited act of God's love.[4]

Doctrinal preaching and emphasis has always been linked to sea-sons of real revival. The Word of God is central to revival, and the central doctrines of Scripture are the features of revival.

There is a modern myth, both widely popular and highly destruc-tive, that hinders our thinking about the vital connection between revival and serious theology. This myth says, "Modern man is not interested in theology. We can gain interest among the masses of people only if we forget doctrine and speak more often of felt needs, especially as these felt needs relate to the actual problems people have."

This myth contains an element of truth mixed with a large dose of error. Of course the church should be *relevant* if by this we mean that "we speak so people will hear and understand us." But if relevant means relevant to mankind's *felt* needs, then we must reconsider. What is more relevant than providing the answer for man's eternal need? What is more interesting than pressing the issue of man being eternally lost before a holy God? Nothing in Freud, Rogers, or Skinner can be truly relevant in the light of man's lostness.

When we pray for revival, as we ought, we need to continually remind ourselves that the Holy Spirit never renews the church through *new words*. The Spirit's work is always to lead the church to remember and obey the truths preserved for all time in Scripture. What the church needs today is to recover the great doctrinal truths that were once highlighted in seasons of true revival.

I would like us to consider four such doctrinal truths in the remainder of this chapter. I believe each of these must be recovered before we can address the problems of our own time. If we want to see God move, these truths must be exalted. The Spirit can use the preaching and teaching of these doctrines to grip the hearts of God's people in a mighty way if we set these truths forth with love and clarity.

God's Holiness

In all of the great revivals recorded in history, the awesome reality of God is an absorbing and pressing interest for the multitudes who attend. True revival exalts God in His omnipotence and omniscience. It confronts the church afresh with both the justice and mercy of a sovereign God. As we have seen, the preeminent element of revival here is always an awareness of God's holines.

The prophet Habbakuk prayed for an old covenant restoration in his time. Before he came to ask God for mercy, he acknowledged, "LORD, I have heard of your fame; I stand in awe of your deeds, O LORD" (3:2). Again and again when the patriarchs and the prophets encountered the living and true God, they were filled with terror or awe.

But what about those who believe under the new covenant? "Has not the terror of the Lord been removed?" some people ask. Here are several New Testament texts which readily answer this notion:

> Since we are receiving a kingdom that cannot be shaken, let us be thankful, and so worship God acceptably with reverence and awe, for our God is a consuming fire (Hebrews 12:28-29).

> Therefore, my dear friends, as you have always obeyed—not only in my presence, but now much more in my absence—continue to work out your salvation with fear and trembling, for it is God who works in you to will and to act according to his good purpose (Philippians 2:12-13).

> He said in a loud voice, "Fear God and give him glory, because the hour of his judgment has come. Worship him who made the heavens, the earth, the seas and the springs of water" (Revelation 14:7).

> *Then a voice came from the throne, saying: "Praise our God, all*
> *you his servants, you who fear him, both small and great!"*
> *(Revelation 19:5).*

Repeatedly when the Lord Jesus displayed His divine power to men and women, the response was awe. We read, for example:

> *When the crowd saw this, they were filled with awe; and they*
> *praised God, who had given such authority to men (Matthew*
> *9:8).*

> *Jesus knew what they were thinking and asked, "Why are you*
> *thinking these things in your hearts? Which is easier: to say,*
> *'Your sins are forgiven,' or to say, 'Get up and walk'? But that*
> *you may know that the Son of Man has authority on earth to for-*
> *give sins. . . ." He said to the paralyzed man, "I tell you, get up,*
> *take your mat and go home." Immediately he stood up in front*
> *of them, took what he had been lying on and went home prais-*
> *ing God. Everyone was amazed and gave praise to God. They*
> *were filled with awe and said, "We have seen such remarkable*
> *things today" (Luke 5:22-26).*

After Jesus raised the son of a widow at Nain we read that the people "were all filled with awe" (Luke 7:16). And when we read of the early church, still living in the days following the great outpouring of Pentecost, Luke records that "everyone was filled with awe" (Acts 2:43).

It is not surprising, then, that when the Spirit is poured out upon people in the New Testament era we read that "everyone was filled with awe." And if we want to see the Holy Spirit work mightily in our time, we must recover a proper focus upon the doctrine of God's holiness.

People will not know and fear God as they ought until they know God properly. And they will not know God properly until they hear more fully the doctrine of God. David Wells is sobering in his analysis:

We, today, are actually on the verge of a fresh theological discovery of a very different kind. It is that God is centrally love and that He is only peripherally and remotely holy. And in so doing we are on the verge of standing Scripture on its head. No, the holiness of God is not peripheral. It is central, and without this holiness our faith loses its meaning entirely. As P.T. Forsyth declared a century ago, "sin is but the defiance of God's holiness, grace is but its action upon sin, the cross is but its victory, and faith is but its worship." And so without a compelling vision of the holiness of God, worship inevitably loses its awe, the truth of God's Word loses its interest, obedience loses its virtue, and the church loses its moral authority. And it is precisely here that modernity, which is more or less synonymous with "the world" in the New Testament, has made its deepest intrusion into the life of the church. Modernity has rearranged our appetites.[5]

The biblical concept of holiness has two meanings. The primary idea is "apartness" or "otherness." When we refer to God as holy we thus refer to His transcendence, or majesty. He is superior to all other beings in every way, and He alone is completely worthy of reverence and adoration. This idea is illustrated throughout the Old Testament. For example, the ground that Moses stood upon, as well as the bush he saw burning in the desert, were both holy because God was present.

The second meaning related to the biblical concept of holiness includes the idea of God's purity and righteousness. God does right in everything because God alone is right. His nature is intrinsically holy, thus all that God does must conform to His holy character.

Those who are earnestly praying for revival must labor to restore the centrality of the holiness of God to their churches and ministries. If we will not exalt this truth, then we will not exalt the God who reveals Himself in true revival. We must not grieve the Spirit and put out the fire of revival by ignoring the centrality of God's holiness.

The Centrality of Christ

Clearly, the theme of the entire Bible is the person of Jesus Christ. The mystery of His person begins to unfold in the Old Testament in both shadow and type, by which the elaborate ceremonies and rituals point worshipers forward to the reality which is yet to come openly. In the New Testament He is revealed to us as "the Word [who] became flesh and made His dwelling among us." John speaks of this revelation as "the glory of the One and Only [Son], who came from the father, full of grace and truth" (John 1:14).

The transcendent glory of God was "veiled in flesh" in the incarnation of Jesus. Only at times did this glory break through so as to be seen more directly. The supreme example of this in the New Testament occurs on the Mount of Transfiguration (see Matthew 17:1-13). This glory is not to be revealed in *direct* ways to believers in the present age (see Revelation 22:4-5).

When the Spirit is poured out in greater measure upon the church, the result is always deeper love for Christ, fuller appreciation of His importance, and deeper worship of Him as the Lamb upon the throne.

The sermons of the apostles illustrate my point. They are full of the person and work of Christ. They tell the wonderful story over and over, with no doubt that the Christ they knew and preached was identical with the Jesus of history.

The first sermon preached during a time of New Testament revival exalted Christ with words clearly conveying the centrality of Jesus:

> Men of Israel, listen to this: Jesus of Nazareth was a man accredited by God to you by miracles, wonders and signs, which God did among you through him. . . . But God raised him from the dead. . . . God has raised this Jesus to life. . . . Exalted to the right hand of God. . . . Therefore let all Israel be assured of this: God has made this Jesus, whom you crucified, both Lord and Christ (Acts 2:22,24,32-33,36).

In revival, both Christ and the blood of Christ are central to the emphasis which precedes the Spirit's work. There seems to be at least one reason here for why the communion service has often been an occasion of deep revival among God's people.

At Cambuslang, Scotland (July 1742), the presence of the Lord at the communion observance was so real to all present that it was agreed to again celebrate the Lord's Supper soon. (This is not common in Scottish church life.) The next communion was held in August and over 20,000 attended. Only a few thousand people partook, but multitudes of awakened sinners sought the Lord for salvation and were converted.

Similar events have taken place throughout church history, such as the revival in Madras, India, in 1940. Interestingly, one writer has concluded that the root of the Methodist revival is to be seen in the Lord's Supper.[6]

When George Whitefield came to Cambuslang to preach during this same season of revival he noted that from the strongest man to the smallest child, people fell down, shaking and trembling. Whitefield said, "Nor does this happen only when men of warm address alarm them with the terrors of the law, but when the most deliberate preacher speaks of redeeming love. . . . Talk of a precious Saviour, and all seem to breathe after him."[7]

The law of God must be preached during revival, as sinner and saint alike must be made to see the holiness of God and His divine standard. But against this black backdrop there has always been the loveliness of the person of Christ and the truth of His dying and rising for our justification. David Brainerd remarked that the greatest work done by his preaching among the Susquehanna Indians in the 1740s came "when I insisted upon the compassions of a dying Saviour, the plentiful provisions of the Gospels and the free offers of Divine grace to needy distressed sinners."[8]

When Jonathan Edwards wrote of the revival in Northampton, Massachusetts, he described the centrality of Christ and His cross in the lives of the revived flock by saying:

In all companies, on other days, of whatever occasions persons met together, Christ was to be heard of, and seen in the midst of them. Our young people, when they met, were wont to spend the time in talking of the excellency and dying love of Jesus Christ, the glory of the way of salvation, the wonderful free and sovereign grace of God, His glorious work in the conversion of a soul and the truth and certainty of the great things of God's Word . . .[9]

A similar testimony was recorded by a minister of Golspie (Sutherland) in 1743 when the Holy Spirit came upon the congregation:

The terrors of the Lord denounced in His Word against the willful transgressors of His holy laws, and the impenitent unbelieving despisers of His gospel grace, the impossibility of salvation on the score of self-righteousness; the absolute necessity of the efficacious influences of the grace and Spirit of God, in order to a vital union with Christ by faith, for righteousness and salvation; that all the blessings of the new covenant, freely given by the Father to the elect, and purchased for them by the sufferings and death of Christ the Son, are effectually applied to them by the Holy Ghost—these were the doctrines insisted on to the people of this congregation.[10]

Justification by Faith Alone

True revival, as I have tried to show, always results in a fresh outpouring of the Holy Spirit. The Holy Spirit comes to exalt Christ and His gospel. If those who minister want to be faithful to the Word and the Spirit's witness, then they must make much of Jesus. They must be preachers of the biblical gospel.

Put another way, revival exalts the truth of divine righteousness—first, in demonstrating that there is a righteousness which is *of* God, and second, in demonstrating that there is a righteousness which is *from* God. As we saw earlier, the righteousness *of* God is displayed through exalting God and His holiness. The righteousness *from* God, however, is that righteousness which Christ gives to those who have saving faith in Him (see Romans 1:17). The law shows mankind his need. It reveals that he stands under God's wrath and judgment. The gospel provides the righteousness that God alone can accept. Through the doing and dying of another, Jesus Christ, God will accept the sinner who flees to Christ for safety.

D. Martyn Lloyd-Jones captures the essence of this:

> There has never been a revival but that this has always come back into great prominence. This doctrine means the end of all thinking about ourselves and our goodness, and our good deeds, and our morality, and all our works. Look at the histories of revivals, and you will find men and women feeling desperate. They know that all their goodness is but filthy rags, and that all their righteousness of no value at all. And there they are crying out to God for mercy and for compassion. Justification by faith. God's act. "If God does not do it to us," they say, "then we are lost." And so they wait in utter helplessness before him. They pay no attention, and attach no significance to all their own past religiosity, and all their faithfulness in church attendance, and many, many other things. They see it is all of no good, even their religion is of no value, there is nothing that is of value. God must justify the ungodly. And all that is the great message that comes out, therefore, in every period of revival.[11]

Faith is the *instrument* through which God brings sinners to Christ for salvation. We are not saved by faith, strictly speaking. We often put it this way but this is simply not true. We are saved by *Christ!* Christ saves us because of the amazing grace of God. Faith is only our empty hand taking what God gives to us. "Nothing in my hands I bring, simply to thy cross I cling." We must understand that the believing sinner would never receive the gift of salvation unless God first gave him the gift of faith (Ephesians 2:8-10).

So why all the stress on "faith" and the "righteousness from God" which saves us? Because by keeping everything else out of the saving process but faith alone, we keep out all "works of the law" and stay focused clearly on the One who alone saves.

When a sinner is saved, the Holy Spirit regenerates that person so that he will be brought into union with Christ. The one who believes in Christ is united to Him and is thereby constituted legally righteous on the *sole* basis of the imputation of Christ's righteousness. When sin condemns me, and Satan then accuses me, what is my plea? "It is enough that Jesus died, and that He died for me," responds the hymnwriter. And so it is. The perfect righteousness of Christ is all I need for God to look with favor upon my poor soul. The life and death of Christ alone is sufficient to redeem me for eternity.

In revival, deep impressions of God and His holiness are made upon those truly visited by the Spirit. Sometimes men and women actually fall down under the weight of it. The terror of the law and the holiness of God is just too much for them to take in without a response that affects their entire being (see Romans 3:19-20). How different those scenes are from our own time, in which we see multitudes falling down in hysterical laughter!

Yet it is not falling down under the weight of the law and the terrors of the Lord that will make a person a follower of Christ. Such response does not constitute saving faith. This is where many people have gone wrong, even during times of real revival. They sometimes think they have become acceptable to God because of the sheer depth of their experience during revival. The right way to address this problem is to ask the simple question: How am I righteous before God? The *Heidelberg Catechism* answers with warm clarity:

> Only by a true faith in Jesus Christ; that is, though my conscience accuse me that I have grievously sinned against all the

commandments of God and kept none of them, and am still inclined to all evil, yet God, without any merit of mine, of mere grace, grants and imputes to me the perfect satisfaction, righteousness, and holiness of Christ, as if I had never had nor committed any sin, and myself had accomplished all the obedience which Christ has rendered for me; if only I accept such benefit with a believing heart.[17]

The amount of faith, the sheer strength of faith, the worthiness of faith, or the deep impressions made in coming into the experience of faith—none of these actually save. It is Christ and His righteousness alone that saves. In true revival, this grand truth is wonderfully exalted through the agency of the Holy Spirit.

As I said a moment ago, during revival people fear that they might not be qualified to believe, or at least they often feel they are not yet ready. They see other people suddenly freed of their heavy burdens of sin and wonder why their own burden still remains. Thus they begin to doubt and struggle with whether they are right with God. It is at times like this that they need to be reminded that saving faith has nothing to do with what they are experiencing, and everything to do with believing in the Lord Jesus Christ. If they are not reminded of this glorious truth they will find themselves in even deeper despair.

We have a marvelous illustration of this in Acts 16 when the Philippian jailer is under distress and cries out, "What must I do to be saved?" The simple answer given has brought relief to more than one distressed soul during great outpourings of the Spirit of God: "Believe in the Lord Jesus, and you will be saved—you and your household" (Acts 16:31).

But what about repentance? Some people point out that repentance is not mentioned in the account of the Philippian jailer. The answer to this objection, I believe, is self-evident. The man was under such profound conviction, crying out at the point of a possible suicide, that the answer inherently includes repentance, given the circumstances.

Repentance, as is true with faith, is a gift of the Holy Spirit (Acts 5:31; 11:18). It is a radical change of mind which results in conversion, or turning, from one way to another. Those who are made aware of their need of God's holiness, and of the way of sin and its effects, will gladly turn in repentance if they see Christ as lovely and desirable to their souls. This transaction is the result of the Spirit's work in a person's life.

Repentance and faith are inseparable, yet different. Repentance is the result of sorrow. It leads us to turn about, to change our mind. But faith brings us into union with Christ. It is for this reason that revival is often a time when hearts are plowed deeply by the law and eyes are opened to the need to repent. This is why faith must be properly set before people as the nonmeritorious response (or instrumental cause) by which they receive the gift of eternal life.

Lloyd-Jones is once again a safe guide:

> . . . in the church there is still a good deal, unconsciously, of
> holding on to works, and of regarding this whole matter of sal-
> vation as something that results from what we do—as if we
> could make ourselves Christian people!

> So, it is essential that we should be clear about this great doc-
> trine. It was the thing that revolutionized the life of Martin
> Luther, and ushered in the Protestant Reformation, the thing
> that was again rediscovered in the eighteenth century by
> Whitefield and the two Wesleys, and by Rowland and Harris
> in Wales, and by all these men who were so used of God. It
> was the realization of justification by faith that really led to the
> outpouring of the Spirit. It has always been the case. And so
> we cannot afford to neglect, or to ignore this crucial doctrine.[13]

Regeneration by the Spirit's Power

As justification by faith alone was the material principle of the Protestant Reformation, so regeneration by the sovereign power of the Holy Spirit was the prominent doctrinal emphasis of the great revivals of the eighteenth century in America and Great Britain. George Whitefield refers to this doctrine at least 46 times in his *Journals*. His first publication came in August of 1737. It was a sermon titled, "The Nature and Necessity of Our New Birth in Jesus Christ, in Order to Salvation." The sermon was printed in three editions before the end of 1737, having, as Whitefield said, "sold well to persons of all denominations and dispersed very much at home and abroad."

We must not insist upon slavishly following any single doctrinal emphasis as an end in itself. What we *must* insist upon is the balance of ministry firmly rooted in Scripture. It is worth noting, regarding the revival times of Whitefield and the Wesleys, that "the fact that preaching on regeneration was so universally blessed of the Holy Spirit secures for it further recognition as a salient doctrine in the revival."[14]

William McCulloch had ministered at Cambuslang for over a decade before he chose to preach on subjects "which tend most directly to explain the nature, and prove the necessity, of regeneration." He proceeded to do this for about a year before the truths of his sermons were made real to his hearers in 1742. Eifion Evans, a revival historian, notes that "the same was true at Kilsyth under James Robe's ministry in 1740, and at Llangeitho, under Daniel Rowland's ministry, in 1781."[15]

In an age when multitudes think they have been born again because they have prayed a prayer to "invite Jesus into their hearts" (a phrase never used in this manner in the New Testament) it would behoove us to consider a fresh doctrinal emphasis upon regeneration if we would exalt this great biblical truth so often highlighted in revival seasons. Again I must allow Lloyd-Jones to have the final word on this subject:

> Regeneration. It stands out in the story and in the history of
> every revival that has ever taken place in the long history of the

Christian church. In other words, everything about a revival emphasizes the activity of this sovereign God. He is intervening. He is working. He is doing things. And this is shown very plainly by the results and the effects of the work of regeneration.[16]

THE NECESSITY OF PROCLAIMING DOCTRINE

Human preparations are no substitute for the working of the Spirit. We must be continually reminded that it is "not by might nor by power, but by my Spirit" (Zechariah 4:6). The latest strategies may seem exciting and even be productive but they simply are not the answer. For a while they may appear to bring great blessing but the judgment of such things is not at the end of a meeting but at the end of the age.

The Holy Spirit has worked mightily in the past through ministers and churches that have dealt with God's truth honestly. Only when God is kept central, and Christ and the grace of God are the focus of believing hearts, will we ever see the Spirit be pleased to blow upon the work of Christ with renewing power.

As we have noted in this chapter, at the heart of every great revival have been several God-centered doctrines. In a sentence we might well say that the grace of a sovereign God is central when God moves in revival!

There is a vital connection between distinctive doctrinal preaching and real revival. Many people today appear to believe that clear doctrinal preaching, especially if it addresses what have been called "hard points," will kill the Spirit's work and the hope of revival. The truth is the exact opposite, as has always been the case. The famous nineteenth-century preacher Charles H. Spurgeon saw that revival and distinctive doctrinal preaching were connected. He spoke of this in a sermon to his congregation:

> In the history of the church, with but few exceptions, you could not find a revival at all that was not produced by the

orthodox faith. What was that great work which was done by Augustine, when the church suddenly woke up from the pestiferous and deadly sleep into which Pelagian doctrine had cast it? What was the Reformation itself but the waking up of men's minds to those old truths? However far modern Lutherans may have turned aside from their ancient doctrines—and I must confess some of them would not agree with what I now say—yet, any rate, Luther and Calvin had no dispute about Predestination. Their views were identical, and Luther's *Bondage of the Will* is as strong a book upon the free grace of God as Calvin himself could have written. Hear that great thunderer while he cries in that book, "Let the Christian reader know, then, that God foresees nothing in a contingent manner; but that He foresees, proposes, and acts, from His eternal and unchangeable will. This is the thunder stroke which breaks and overturns Free Will." Need I mention to you better names than Huss, Jerome of Prague, Farel, John Knox, Wickliffe, Wishart, and Bradford? Need I do more than say that these held the same views, and that in their day anything like an Arminian revival was utterly unheard of and undreamed of?

And then, to come to more modern times, there is the great exception, that wondrous revival under Mr. Wesley, in which the Wesleyan Methodists had so large a share; but permit me to say that the strength of the doctrine of Wesleyan Methodism lay in its Calvinism. The great body of Methodists disclaimed Pelagianism, in whole and in part. They contended for man's entire depravity, the necessity for the direct agency of the Holy Spirit, and that the first step in the change proceeds not from the sinner, but from God. They denied at the time that they were Pelagians. Does not the Methodist hold, as firmly as ever we do, that man is saved by the operation of the Holy Ghost, and the Holy Ghost only? And are not many of Mr. Wesley's

sermons full of that great truth, that the Holy Ghost is necessary
to regeneration? Whatever mistakes he may have made, he continually preached the absolute necessity of the new birth by the
Holy Ghost, and there are some other points of exceedingly
close agreement; for instance, even that of human inability. It
matters not how some may abuse us, when we say man could
not of himself repent or believe; yet, the old Arminian standards
said the same. True, they affirm that God has given grace to
every man, but they do not dispute the fact that apart from that
grace there was no ability in man to do that which was good in
his own salvation. And then, let me say, if you turn to the continent of America, how gross the falsehood that Calvinistic doctrine is unfavourable to revivals. Look at that wondrous shaking
under Jonathan Edwards, and others which we might quote. Or
turn to Scotland—what shall we say of M'Cheyne? What shall we
say of those renowned Calvinists, Dr. Chalmers, Dr. Wardlaw,
and before them Livingstone, Haldane, Erskine, and the like?
What shall we say of the men of their school but that, while
they held and preached unflinchingly the great truths which we
would propound today, yet God owned their word and multitudes were saved. And if it were not perhaps too much like
boasting of one's own work under God, I might say, personally, I
have never found the preaching of these doctrines to lull this
church to sleep, but ever while they have loved to maintain these
truths they have agonised for the souls of men, and the 1,600 or
more whom I have baptized, upon profession of their faith, are
living testimonials that these old truths in modern times have
not lost their power to promote a revival of religion.[17]

But why is this so? First, I answer that truths which glorify God
convict sinners deeply. To know that I am utterly sinful and totally
incapable of coming to God on my own lays the foundation for a
work of grace. Second, the grace of God, understood in the manner
we have seen, lifts up the cross of Christ as indispensable for the salvation of sinners. When the law condemns and the self-righteous see

their need for the grace of God the Spirit leads men and women outside themselves to Calvary. Finally, the truth of grace honors God. These exalted truths give to God all the glory for the salvation of the sinner and for the great mercies of revival.

Knowing these things, I must wonder—is our generation, which hears so little of these exalted truths, truly ready for a genuine outpouring of the Spirit?

Part Three

PRACTICAL AND PASTORAL ISSUES

<u>Seven</u>

REVIVALS: THEIR RISE, PROGRESS, AND DECLINE

Man can no more organize revival than he can dictate to the wind.

—John Blanchard

While revivals do not last, the effects of revival always endure.

—F. Carlton Booth

VERY LITTLE THAT happens during seasons of revival is new. All the elements that are powerfully present when God moves across churches and communities can be seen both within Scripture and the history of the Christian church. In a day where confusion regarding revival abounds it is important to note this fact: Revival does not usher people into some new dimension—a kind of twilight zone of deeper, unusual spirituality. Rather, revival brings increased blessing upon the normal ministries of a New Testament church. Preaching, the celebration of the sacraments, outreach and evangelism, clear calls to repentance and faith, God-centered worship—all of these elements should be present throughout this age. During revivals these are present as well. The difference is that during revival the attending power of God upon these elements becomes very evident.

93

Further, we need to understand that a church without the preached Word, without biblical discipline, without the New Testament sacraments of baptism and the Lord's Supper, and without prayer and congregational worship is simply not a church. What is needed when these salient elements are absent—or even in decline, as in thousands of conservative churches in our generation—is serious God-centered reformation. Revival *without* such reformation may bring an increase in mysticism and thus a deepening of problems.

During revival these essential elements of the church are intensified in their effect. A deep impression is made by them upon the lives of worshipers. (Sometimes revival actually brings reformation, but without reformation, as we shall see later, revival will eventually come to little in the long run!)

God expects the church to be obedient in regard to these constituent elements of church life whether we see "showers of blessing" or not. This truth is important to grasp. We may well be faithful to God and never see revival, even though we deeply long for it. We must earnestly pray for heaven-sent abundance in our ministries but we must never quit or give in to the world's agenda in our desire to see mighty harvesting seasons. All of this is said to underscore this point: "Revival is not normal any more than spiritual decline and backsliding are normal. These are opposite ends of the normal life of the church. Revival is supernormal and backsliding is subnormal."[1]

THE NATURE OF TRUE REVIVAL

As I have previously mentioned, both in defining revival and in observing the theological issues that surround it, revivals do not differ in *nature* from the church's experience during nonrevival days. What differs is degree, not kind. We have noted that "what happens in revivals is only a heightening of normal Christianity."[2] Conviction of sin will be deeper in revival. Feelings for Christ and His cause will become quite intense and repentance will become open and dramatic.

At the same time the saving and sanctifying work of the Holy Spirit is not fundamentally different than under normal circumstances. The words of Jesus regarding the Holy Spirit's ministry throughout this age help us to understand this point:

> When he comes, he will convict the world of guilt in regard to sin and righteousness and judgment: in regard to sin, because men do not believe in me; in regard to righteousness, because I am going to the Father, where you can see me no longer; and in regard to judgment, because the prince of this world now stands condemned (John 16:8-11).

The Holy Spirit convicts the mind by the truth. He leads people to confess sin and to trust in the righteousness of Christ alone. He also stirs longings for holiness and love to Christ. These are normal. These form the biblical pattern for the church until the end of this present age. What revival brings is the *intensification* of these normal operations of the Spirit.

SEVERAL NOTES OF CAUTION

A note of caution, sounded by Iain Murray, is greatly needed in this day of confusion:

> It is, therefore a dangerous error to suppose that revivals have some unique ingredient by which their authenticity is to be judged. In times of alleged revival there may be extraordinary excitement; there may be many professions of faith; there may be striking physical phenomena and much emotion; strong men weep or fall to the ground like the jailer at Philippi; but not all these things together are, in themselves, proof that a revival is genuine. Something more is needed. The biblical tests by which the normal work of the Spirit is recognized have to be applied and if that normal work is not found to be present it is certain that, whatever men may claim, there is no biblical revival.[3]

Let me illustrate Murray's point simply. One of the greatest periods of revival in our nation's history was The Great Awakening. Historically there is some warrant for the term. Moral breakdown and religious sleepiness pervaded the churches and the general society in the years before this time. Spiritual fervor and lasting repentance did follow a season of harvest, both in and out of the visible churches. Yet the designation "The Great Awakening" could be considered a misnomer for several reasons. Why?

The term *awakening* is useful. It describes accurately what happens when a person who is spiritually asleep, or "dead in . . . transgressions and sins" (Ephesians 2:1), is aroused to life by the sovereign intervention of the Spirit of God. The term great was used, at least in this instance, because the *number* of souls awakened was large. But we must remember that an awakening is great, in the proper use of the word theologically, even if only one soul is savingly brought to Christ. It was our Lord who said, "I tell you that in the same way there will be more rejoicing in heaven over one sinner who repents than over ninety-nine righteous persons who do not need to repent" (Luke 15:7).

This brings us to one of the inherent dangers so much of the language used in discussion about revivals. If we continually speak about The Great Awakening, do we not run the risk of inferring that when only a few souls come to Christ it is a trivial awakening? The Great Awakening is accurate and useful. I am content to keep the term for historical reasons. But at the same time I am not content to allow the error of incorrect language to remain if it keeps God's people from giving proper glory to the Lord for the "small things" that happen week by week in our midst.

Another danger in any discussion about revival is our tendency to turn our attention from Christ Himself to the servants of Christ. We have seen that every awakening, whether of an individual or of a multitude, flows from the finished work of Christ and the sovereign work of His Spirit. If this is true, then the glory for the awakening properly belongs to the Lamb of God. The natural human tendency, and this is true in awakenings as in other times, is to turn our attention from Christ as the giver of the Spirit, to the servants of Christ.

Samuel Davies, a faithful servant of God who was used widely during the southern awakening in Virginia in the eighteenth century, was much admired. In one of his sermons Davies warned his beloved flock against people's tendency to attribute too much to a servant of God or to a revival itself:

> I must tell my dear friends, that I hope religion in this place is supported by a stronger pillar than such a feeble mortal as I: otherwise, it is a very sorry religion indeed. The eternal God, the rock of ages, is the foundation that supports it; and we should always remember, even in the ardor of friendship, that he is a jealous God; jealous of His honor, and warmly resents it, when any of His poor servants are made the idols of His people, and draw off their regard from Him. And I am afraid, some of you are in danger of this idolatry. I have indeed been shocked at the high character I have heard of myself on this occasion. What am I at best, but an unworthy minister of Christ, by whom some of you have believed?[4]

Unfortunately, many believers today are too quick to praise a human instrument who is said to have brought revival and forget the One who truly made revival possible. What's more, we hear many claims of revival taking place, yet we see little true evidence of the Spirit's working. Davies, quoted above, lived through one of the most wonderful seasons of true revival in American history. At one point he noted that "there has not been of late any such general outpouring of the Spirit, as is necessary to produce a public national reformation. . . ." His honesty is refreshing when put alongside the claims made by so many today. We have far less reason to speak of a widespread revival today, yet the talk of such is heard almost daily. Davies, who knew profound effusions of the Spirit upon his own life and ministry, wrote of himself and his ministry:

> I have but little, very little, true religion. . . . Perhaps once in
> three or four months I preach in some measure as I could
> wish. . . . It is really an afflictive thought that I serve so good a
> Master with so much inconstancy. . . . I am at best smoking
> flax; a dying snuff in the candlestick of his church. . . . The
> flame of divine love, sunk deep into the socket of a corrupt
> heart, quivers and breaks, and catches, and seems just expiring
> at times.[5]

When God moves in revival, a sense of His holiness and majesty inevitably fills mortals with awe and solemnity. Whereas evangelicals in our day are eager to say that they are seeing revival and often quick to promote their personal role in such, evangelicals like Samuel Davies were extremely reticent to claim anything. We could stand to learn from men like Samuel Davies, who knew God with such an enlarged heart and mind.

THE RISE OF TRUE REVIVAL

True revival often begins where there is little or no expectation. Sometimes revival results when Christians see the need and take time to seek God in earnest prayer. At other times, revival breaks out even though few people seem concerned at all. In either case it is God who interrupts the flow of history and sends a new outpouring of His Spirit to "revive us again in the midst of the years." This latter fact should serve as an encouragement to us, for it appears that the need for revival is great and people's real interest in true revival still quite small.

The Rise of Revival Biblically

Descriptions of revival abound throughout Scripture, especially in a number of prophetic statements that look ahead to the days of this peresent age. A good example can be seen in the prophecy of Amos: "'The days are coming,' declares the Lord, 'when the reaper will be overtaken by the plowman and the planter by the one treading grapes'" (Amos 9:13). This prophecy recalls the promise of Leviticus 26:3-5 and points to a true solution to the miseries wrought by Israel's famine. The following comments on this text are helpful:

> These promises are not primarily, far less exclusively, about the agricultural effects of the Fall. The primary focus is upon the abundant life—spiritual and temporal—of the kingdom of God. This applies to the church in the present age and to the church in the glory of the heavenly kingdom. It is the church preaching Christ to a world in deep trouble. It is the Lord adding to the church daily those who are being saved (Acts 2:47). It is the establishment of Christian families and covenant life in the home (Deuteronomy 6:6-9; Ephesians 6:1-4). It is God-honouring industrial relations (Ephesians 6:5-9; 1 Peter 2:13-25). It is government upholding national righteousness (Proverbs 20:26; Romans 13:1-7). It is Jesus Christ converting sinners to Himself and leavening His world with the light of the gospel—put into practice through a lively obedience to the whole Word of God. This will continue till the end of our age and issue in the perfect glory of the church in heaven.[6]

What Amos described is the glory of the new covenant. Amos had in view, prophetically, the age of the New Testament. This is the age which will culminate in the future glory of the new heavens and the new earth. This age is pictured by Amos's prophecy in terms of both its *present* and *future* state. (This was a common trait in the prophetical writings of the Old Testament.) The gospel advances in a hostile and unbelieving world. This will be true till the end of the age. At the time of Christ's crucifixion gross spiritual darkness pervaded the entire planet, and the knowledge of God was limited to only a handful of people in a very small area of the globe. But from this tiny beginning of 120 believing disciples the gospel spread powerfully throughout the Roman Empire in just a few decades. "The fullness of time" had arrived. Eventually the message of the cross spread onward to the ends of the earth, and is still spreading today. The kings of this earth have made their war against the Lamb and against His "called, chosen and faithful followers" but "the Lamb will overcome" them all (Revelation 17:14). This spiritual battle continues (2 Corinthians 10:4), but it will culminate in the victory of the King when He comes in His glorious advent at the end of the age. The present battle ebbs and flows, but as one commentator observes: "There are times of spiritual revival and reformation and periods of relative decline, all varying with time and place. But the spread of the gospel continues on towards the goal. . . ."[7]

Now, the prophecy of Amos underscores a central truth regarding revival that is one of its great distinguishing marks: True revival is completely beyond the control of human beings! We cannot start a revival, and we can never determine where the next one will take place. There is, simply put, a mystery about these "effusions." Where ministers and missionaries have labored for years, with little or no harvest, all of a sudden God sends a shower and the growth is so great the churches can hardly contain the blessing.

As Amos indicates, the seed must be sown at all times. The church does this when she preaches the Word of God faithfully (see Matthew 13:1-23). Note, however, that the response to this seed is never in the hands of the sower. It is God who must give the increase. In revival, the increase, as we have seen, is truly plenteous—to the point of being staggering. In Amos's analogy, the sower sows the seed, then the reaper reaps the harvest. But note that even after the harvest is gathered in and the plowman returns to the field again, the harvesting still continues. As one observed: "An ordinary sowing results in an extraordinary reaping! It is immediately obvious that such a transformation is the work of God and is beyond all human control."[8] This point is profoundly true in the rise and progress of true revival. The harvest is often unexpected. The size is beyond any plans. And the origin of the blessing is clearly God. Planning committees, no matter how earnest, cannot decide when to *initiate* a visitation of God!

The Rise of Revival Historically

Some years ago I heard a theologian say, "No one living in the West who was born after World War II has witnessed a genuine revival." I thought about this comment for some time and concluded that he was essentially correct. Unless you have lived or traveled widely outside of the western nations, you have not witnessed a large-scale national awakening. (In Canada, the United States, and even in Great Britain, *some* Christians have witnessed regional and at times group revivals, such as Saskatchewan [1971-72], the "Jesus Movement" [the early 1970s], the revival on the Isle of Lewis [1949-53], and so on). But the large and expansive revivals that clearly marked the progress of the church in North America and Europe for centuries have not been witnessed in recent decades. However, outside the western nations, revivals still occur.

THE FIRST GREAT AWAKENING

True revivals came frequently to the churches of New England in the first few generations of Christianity on this continent. Jonathan Edwards, in writing about The Great Awakening, noted that his grandfather's church in Northampton, Massachusetts, had experienced five different moves of the Holy Spirit before the one so distinctly noted by church historians (1679, 1683, 1696, 1712, and 1718). In the 1730s and 1740s America's so-called First Great Awakening swept through many churches with great force and effect. God used marvelous preachers such as Jonathan Edwards, the brothers William and Gilbert Tennent, and the itinerant evangelist George Whitefield to arrest the people's attention and to passionately put before them their need for true repentance. Before this season of awakening, the American colonies stood at a very low ebb morally and spiritually. Family life was breaking down at alarming rates. Drunkenness and drug use were at an all-time high and sex outside of marriage was considered acceptable by alarming numbers of people. Occultism was rampant and the church's response to it very often unbiblical (e.g., the response to witches, the infamous Salem trials, and so on).

After the season of revival things changed dramatically. How did this marvelous revival begin? What was the actual progress of this move of God? The answer to those questions provides some interesting material for thought regarding the *how* of God's moving in true revival.

Jonathan Edwards, the great theologian and preacher of Northampton made it his practice to preach the law and the gospel in typical Reformation and Puritan fashion. What do I mean?

Though the law of God is useful for guarding against crime and protecting society in the public sphere, its primary *theological* use has always been to intensify the will of God (e.g., Sermon on the Mount) so that the sinner cannot stand before God confident in his own righteousness. The law, used in this manner, reveals the "exceeding sinfulness of sin" and accuses us. It has the effect of delivering us over to wrath, judgment, and spiritual death. To some extent every person has some knowledge of this reality (see Romans 1:18-32), yet at the same time most people do not experience this "accusing work" unless the Holy Spirit moves upon their heart through the preaching of the law. The law shows human beings the actual extent of their estrangement from God. If preachers only give people the gospel, as is commonly done in evangelical churches in our time, then people will never understand their true need. (Ministers often avoid saying anything about the law because they are afraid they will frighten their flock and keep them from the gospel. The truth is that people will eventually refuse to hear the gospel without the proper preaching of the law.)

We can illustrate this spiritual problem using a medical scenario. Consider a person who has a radical cancer. The doctor, who very much wants to avoid frightening the patient, decides to pursue a significant plan of treatment without telling the person the reason for the treatments. The medical problem is life-threatening, but the doctor is "too nice" to tell the truth and warn the patient about the effects of chemotherapy. Without the doctor's warnings, the patient will experience all types of problems resulting from chemotherapy and will have no knowledge as to why they are happening.

I'm sure you'll agree with me that for a doctor to act in such a way is medically and psychologically absurd. To preach repentance and faith in Christ without proclaiming the problem of sin is to hide important facts from the "patient."

When early American pastors preached the Word, they did not hesitate to point out specific sins that were a violation of God's holy character as revealed in the law. Edwards, for example, clearly cited irreverence for the household of faith, desecration of the Lord's Day, disobedience to parents, neglect of family worship and prayer, quarreling, sensuality, greediness, and hatred for one's neighbor as sins that condemn those who engage in them. He challenged the dullness of his people directly and earnestly pleaded with them to repent. The ground of people's hearts was plowed through such preaching and serious pastoral labor, and it's this kind of labor that is often the precursor to authentic revival.

Edwards also encouraged his young people to form small groups for serious prayer. Some adults joined these meetings as well. After two young people died in separate incidents, a growing seriousness touched the lives of many. And in the year 1734 Edwards began a series of sermons on the doctrine of justification by faith alone. (This doctrine has often been at the heart of true revival!)

As his sermons progressed, one lady in the Northhampton church came under profound conviction. In a powerful way she saw her need for becoming rightly related to God on the sole basis of Christ's imputed righteousness, received by faith alone. She was wonderfully converted. A spark was lit that kindled a fire which spread quickly throughout the Connecticut River valley. Over the next six months Edwards saw nearly 300 people converted in Northampton. (This was a town of only 1,200 people!) He was so amazed at this rise of true and vital religion among his people that he coined this helpful description of revivals: "surprising works of

God." Soon the story of the Northampton revival spread. The news of the events in Northampton was used to kindle further interest elsewhere. The Spirit of God seemed to come frequently with amazing power upon different groups of people, much as the tides of the seas keep coming upon a shoreline during seasons of high tide.

Thousands of people were soon added to churches all across New England. The revival reached its climax in 1740-42. In October 1740, George Whitefield came to Northampton after he read Jonathan Edwards's famous account of the events of 1734-35 in his book *Narrative of Surprising Conversions*. Edwards would later write a letter to a Boston minister explaining how a fresh awakening had once again come to his flock. He noted that the entire town seemed transformed by an unusual consciousness of God's presence. (Which is one of the marks of true revival, as we saw earlier.) During the summer of 1741, meetings sometimes went right through the night.

It was during that summer that Edwards would preach what eventually became the most famous sermon in American history: "Sinners in the Hands of An Angry God." Edwards had actually preached from the same text several times previously. In fact, he had preached virtually the same sermon in June of 1741 to his own congregation in Northampton. But in July, while serving as a guest preacher in Enfield, Connecticut, he preached this sermon again. This time it came with remarkable effect. The Holy Spirit attended this meeting with an "effusion" of "unction." One listener wrote, ". . . before the sermon was done—there was great moaning and crying out through the whole house—What shall I do to be saved?—the shrieks and crys [sic] were piercing and amazing—amazing[ly] and astonishing[ly] was the power of God seen. . . ."

Edwards's sermon became almost synonymous with the awakening itself. (It must be noted that this sermon was only one small part of the whole of what was preached during these years of revival.) Isaac Watts wrote in his printed copy of this famous sermon words that I think still carry profound balance and insight: "A most terrible sermon which should have had a word of Gospel at the end of it, though I think 'tis all true." Even in the rise and progress of true revival, mistakes in both content and balance are often made. As long as there is a human element, which there always must be, this should be expected.

During the years that followed the Northampton visitation, revival fire spread across the East. The effects of the ministry of the brothers Gilbert and William Tennent and the labors of the English itinerant George Whitefield were both marvelously used by God to ignite the further rise of revival interest.

THE SECOND GREAT AWAKENING

By 1770 the tide of The Great Awakening had gone out. The country was again in a declining state morally and spiritually. It has been noted that less than 5 percent of the population attended church on the eve of the American Revolution. The war for independence drained the people both financially and spiritually. The pioneering of the western frontier added to the social upheaval and morality took a serious downturn. The rugged individualism of the new frontier movement caused a breakup of family life as well as commitment to the church.

The Revolutionary War effort brought great social changes and strange new philosophies that threatened to blanket the American colonies with open and aggressive infidelity. The writings of Thomas Paine, made available through new publishing ventures, reached growing numbers of readers, spreading both deism and rank unbelief. Robbers and slaves traders were a rough and ready lot who added to the increased social decay.

Colleges, once Christian in their orientation, were now staffed with prominent faculty members who were "freethinkers." These popular professors regularly attacked biblical faith. Christianity was in such disregard that most believers on campus—and there were only a few of them—met in secret and in some cases kept minutes of their gatherings in code in order to avoid persecution. In some instances rebellious students actually disrupted worship services with their profanity. As was done during the Vietnam era, students blocked the entrance to some college buildings, burned others, and in general wreaked havoc. Several college presidents were forced to resign under the stress of the times.

By 1795 Yale, a previously strong Christian institution, had only 12 students who openly professed their faith in Christ. This sad situation was the same all across the colonies. But at Yale a change would shortly ensue. Timothy Dwight, the grandson of Jonathan Edwards, was inaugurated as president of Yale in September of 1795. The student body was afraid that their right to free speech might be curtailed by Dwight. They decided to challenge the president to a debate with them. He agreed, and they chose as the topic: "Are the Scriptures the Word of God?" Dwight powerfully and logically took each of their arguments and destroyed them. In 1796 he preached a noted sermon: "The Nature and Danger of Infidel Philosophy." He strongly encouraged the students to turn back to biblical Christianity. In the providence of God the situation began to turn. God stirred many hearts and the mercies of a divine interruption touched Yale again. By 1802 it is noted that one-third of the student body professed faith in Christ openly. This, in effect, was the beginning of a new wave of spiritual awakenings that touched Andover, Princeton, Amhurst, and other colleges. Waves of this rising tide swept across campuses for the next 40 or 50 years! The trustees of these schools appointed presidents who were ardent believers. These presidents helped to change the faculties by replacing unbelievers with godly men. Many of these new leaders facilitated major changes in policy and campus outlook. Campus days of prayer and college meetings (during which students would hear preaching) became regular features for decades to follow. The "Day of Prayer" became a feature of college life.

These college meetings also resulted in the spread of revival to the churches. A new itinerant evangelist, Asahel Nettleton, was greatly used to bring awakening to many of the same areas that had been visited 60 years earlier. Ministers promoted prayer meetings at their churches, and large numbers of converts were often born at those meetings! The spiritual tide of these visitations spread to the western frontier, especially through the new Methodist movement. Camp meetings followed, drawing huge crowds on the Kentucky frontier for days of meetings which included direct and powerful preaching. At times anti-Christian sorts would come to interrupt these meetings only to become powerfully converted.

Many historians, both secular and Christian, have noted that this new wave of revival, sometimes called The Second Great Awakening, put the young nation solidly upon a moral and religious footing that kept it from falling into a pit of lawlessness that might have destroyed it before it became strong and prosperous in the decades ahead. During the first half of the nineteenth century the nation's population increased fourfold. During these same years the church increased *tenfold!* Amazingly, by 1834 the total annual income of all the benevolent societies rivaled the budget of the entire federal government. We cannot say that the nation was converted; it never will be. Yet the effects of decades of divine visitation upon the churches were felt in every corner of society.

REVIVAL IN THE LATE 1850S

Another great revival began in the late 1850s, just prior to the Civil War. By this time materialism and greed had gripped many people, including professing Christians everywhere. The Industrial Revolution had made its mark. Slavery and related issues (prison reform, temperance, and so on) had badly divided people. Political and social agitators of all sorts had arisen north and south. Families were divided and the nation was on the brink of its greatest disruption ever. When the appalling gloom was at its worst, a new emphasis upon prayer arose. The story is again indicative of how revival rises and grows.

Jeremiah Lanphier, a Dutch minister, started a prayer meeting in the old Dutch Reform Church in New York City in September 1857. On the first day, after a prolonged wait, six people came to pray with Lanphier. Then, during the next week, 23 businessmen showed up. The third week there were 40, and by October 14 over 100. This was the day of the great economic collapse. The nation entered a prolonged and deep depression. Within the next month every room in the church was filled with praying businessmen. Within six months 150 such meetings were taking place across New York City, with 50,000 men in attendance. In due course every major city of the nation had similar prayer meetings going on. Many reports suggest that conversions numbered as many as 50,000 people per week, at least during part of this time. The Spirit of God was moving in revival. It has been estimated, conservatively, that over one million people were converted during this two-year period from late 1857 to late 1859. If this is accurate, then 1 in 30 adults were savingly joined to Christ in this short space of time. All the orthodox Protestant denominations benefited remarkably from this blessing as the records of the time indicate. To get an idea of how this would compare to our day, imagine about 8-10 million people experiencing true conversions in a matter of a few weeks—without the programs and plans and the massive human engineering of our age.

A whole new generation of preachers was called into service. Seminaries were again on the rise and almost every denomination in America planned new schools. Missionary candidates came forward as never before because large numbers of college students were soundly converted and eager to obey Christ as their Lord. In the next few years another wave of revival would sweep through the South during the bloody Civil War. This revival especially touched thousands of soldiers in the Southern armies. (This appears to be one of several reasons for the maintenance of a stronger Bible-based faith in the South for a longer period of time than was known in the more industrial North. Only since Vietnam has the "Bible Belt" begun to look much more like the rest of the nation religiously.)

THE TEMPORARY NATURE OF REVIVALS

No revival lasts forever. This is as it must be. But why? Well, as we have seen, revival is a shower, an effusion. Showers do not last; they are not meant to last. But the *effects* of a shower does last.

Though many people are skeptical of the fruit that results during revivals, the evidence is that authentic revivals bring real blessing and lasting fruit. Let me illustrate personally.

I was affected by the revival showers that visited several college and seminary campuses in 1969-70. This was a season in which revival touched part of the wider youth culture ("The Jesus Movement") as well as Christian young people in college and seminary. The times were tumultuous and society was in upheaval. God came upon a number of us with great blessing. The revival shower was brief, but the effects in my life have been lasting. The beginning was unplanned and the ending was almost as sudden. The "dew of heaven" remained but the showers lasted for only 72 hours.

Several years ago I attended the twenty-fifth reunion of my graduating college class. A number of people from that class gave witness to lasting life changes that came in early 1970. Others, who appeared to be passed by during those few unusual days, seemed almost oblivious to the whole matter. I could not help but note the differences God's Spirit had made in the lives of many of us. The 1960s were a decade during which my college, like many of that time, had reached the lowest spiritual point in its history. This could be seen in a number of ways. For example, a continually declining number of students were interested in missions and Christian service all through the 1960s. But in 1970 the numbers began to climb again. Before the revival came there was little concern for "Christ and His Kingdom," but after the showers of blessing many students expressed new interest in matters related to eternity and the claims of Christ.

Revivals, then, do not last. Sometimes revival transforms a church, a college, or even a community. The activity lasts for several weeks only to be all but forgotten within a few months or years. Yet those whose lives were touched have been changed for life. There have been some exceptions to this pattern of brief showers where sweeping revivals have lasted for years, as in some of the accounts I have given. Whatever the case, one thing is certain:

The collective value of revivals in terms of godless lives changed for time and saved for eternity, godless communities "cleaned up," missionaries sent out and God honoured in the worship of hundreds and even hundreds of thousands of new converts, cannot be disputed.[9]

Sometimes revivals fail to make progress and even end abruptly because leaders fail to lay a solid foundation in the Word of God. Other times they fail because people become so preoccupied with the phenomena of the revival—the noise and the physical effects— that they lose sight of the glory of Christ. At still other times no clear human reason for the decline or the end of a revival can be discovered. William Haslam correctly noted that "as a fact, it is well known that revivals begin and continue for a time, and then they cease as mysteriously as they began."[10] Brian Edwards adds, "A gradual slowing down in any revival is inevitable and is no necessary criticism of revival itself. After all, the full force of Pentecost did not last for ever."[11]

Though human error and failure may cause some revivals to wane or die, the simple fact is that revival doesn't last because revival, as we have seen, is not the *normal life* of the church. D. Martyn Lloyd-Jones made this observation:

> There are not only the great experiences but also the ordinary, everyday experiences, and a church that is always praying for a continual revival is a church that has not understood her mission. The church is not meant always to be in a state of revival but is also to do ordinary, everyday work. But some remember this fact so well that they forget that the church is meant to have special occasions![12]

Dr. Lloyd-Jones understood that there is mystery in God's ways of grace, especially in those special seasons called revival. The commencement, duration, and termination of revival is all in God's hands. We can no more end a revival than we can begin one! "Only those profoundly ignorant of the working of the Holy Spirit speak of revival in this way."[13]

Since we cannot organize revival, are we left to "wait" and do nothing? The answer lies just below the surface of the question. Never does the great sovereign of the church encourage inactivity but rather believing, hope-filled anticipation which considers the greatness of His promises. A careful consideration of the richness of God's mercy joined with the wideness of His plan for the nations (see Romans 11) can only fill worshiping saints with great hope for tomorrow.

Eight

PRAYER: THE CATALYST OF REVIVAL

Every true prayer is a variation on the theme "Thy will be done."

—John R.W. Stott

When prayers are strongest, mercies are nearest.

—Edward Reynolds

That which God abundantly makes the subject of His promises, God's people should abundantly make the subject of their prayers.

—Jonathan Edwards

Prayer flows from doctrine.

—John Calvin

THE LATE YALE professor Kenneth Scott Latourette, one of our century's most eminent church historians, demonstrated that the progress of Christianity has always been marked by stages of advance followed by periods of decline.[1] These periods of decline are generally followed by periods of recovery and blessing. Latourette compared this historical pattern to the ocean, which comes up on the earth's shorelines during high tide and then retreats during low tide. Whether it is advance or retreat, there is always movement. Because the church is not a static institution but a living organism, this is exactly what we should expect.

Professor Keith Hardman, a modern student of revival movements, has made this observation:

113

> The great awakenings over the centuries—the amazing spread of
> the early church despite persecutions, the Franciscan move-
> ment, the reformation, the Puritan awakening in England, the
> great awakenings in America and Britain, the worldwide mis-
> sionary movement of the nineteenth century, and the Welsh
> revival [1904]—are all examples of the periodic nature of
> Christian advance.[2]

Revivals are periodic historical recoveries of the people of God after seasons of judgment. These seasons of judgment are marked by spiritual decline, even apostasy. The principle of revival, as we have discovered, is taught throughout the Bible. But such revival never comes in a vacuum. In every biblical account we might survey it is to be distinctly noted that God always employs *means* in His operations in the world.

The means that God uses to ignite a revival are simple. There are only two, and both can be observed continually throughout the New Testament. In fact, these means are so very simple that we run the risk of thinking there has to be more for us to do in terms of human responsibility.

First, when you study revival long enough you inevitably find that there were people praying for revival when God poured out His Spirit upon the church. Sometimes there were only a few people praying, even just one or two. At other times there have been large numbers of earnest intercessors. Because this varies, we can know that the number of people who are praying is not the real issue. (A danger in our time might well be our tendency to think that the more intercessors we can enlist to pray together, the more likely it will be for God to pour out His Spirit upon us.)

Second, God has always used a variety of people in revival. Most of the central figures in a divine visitation have been people who are engaged in some form of preaching or speaking. This preaching might have been on a college campus, in the open air, or in the pul-pit of a local church. Some of these preachers were great scholars and college presidents; others were settled ministers in local churches. More often than not these preachers were itinerant ministers who traveled from place to place and engaged in apologetics and evangelism. No matter what the backgrounds of these speakers, they all had one thing in common: They preached the Word of God with clarity, simplicity, and great boldness!

In revival, then, God does not act in "bare" divine sovereignty. When God "rends the heavens" (Isaiah 64:1-2) with a great extension of grace He always accomplishes this work through human agents. For this reason it is very beneficial to look at several revival leaders and to observe how the two principal means of igniting revival were part and parcel of their labors. Such consideration may well fuel the fire of a new generation of praying believers who will cry night and day, "Do it again, Lord. Revive Your people according to Your Word!"

Prayer's Connection with Revival

Dr. A.T. Pierson once said, "There has never been a spiritual awakening in any country or locality that did not begin in united prayer." That might well be true, but wrong conclusions are often drawn from this fact by modern evangelicals. They hear that prayer always preceded past revivals, so they go out and organize large groups of people with the intention of bringing revival through the commitment to prayer by large numbers of intercessors.

The assumption is that if the prevalence and effect of true prayer is intimately connected to the rise and progress of true revival, then surely revival will come if we bring together a large number of people who pray earnestly. The theology behind this thinking is generally not spelled out, but Charles G. Finney reasoned in the last century that millions of people were in hell because "the prayer of faith was not prayed."[3]

We must understand: The effects and results of the work of Christ are not determined by our efforts. God does ordain that prayer will be a means of divine blessing, and the Holy Spirit Himself stirs up the very same prayer He intends to answer (see Romans 8:26-27). He is the true intercessor, and our hearts are His altar. Yet we must never think of our prayer as a means to get what we want from God. Prayer is best understood as "an offering up of our desires unto God for things agreeable to his will, in the name of Christ, with confession of our sins, and thankful acknowledgment of his mercies."[4]

Why, then, is prayer necessary for Christians? "Because it is the chief part of the thankfulness which God requires of us, and because God will give His grace and Holy Spirit to those only who with hearty sighing unceasingly beg them of Him and thank Him for them."[5]

We are to continually ask God for His grace and for the Holy Spirit, and that "with hearty sighing." In addition we should "unceasingly beg" these gifts from God, for this is God's clear appointment (see Luke 11:9-13). What counts in our praying is not our organizing or our planning. What really counts is the presence and divine influence of the Holy Spirit. If we organize to pray, even gathering huge assemblies for concerts of prayer, and do not understand the nature and purpose of prayer, we are misguided from the outset. And if we gather to display our oneness yet can't even define and defend the gospel itself, then for what are we actually praying? If the modern church desires to pray aright for revival, we must regain a proper understanding of prayer's true role in revival.

A Brief History of Prayer and Revival

Consistent Pattern

The early church was "birthed" in a prayer meeting and prospered in the same air. A simple reading of the book of Acts shows that time and again prayer preceded the outpouring of a fresh enduement of power (termed "boldness") by the Spirit.

This pattern can be observed throughout church history. One of the greatest periods of church growth in the first centuries of Christianity came between A.D. 260-303. During these decades the church suffered wave after wave of persecution. Every believer was a witness, a word which literally meant "martyr." Every situation was an opportunity for preaching the gospel, whether formally or informally. The truth of Acts 1:8 was experienced afresh as faithful disciples of Christ received power and became "witnesses in Jerusalem, and in all Judea and Samaria, and to the ends of the earth." The number of believers in Asia Minor is reported to have been half of the total population of the area! While the social/political structures of the world were failing the church was prospering and reaching out to the remotest parts of the Roman Empire.

In the twelfth century, Peter Waldo, a remarkable leader and man of prayer, was used by God in the outbreak of a revival among the people of Italy and the Alps. His followers were known as Waldensians and the seeds for great missionary recovery were once again sown in times of prayer. This movement had a much wider effect than many people have recognized.

By 1315, still 200 years before the Reformation, there were as many as 800,000 believers in the region of Bohemia alone. These Bohemian evangelicals—profoundly influenced by John Huss, a man of deep personal prayer—planted churches, preached widely, and prepared the ground for the outpouring of the Spirit that would come during the time of Martin Luther.

In the fourteenth century it was John Wycliffe who gave the Bible to the people of England. Wycliffe used Scripture alone to expose the heresies of the Roman Catholic Church and founded a society of witnesses known as the Lollards. These men, along with Wycliffe, were known for their remarkable commitment to prayer.

In 1489 Savanarola, one of the greatest preachers ever to grace the Christian church, was converted in Florence. Savanarola began to preach the doctrines of heaven and hell with great conviction. So widely known was his preaching that the Turkish Muslim Sultan had the sermons translated so that he could read them. A man of prayer, Savanarola sometimes spoke to crowds as large as 10-20,000 people. When he was persecuted by corrupt church leadership, his motto became, "As for me, prayer."

Martin Luther, the greatest reformer of all time, was a great theologian. He was also a great man of prayer. Sometimes he prayed for two or three hours in a single day. When he faced the Diet of Worms in 1521, his life was on the line. He was instructed to recant his writings which spoke against the Roman Church. He spent the evening alone, pondering what he should say and do. A spy observed that he was on his knees until daybreak. The spy, so we are told, returned to his masters saying, "Who can overcome such a man who prays thus?"

John Calvin, the master of Geneva, would study into the evening and then rise to pray as early as 4:00 A.M. John Knox, the Scottish reformer, cried out to God in earnest prayer, "Give me Scotland, or I die!" The story of one reformer after another follows this same pattern. They studied the Word, prayed, and preached. The mercies of heaven fell with frequent blessing upon their labors.

Richard Baxter, the famous minister of Kidderminster, England in the seventeenth century, gave to the church one of the greatest models of pastoral care ever devised by a parish minister. When he arrived at his new church he found that the spiritual health of the people was extremely poor. Only a few in the little village bothered with Christianity at all. Baxter began to pray. It has been said that "he prayed until the walls of his study became stained with his breath." He then began a visitation ministry, calling upon every home in his area. He encouraged each home to establish a family worship time. He showed them how to do this and then invited each family to attend the parish church. Within a few years the church was again crowded. Scores of people were converted and his classic work, *The Reformed Pastor*, has since touched generations of ministers with the hope of true revival in the local church.

In 1630 a wonderful revival came to the Scottish town of Shotts. John Livingstone, a young minister, was asked to speak. He became so afraid that he fled. As he hid in the wheat fields during the night he prayed on his face before God. A group searched for him and upon finding him set up an open air pulpit and asked him to preach. At one meeting, about 500 people were converted.

Moving onto the eighteenth century, we find that men such as John Wesley, Charles Wesley, George Whitefield, Howell Harris, and Daniel Rowland were all men of prayer as well. The power conveyed in their preaching was beyond anything their hearers had previously known. Though they had some doctrinal differences, one thing held true for all of these evangelists: They prayed and continually urged others to pray with them.

Jonathan Edwards spent whole days—and sometimes entire nights—in prayer. His record of heartfelt dealings with God are still a treasure to people today. His pulpit ministry, mightily used by God in revival, was always a ministry of the Word that knew the power of the Spirit. For him, the connection of power with sound preaching was clearly linked by prayer.

A great revival came to Cambuslang, Scotland, in 1742. The pastor of the church, William McCullough, had heard about the revivals that had taken place in America and England. He prayed and asked God to visit his parish. Later, George Whitefield came to Scotland and was used by God in Cambuslang. A great awakening occurred and so many people came that it was necessary to conduct open-air meetings, with 10-12,000 in attendance.

In the nineteenth century revival came once again. A visitation took place in Scotland at Kilsyth in 1839. The pastor was a young man named William Chalmers Burns. He told his people the story of the revival in nearby Shotts in 1630. He stood before the people and then lifted his hand to heaven to plead with God to do it again. As he prayed God was pleased to come upon the people with remarkable effect. Many were soundly converted and revival blessings began to flow once again. When Burns visited Dundee the mercies followed there as well.

An Illustration from One Denomination

In later-seventeenth-century Britain one of the most thriving fellowships was the Calvinistic Baptists. From the early 1640s, with only seven churches, they had grown to nearly 300 congregations by

1689, which was when they issued The London Confession of Faith. These growing Baptist churches were marked with a passion for the lost. John Bunyan, a part of this denomination, had been used mightily to kindle a fire among his fellow ministers. A slice of the history of this denomination will help to illustrate for us the relationship between prayer, revival, and mission.

From 1660 to 1688 England enforced laws against all religious groups that were outside the state church. When Bunyan was arrested for violating this law he was put on trial and accused of having "devilishly and perniciously abstained from coming to Church to hear Divine Service" and of "being a common upholder of several unlawful meetings and conventicles, to the great disturbance and distraction of the good subjects of the kingdom, contrary to the laws of our sovereign lord the king." Bunyan was told that if he would simply desist from preaching he could go free. He refused, and as a result remained in prison for years. For John Bunyan, the ultimate authority was not the King of England but rather the King of Kings! As one historian writes:

> Bunyan . . . also knew that the Spirit of God had given him a
> gift for preaching, a gift that had been confirmed by the con-
> gregation of which he was a member. For Bunyan, the claims
> of God and his belief that he is called to preach outrank his
> loyalty to his earthly monarch. Bunyan had to obey his God,
> otherwise on the day of judgment he would be "counted a trai-
> tor to Christ." And because Bunyan would not waver in his
> convictions he spent roughly twelve years in prison, from
> 1660-1672.[6]

Amazingly, when freedom and toleration came to the Baptists in 1689 the denomination began to plateau in its growth. By 1750 the number of churches had declined to only 150. Several reasons may have prompted this decline, but none had such chilling effect as the rise of a new theological position known as High Calvinism. The

Baptist ministers who held to this position would not urge the lost to come to Christ. They were so afraid of interfering with the Holy Spirit's work in regenerating dead sinners that they did not wish to urge people to do what they were powerless to do without effectual grace.

When the revival showers of the 1730s descended upon hundreds of churches in Britain, these same Baptists were both cautious and critical. Not only were the two Wesley brothers Arminian in their doctrine but revival leaders such as the Wesleys openly criticized these Baptists. Charles Wesley, for example, once commented that these confessional Baptists are "a carnal . . . contentious sect, always watching to steal away our children, and make them as dead as themselves." Though Whitefield was himself a Calvinist, a number of his critics who were Baptists saw him as weakened by what they termed his "Arminian accent."

For many decades these Baptists resisted the revival of their time because they saw the Church of England as having, in John Gill's words, "neither the form nor matter of a true church, nor is the Word of God purely preached in it." Their chief interest was in preserving what they saw to be proper church life.

In the words of historian Michael Haykin:

> The Baptists did not emerge from their spiritual "winter" until the last two or three decades of the century. Again, there were a variety of reasons for what amounts to a profound revival among their ranks. There was theological reformation, in which the High Calvinism of the past was largely rejected in favor of a truly evangelical Calvinism. Then there were calls for repentance.[7]

In the previous century the Puritans had developed a practice in which they sought to regularly "give themselves wholly to God." Among the Baptists, this had been lost by the eighteenth century. But something was about to change. Andrew Fuller, a pastor who prayed much and had a deep love for both God and the lost, began to challenge the Baptists theologically and personally. Fuller spoke of five ways in which fellow Baptists could prepare themselves for revival. (This idea of "preparing for revival" was almost unheard of at this time!) He exhorted his fellow Baptists to cultivate Christianity in the home, to witness to unbelievers, to honestly examine their character for changes that were needed, and to develop a spirit of generosity toward those in need. He especially stressed the attitude of a person's heart: "Think it not sufficient that we lament and mourn over our departures from God. We must return to Him with full purpose of heart."[8]

Above all else, Fuller urged his fellow Baptists to seek God in prayer. Here is a part of what he said:

> Finally, brethren, let us not forget to intermingle prayer with all we do. Our need of God's Holy Spirit to enable us to do anything, and everything, truly good should excite us to this. Without this blessing all means are without efficacy and every effort for revival will be in vain. Constantly and earnestly, therefore, let us approach His throne. Take all occasions especially for closet prayer; here, if anywhere, we shall get fresh strength and maintain a life of communion with God. Our Lord Jesus used frequently to retire into a mountain alone for prayer, he, therefore, that is a follower of Christ, must follow Him in this important duty.[9]

One year before Fuller wrote these words, regular meetings for prayer had commenced among the Baptists. The purpose of these meetings? To pray for biblical revival in their churches. When the origin of this call for prayer is traced to the fountain, we arrive at the meeting of the Northampton Association of Baptist Churches. Here, Jonathan Edwards's treatise *A Humble Attempt to Promote Explicit Agreement and Visible Union of God's People in Extraordinary Prayer for a Revival of Religion and Extension of Christ's Kingdom* had come to the attention of John Sutcliff, who had been so moved by Edwards's plea that he encouraged Baptist pastors to pray for a fresh outpouring of the Spirit of God upon their churches and labors. Sutcliff's proposal read, in part, as follows:

Upon a motion being made to the ministers and messengers of the associate Baptist churches assembled at Nottingham, respecting meetings for prayer, to bewail the low estate of religion, and earnestly implore a revival of our churches, and of the general cause of our redeemer, and for that end to wrestle with God for the effusion of His Holy Spirit, which alone can produce the blessed effect, it was unanimously RESOLVED, to recommend to all our churches and congregations, the spending of one hour in this important exercise, on the first Monday in every calendar month.

We hereby solemnly exhort all the churches in our connection, to engage heartily and perseveringly in the persecution of this plan. . . .

The grand object of prayer is to be that the Holy Spirit may be poured down on our ministers and churches, that sinners may be converted, the saints edified, the interest of religion revived, and the name of God glorified. At the same time, remember, we trust you will not confine your requests to your own societies; or to your own immediate connection; let the whole interest of the Redeemer be affectionately remembered, and the spread of the gospel to the most distant parts of the habitable globe be the object of your most fervent requests. We shall rejoice if any other Christian societies of our town or other denominations will unite with us. . . .

Who can tell what the consequences of such an united effort in prayer may be! Let us plead with God the many gracious promises of His Word, which relate to the future success of His gospel. He has said, "I will yet for this be enquired of by the House of Israel to do it for them, I will increase them with men like a flock." Ezek. xxxvi.37. Surely we have love enough for Zion to set apart one hour at a time, twelve times in a year, to seek her welfare.[10]

The focus of this call was revival, or what is termed by Sutcliff as "the effusion of His Holy Spirit." There was recognition here—as had been the case throughout church history when believers became exercised about true revival—that revival is solely in the hands of God. Those who prayed were convinced that God honors the means (that is, believers praying for revival), but they also based their intercession upon the firm belief that God alone sent the blessing.

Professor Michael Haykin concludes:

> There is little doubt from the record of the history that God heard the prayers of Sutcliff and his fellow Baptists. As they prayed, the Calvinistic Baptists in England began to experience the blessing of revival, though, it should be noted, a change was not immediately evident.[11]

The first fruit of John Sutcliff's call to prayer was the formation of the Baptist Missionary Society in 1792. (This is a marvelous story in itself.) This led, in the following year, to William Carey being sent out as the Society's first foreign missionary. Thus the modern missions movement had its beginnings in a prayer meeting for revival.

By 1810 more evidence of fruit could be seen in the English churches themselves according to a letter Andrew Fuller wrote to William Carey. He noted that meetings in his church were thronged with people who were deeply concerned about their souls. The harvest was now beginning to come in, but only after years of prayer for the blessing of heaven.

When Sutcliff lay dying in 1814, one of the last things he uttered to his family was, "I wish I had prayed more." Andrew Fuller speculated that by this Sutcliff meant "more spiritually." Fuller tested his own prayer life and found it wanting as well. What did these men of such earnest prayer feel when they spoke in this manner? Haykin answers accurately, "A profound awareness that the Spirit's blessing and empowerment in personal and corporate revival is *the* most important aspect of the believer's life and the church's life."[12]

These men prayed for revival believing that they should not cease their earnest crying unto God "till the Spirit is poured upon us from on high, and the desert becomes a fertile field, and the fertile field seems like a forest" (Isaiah 32:15). They believed with all their heart and soul that the work of God must be advanced using spiritual means, not carnal. They understood the words "Not by might nor by power, but by my Spirit" (Zechariah 4:6) to refer to prayer. They saw that their only contingency for the battle was to be found in asking for and receiving greater effusions of the Holy Spirit. This is nothing more nor less than revival in a New Testament sense.

Edwards's message promoting prayer for revival not only reached into Great Britain and touched the Baptists, as we have witnessed, but it also reached back across the Atlantic to America as well. Before The Second Great Awakening, churches were in desperate straits. Latourette wrote, "It seemed as if Christianity were about to be ushered out of the affairs of men."[13] But prayer for a mighty outpouring of God was lifted in England and among a host of believers the world over. All across America the idea of "The Union of Prayer" caught on and Congregational, Presbyterian, Methodist, Baptist, and Reformed churches all adopted the plan. Before long both Britain and America were "interlaced with a network of prayer meetings, which set aside the first Monday of each month to pray. It was not long before revival came."[14]

So we must take note of church history. It is a fact beyond any reasonable doubt: When God is pleased to bless His people with fresh effusions of the Holy Spirit, He first prompts them to pray and ask Him for the blessing.

SHOULD WE PRAY FOR REVIVAL?

The decline of society in the West is beyond serious question. Every leading cultural and religious indicator tells us that we are presently witnessing the collapse of civilization as we have known it. We are quite prone to think that the way things are is the way they always will be. We seem to have already forgotten that in only a matter of a few days the once impregnable "Iron Curtain" came down in the late 1980s. We so easily forget the truth of these solemn words:

> Not to us, O Lord, not to us
> but to your name be the glory.
> because of your love and faithfulness.
> Why do the nations say,
> "Where is their God?"
> Our God is in heaven;
> he does whatever pleases him (Psalm 115:1-3).

What possibility is there for a mighty awakening in our time? To read some of the things we have noted in this chapter is thrilling, but is our time any worse, in the most basic human sense, than any previous age? My friend Erroll Hulse has written:

> We must not forget the situation that preceded the eighteenth-century awakening. We have liberalism; they had deism. We have the drug menace; they had rum. We have abortion; they had the degradation of the slave trade. We have contempt for the gospel, especially in places of influence; so did they. We have bishops who tolerate practicing homosexuals in the ministry and the blatant public denial of the deity of Christ by one of their number; eighteenth-century Britain also suffered a supine clergy. Yet in spite of all the obstacles the Holy Spirit intervened in a marvelous way, using humble prayers and a handful of godly leaders.[15]

Jonathan Edwards noted that "when God has something very great for His church, it is His will that there should precede it the extraordinary prayers of His people." This is as it should be, for the psalmist writes:

Blessed are those you choose
and bring near to live in your courts!
We are filled with the good things of your house,
of your holy temple.
You answer us with awesome deeds of righteousness,
O God our Savior,
the hope of all the ends of the earth
and of the farthest seas (Psalm 65:4-5).

And how can we not be encouraged to pray for revival when we hear the Lord's words to the prophet Jeremiah: "Call to me and I will answer you and tell you great and unsearchable things you do not know" (33:3)? Further encouragement can be found in the words of Isaiah: "Surely the arm of the LORD is not too short to save, nor his ear too dull to hear" (Isaiah 59:1). When God's Word abounds with promises regarding the Spirit and the present age we must reason, with regard to the possibility of new effusions in such dark times, "Is anything too hard for the LORD?" (Genesis 18:14).

We must be swept along by the realization that there really is nothing "too hard for the Lord." Revival, being God's way, is not difficult for Him to bring about. Our problem is that we reason as mere mortals and we fail to reckon on the greatness of the Giver and His plans for good. The words of one widely used revival minister, Horatius Bonar, are worth careful reflection:

> When man proceeds to the accomplishment of some mighty
> enterprise, he puts forth prodigious efforts, as if by the sound
> of his axes and hammers he would proclaim his own fancied
> might, and bear down opposing obstacles. He cannot work
> without sweat, and dust, and noise. When God would do a
> marvelous work, such as may amaze all heaven and earth, He
> commands silence all around, sends forth the still small voice,
> and then sets some feeble instrument to work, and straightway
> it is done! Man toils and pants, and after all effects but little:

the Creator, in the silent majesty of power, noiseless yet resist-less, achieves by a word the infinite wonders of omnipotence!

In order to loose the bands of winter, and bring in the verdure of the pleasant spring, He does not send forth His angels to hew in pieces the thickened ice, or to strip off from the mountain's side the gathered snows, or to plant anew over the face of the bleak earth, flowers fresh from His creating hand. No! He breathes from His lips a mild warmth into the frozen air, and forthwith, in stillness, but in irresistible power, the work proceeds; the ice is shivered, the snows dissolve, the rivers resume their flow, the earth awakes as out of sleep, the hills and the valleys put on their freshening verdure, the fragrance of earth takes wing and fills the air, till a new world of beauty rises in silence amid the dissolution of the old!

Such is God's method of working, both in the natural and in the spiritual world—silent, simple, majestic, and resistless! Such was the Reformation! Such were the revivals in Scotland under our fathers of the Covenant! Such was the Kirk o' Shotts on that memorable Pentecost, when the unstudied words of a timid trembling youth carried salvation to five hundred souls. Such was Ayr in its Pentecostal days, when from the lonely church at midnight, there went up to heaven the broken sighs of that man of prayer, John Welsh. And such was Northampton in later times, when Jonathan Edwards watched and prayed for its citizens, and when, from the closet of that holy man, there went forth the living power that wrought such wonders there![16]

But can we expect great revivals like these again? Aren't we now living in "the last days," as many insist? Well, yes, we are living in "the last days." But the church has lived in the New Testament period known as "the last days" since Pentecost (see Acts 2:17; 2 Timothy 3:1), according to the biblical language used to describe this age. The writer of Hebrews leaves us with no doubt regarding this:

> *In the past God spoke to our forefathers through the prophets at many times and in various ways, but in these last days he has spoken to us by his Son, whom he appointed heir of all things, and through whom he made the universe (1:1-2).*

But some persist by saying, "Well, these are the *last* of the last days." I ask, "How do you know this?" Where is the scripture which clearly states that this is true of our time? The best anyone can do is speculate, which, according to our Lord, is both dangerous and unwise (see Matthew 24; Mark 13; Luke 12). Anyone who reads the history of Christian "predictions" regarding the last days will immediately draw one conclusion: Multitudes of Bible teachers have failed in their efforts to pinpoint which generation will be the last before Christ's return. Surely to refuse to ask for effusions of the Spirit on the basis of last-days speculation will be a lame excuse before Christ on the day of judgment.

The church in America has been paralyzed by a kind of pessimism that nearly eats the life out of earnest believers. Would it not be better to continue these discussions regarding the age that precedes Christ's coming in a charitable spirit while simultaneously asking the Lord to grant us new measures of blessing for the spiritual battles of our time? Could we not put aside our endless debates about the exact timing of Christ's return in relationship to other events and follow the example of both Scripture and church history regarding prayer for revival? It seems to me that no generation in the history of the American church has been more exercised about the timing of the Lord's coming and less prepared for Him to come. This overemphasis upon the future, with a near-complete abandonment of the present, cannot be the balance of scriptural truth regardless of a person's views of eschatology.

Whether or not the church has a promise of revival in prophetic Scripture is a point to be considered. Suffice it to say that the church actually needs no biblical prophecies to pray for revival. She surely needs no private and personal revelations to pray for what God has repeatedly given. Praying congregations in the past had no such mystical enlightenment. The church will always have the same provision of the Holy Spirit right to the end of this age. Even if the days ahead are filled with apostasy, and the conditions of the world grow much worse, should not the church pray for a divine enduement of power so she can face such challenging and difficult days?

There is simply no warrant for us to accept "lukewarmness" in the church as normal. Though some individuals insist we are living in the Laodicean age (see Revelation 3:14-22) and thus should not expect another great awakening, there is nothing in the text of Revelation 2 and 3 that would lead us to draw such a conclusion. What we desperately need to hear in Revelation 2 and 3 is the voice of God through Scripture. We can begin to listen to His voice by repenting and opening the door of the church to Christ (Revelation 3:19-20)!

Come, let us pray together for a great spiritual awakening in our generation. Such a work of heavenly grace would surely glorify God. "Who knows? He may turn and have pity and leave behind a blessing" (Joel 2:14).

Nine

PREACHING:
THE FUEL OF REVIVAL

Preaching has divine authority only when the message comes as a word from God Himself.
—James I. Packer

A burning heart will soon find for itself a flaming tongue.
—Charles H. Spurgeon

Give me one hundred preachers who fear nothing but sin and desire nothing but God, and I care not a straw whether they be clergymen or laymen, such alone will shake the gates of hell and set up the kingdom of God on earth.
—John Wesley

Accuracy in exegesis is no substitute for reality in experience.
—John Blanchard

What a dreadful thing it would be for me if I should be ignorant of the power of the truth which I am preparing to proclaim!
—John Wesley

THE ACCOUNT GIVEN in the first chapter of the book of Acts tells us that immediately after Jesus had appeared to His disciples and promised them "power when the Holy Spirit comes on you" (1:8), He was taken up into heaven before their very eyes. The event reads simply: "After he said this, he was taken up before their very eyes, and a cloud hid him from their sight" (1:9). Following an angelic announcement regarding His return ("This same Jesus . . .

131

will come back in the same way"), the amazed group of disciples returned to Jerusalem, a short walk from the Mount of Olives.

Prior to Jesus' ascension, these early believers had been through an incredible 40 days with the resurrected Lord. But now He had departed. What would they do next? How were they to respond to what Jesus had told them? What had He given to prepare them for these eventualities? And what would fuel the fire that would soon be given as He had promised (1:8)? We don't have to read for long in Luke's account until we find our answer:

> In those days Peter stood up among the believers (a group num-
> bering about a hundred and twenty) and said, "Brothers, the
> Scripture had to be fulfilled which the Holy Spirit spoke long ago
> through the mouth of David concerning Judas, who served as a
> guide for those who arrested Jesus—he was one of our number and
> shared in this ministry." . . . Therefore it is necessary to choose
> of the men who have been with us the whole time the Lord Jesus
> went in and out among us" (1:15-17,21).

The immediate problem that faced these disciples was what to do regarding the office of Judas. (This underscores the *uniqueness* of the apostolic office and function.) As they considered this matter, two of the disciples reflected upon their walk to Emmaus a few days earlier. They remembered how Jesus "explained to them what was said in all the Scriptures concerning himself" (Luke 24:27). Because of the way Jesus had used the Scriptures these disciples understood that when the written Scriptures spoke, God spoke! There was no room for doubt here, as I.D.E. Thomas observes:

> Again and again in the Acts we find the apostles having
> recourse to the Scriptures, and finding in them light for their
> problems and authority for their assertions. This was the basis
> on which Paul always reasoned: he "reasoned with them out of
> the Scriptures" (Acts 17:2). To the apostles the Scriptures were

God's Word: when the Scriptures spoke, God spoke. Every line was stamped with the autograph of the only true God. The apostles showed none of the hesitancy and diffidence of so many present-day theologians and preachers. Their preaching was always positive and full of assurance, in the great tradition of the Hebrew prophets. But, whereas the prophets would say, "Thus saith the Lord," the apostles would say "Thus saith the Scriptures."[1]

This perceptive observation leads us to the second of the two great means the Spirit of God uses in quickening the life of the church: the Scriptures. As prayer precedes and accompanies true revival by being an instrument of ignition, so preaching feeds and nourishes revival as the voice of God to the awakened church. Anointed preaching and teaching is always at the forefront of true heaven-sent revival.

Preaching's Connection with Revival

Several Old Testament accounts affirm for us the role preaching has in revival. For example, 2 Chronicles 34 tells us that when the high priest "found the Book of the Law of the LORD that had been given through Moses" he had it brought to King Josiah (verse 14). Upon hearing the words of this Book the king began a process of deep repentance. We read that "he had everyone in Jerusalem and Benjamin pledge themselves to it" (34:32), and Josiah, taking steps of true reform, "removed all the detestable idols from all the territory belonging to the Israelites" (34:33).

Our Lord plainly promised power to His disciples (Acts 1:8) before He ascended to His throne in heaven. The disciples might well have imagined that this would be some type of political power or power for social accomplishment. But what our Lord clearly had in mind was the enablement of the Holy Spirit, the power which would bring them boldness in witness and preaching.

The book of Acts repeatedly demonstrates that this is the same power involved in spiritual awakenings. Indeed, until the twenty-first chapter we read of one revival experience after another, beginning with Pentecost in Acts 2.

Unfortunately, many contemporary evangelicals miss this. It seems that Acts has been used to either teach a distinctive theological position that does not line up easily with the more didactic passages in the epistles (as in Pentecostalism or charismatic theology), or it has been treated as a simple record from the transition period from the age of the old covenant to the age of the new. Erroll Hulse is helpful in correcting both errors:

> The book of Acts occupies a unique position in the New Testament. It is the only account of the establishment and growth of the apostolic church. It provides the key to understanding the background of Paul's letters and is the link between the four Gospels and the rest of the New Testament. It would seem that most commentators concentrate on the exegesis of the text and miss the main thrust of the message of Acts. Why is so little attention given to exposition of the progress of the church and missions?[2]

The great themes of Acts—especially those related to the power of the Spirit enabling the preaching of the gospel, and the attendant expansion of the young church in the face of impossible odds—are often overlooked in the hermeneutical debates that surround the critical passages in the text. The loss, to today's church, is huge.

The preaching seen throughout Acts is both powerful and urgent. It is also distinctively Christ-centered. On the Day of Pentecost, 120 disciples were "filled with the Holy Spirit" (Acts 2:4) and immediately began to praise the great works of God in several languages. But this was only the beginning. Next we see Peter, anointed with unction, preaching "Christ and him crucified" (1 Corinthians 2:2). If we look carefully at his sermon we see that it is an extremely simple one. The content is neither striking nor profound. What is striking is how direct Peter is in his application and how powerfully the Holy Spirit drives the message home to the hearts of his hearers. Before Peter finished his message, people already "were cut to the heart" (Acts 2:37). They interrupted Peter and the other apostles with the question "Brothers, what shall we do?" We then read that 3,000 people were converted due to this powerful operation of the Spirit.

This work of witnessing and preaching, begun by the Spirit at Pentecost, continued in much the same manner in the days that followed (Acts 3). In Acts 4:31 we read, "After they prayed, the place where they were meeting was shaken. And they were all filled with the Holy Spirit and spoke the word of God boldly." These early chapters provide us with a pattern that can be traced out in the days that followed—the church prayed, God gave boldness to His servants who preached, harvests were brought in though great waves of blessing, and the people rejoiced and praised God with one heart!

THE HOLY SPIRIT AND PREACHING

In the New Testament we also see a vital connection between the coming of the Holy Spirit and the preaching of the Scriptures. In Luke-Acts, a specific phrase regarding the Spirit's fullness occurs eight times. In each case this specific phrase is related to a prophetic form of speech. The verb used in each instance means "that which fills or takes possession of the mind."[3] The phrase is best rendered, because of the tense used, as "having been filled with the Holy Spirit." The case for a distinctive work of the Spirit connected to preaching becomes even more compelling when we realize that "in each of these eight occurrences the filling of the Spirit is presented as an *event*, a sovereign and spontaneous act of God related to the proclamation of truth."[4]

In Acts 2 the filling of the Spirit results in a supernatural kind of speech. The languages spoken are understandable and the content of the communication is clear (Acts 2:6,8,11). Through the Pentecostal manifestation of "tongues," people of different languages heard about the redemptive accomplishments of the triune God. Peter legitimized this manisfestation by quoting from Joel 2:28-32. The point to be observed here is that the effect of the coming of the Spirit at Pentecost would be the "making known of the Word of God in a greater and more profusive fashion."[5]

In Acts 4:8 we again see the phrase "filled with the Holy Spirit." Often I have heard people ask, "But wasn't Peter filled with the Holy Spirit in Acts 2:4? How can he be filled again?" As noted, all believers are permanently indwelt by the Holy Spirit (see John 14:16; Romans 8:9) and all true believers experience that same Spirit doing the work of sanctification in them, to greater or lesser degrees (see Galatians 5:16-24). But what is going on in these passages in Acts is *unique*. What we see is a distinctive filling which results in an access of power from on high. This unique filling grants boldness and power for witness and for proclamation. It is a sovereign work of God, in which He attends the preaching of His Word; it is more than Him being present simply because the speaker is faithfully preaching what he sees in the written text.

In Acts 4:31 this phrase appears again; this time we read that all the disciples are "filled with the Holy Spirit" and thus all began to speak "the word of God boldly." When Ananias goes to the newly converted Saul of Tarsus in Acts 9 he tells him that "the Lord . . . has sent me so that you may see again and be filled with the Holy Spirit" (verse 17). This is again the exact same phrase used in Acts 2 and 4. But what is the reason for this particular "filling" in Saul's life? We find the answer in verse 15, where God told Ananias, "This man is my chosen instrument to carry my name before the Gentiles and their kings and before the people of Israel" (verse 15). Immediately after this "filling," Luke records that "at once [Paul] began to preach in the synagogues that Jesus is the Son of God" (verse 20).

One other occurrence of "filled with the Holy Spirit" appears in Acts 13. Here Paul and Barnabas are preaching the gospel on the island of Salamis. A Roman proconsul by the name of Sergius Paulus requests that they come to preach to him, and Luke records what happened:

> But Elymas the sorcerer (for that is what his name means) opposed them and tried to turn the proconsul from the faith. Then Saul, who was also called Paul, filled with the Holy Spirit, looked straight at Elymas and said, "You are a child of the devil and an enemy of everything that is right! You are full of all kinds of deceit and trickery. Will you never stop perverting the right ways of the Lord? Now the hand of the Lord is against you" (verses 8-11).

What exactly is the filling of the Spirit spoken of in these various texts? The answer is not novel nor hard to discover. It is actually very clear. A careful reading of the text, and the immediate context, provides the answer:

> An examination of these eight passages reveal it to be an instantaneous, sudden, and sovereign operation of the Spirit of God coming upon a man so that his proclamation of Jesus Christ might be attended by holy power. This, then, appears to be the emphasis of Paul's words when he says to the Corinthians: "And my message and my preaching were not in persuasive words of wisdom, but in demonstration of the Spirit and of power" (1 Corinthians 2:4). The Spirit, by the means of His power, through the words of a preacher, establishes, verifies, and confirms the gospel in the heart of a man so that he must respond to the truth he hears.[6]

I would submit that this work of the Spirit is exactly what is missing in most preaching today. I would also submit that this is exactly what is given to the church when the Spirit of God comes with reviving mercies "in the midst of the years" (Habakkuk 3:2 KJV). This is what takes preaching from mere *words* to *power*. That is why this kind of preaching is the fuel needed to both prompt revival as well as direct it.

THE CONTENT OF REVIVAL PREACHING

Make no mistake about this: The early church and its leadership had complete confidence in preaching as the *primary* vehicle of the Spirit's work. The apostle Paul expresses this confidence boldly when he writes:

> When I came to you, brothers, I did not come with eloquence or superior wisdom as I proclaimed to you the testimony about God. For I resolved to know nothing while I was with you except Jesus Christ and him crucified. I came to you in weakness and fear, and with much trembling. My message and my preaching were not with wise and persuasive word, but with a demonstration of the Spirit's power, so that your faith might not rest on men's wisdom, but on God's power (1 Corinthians 2:1-5).

But preaching today has fallen upon hard times. People seem to think that there are far more effective ways of communicating the message of Christ in this visual age than by merely preaching it.

Much modern evangelical preaching has actually degenerated into a kind of moralism in which the gospel is made into a list of do's and don'ts which replace God's holy law. In this setting a moral homily ends up taking the place of real biblical proclamation, which is centered in the person of Christ. In addition, we have recently seen a rise in Gnostic preaching, which focuses on enlightening people so that they might untap their "full human potential." Even orthodox theology, in conservative circles, has degenerated in the past 50 years or so into a kind of orthodoxism—a type of preaching in which the bare communication of accurate content replaces the spiritual act of preaching "Christ and him crucified" (1 Corinthians 2:2).

THE NATURE OF BIBLICAL PREACHING

Historically, whenever true biblical preaching has made a come-back, revival has quite often followed. In a real sense revival restores such preaching. In another sense such preaching will always be a precursor of revival. It can be said that Spirit-empowered preaching *often* brings revival. It can also be said that revival *always* brings Spirit-empowered preaching. New Testament scholar Robert Mounce sums up my personal observations well when he says, "One thing is certain—they [listeners to this kind of preaching] could not remain neutral. Wherever apostolic kerygma was proclaimed there was either a revival or a riot."[7]

We gain additional insight on the role of empowered preaching when we look at the biblical perspective on spiritual warfare. Paul's argument in Ephesians 6 is that the church, standing in unity as one person, must "stand firm" in the faith, armed for battle, so that together everyone may fight against "the spiritual forces of evil in the heavenly realms" (verse 12). The one offensive article in the congregation's arsenal is "the sword of the Spirit, which is the word of God" (verse 17). But the sword will not have its effect, Paul concludes, unless the church prays for the one who wields the Word in the battle. Paul thus appeals to the Ephesians to "pray also for me, that whenever I open my mouth, words may be given me so that I will fearlessly make know the mystery of the gospel. . . . Pray that I may declare it fearlessly, as I should" (verses 19-20).

Paul makes the same request to the Colossians when he encourages them to "pray that I may proclaim [the mystery of Christ] clearly, as I should" (4:4). As in Ephesians 6, Paul was requesting that the congregation offer intercession on his behalf as he preached the Word of God. In particular Paul desired "boldness" or "fearlessness," as the NIV translates the Greek text here. The word grouping in Paul's letters is the same as that already observed in the book of Acts—it describes what is granted when the Spirit comes with power upon the preaching of Christ. The older English word for this was *unction.* (Some referred to this as "that certain unction.")

When was the last time your church conducted times of prayer in which the people beseeched God to grant this "unction" to the preacher? When this unction is present in preaching, people are profoundly moved. They are gripped. They become serious about matters related to eternity. The general scene, as recorded by many who have witnessed revivals, is often one in which an uncommon quietness moves across the congregation. Those of us who preach may see something like this once in a while. We ought to know it more often. And the people of God need to earnestly ask God to give it to preachers. Lloyd-Jones noted that when this was granted the people "delight in the things of God." The experience of the psalmist truly becomes the experience of the church:

> O God, you are my God,
> earnestly I seek you;
> my soul thirsts for you,
> my body longs for you,
> in a dry and weary land
> where there is no water.
> I have seen you in the sanctuary
> and beheld your power and your glory
> (Psalm 63:1-2).

THE PRIORITY OF BIBLICAL PREACHING

There is no doubt that revivals have very often arisen in the darkest moments of church history. Revivals usually came when God gave back to His people bold and faithful preachers of the gospel. Eifion Evans, who has spent a lifetime studying revival movements and the men who preached in them, concluded:

> Revivals thus display great variety in the manner of their beginnings, but preaching seems to be prominent in each case. God's dealings—sometimes drastic—with the parish or local minister often brought about a radical change in the success of the gospel at the place. . . .[8]

Peter Waldo, mentioned in the previous chapter for his ministry of prayer, was converted to Christ around the year A.D. 1170. One of

Waldo's first actions was to send preachers out two by two with a clear and authoritative message from the Bible. For John Wycliffe the approach was much the same. His "Poor Preachers" were equipped only with English Bibles but they "turned the world upside down." In the time of the Reformation, 100 years later, Hugh Latimer became a great candle for the Lord as he preached the truth in compelling and powerful ways. Throngs of people flocked to hear him.

In the seventeenth century Puritan ministers insisted that preaching was their greatest and most important work. Their sermonic remains, in the form of countless rich volumes recently reprinted, testify to the importance of preaching with the Spirit's power. In the eighteenth century John Wesley, George Whitefield, Daniel Rowland, and Howell Harris all discovered that preaching was the method God singularly owned in converting multitudes. Preaching was the fuel that fed the great blessings of true spiritual awakening.[9]

The same was true in the nineteenth century. Robert Murray McCheyne notes this regarding people's attention to his own preaching during the revival times in 1839: "I have observed at such times an awful and breathless stillness pervading the assembly, each hearer bent forward in posture and of rapt attention."[10]

In this century a revival at Carloway, on the Isle of Lewis in Scotland, occurred between 1934 and the outbreak of World War II. What has sometimes been noted about this particular revival was "the eager attention with which young and old listened to the preaching of the Word." There are many more such accounts, but these few must suffice to demonstrate my point: The Spirit of God always attends to the preaching of the Word of God before and during authentic revival. If we would pray for revival, as we must, then let us then make provision for the preaching of the Word. And let us beseech God more earnestly to send His Spirit upon both preachers and hearers.

May our corporate and private prayer be as follows:

*O God, would You be pleased to give back to Your people, in
these dark times, a true and powerful preaching of Your Word.
Grant that Your servants may be filled with the Spirit and grant
also that we may hear those who preach not as mere men but as
those who speak the word of God (see 1 Thessalonians 1:5).*

Ten

SHOWERS OF BLESSING

Divine omnipotence is the doctrine of revival.
—Charles H. Spurgeon

There will be showers of blessing.
—Ezekiel 34:26

TRUE REVIVAL IS always a season of great blessing. This is true because revival is a season in which God is moving with gracious power. The blessings of Pentecost brought amazing growth and fruitfulness to the early church. True revival, as an extension of the Spirit's dynamic Pentecostal work throughout this present age, also brings amazing growth and fruitfulness.

A basic pattern can be seen, to a certain extent, throughout church history. The Spirit renews the church, enlivens her efforts, attends her services with divine power, and leads her out into the harvest fields where multitudes are born of the Spirit. The spiritual fields are ready to harvest, ready for a massive ingathering. This harvesting often follows times of great darkness and weakness in the church. Yet revivals do decline. Carlton Booth, once a professor of evangelism, correctly noted that though "revivals do not last, the effects of revival always endure." As we saw earlier, revivals are not

meant to last. They are showers and we cannot live in the showers forever. The mystery of why this is so is frankly beyond our comprehen-
sion.

In a later chapter we will see that oftentimes right behind the
massive harvest, or even right in the middle of it, there will spring
up a crop of weeds. These weeds include problems rarely encountered by harvesters in nonrevival times. These problems are not so
much in the world, but in the church. Yes, revival brings blessings,
but if we are not careful problems arise. If we want to be wise in our
prayers for revival, we also need to be aware of both the blessings and
the problems that can be brought by revival.

Revival can be like fire or water. Both fire and water can be beneficial and destructive. For example, fire helps us to heat our homes,
cook our meals, and process valuable resources. Water is likewise
essential. We drink it, clean with it, and enjoy it in a myriad of ways.
Yet a fire that is out of control burns and destroys. And an abundance of water in the wrong place at the wrong time moves mountains, washes away homes, and destroys life. Now, we cannot
dispense of fire or water simply because of their inherent dangers.
Rather, we should seek to find ways to preserve the benefits and deal
with the problems.

That principle applies to revival. As one wrote, "In thinking
about revival, we must recognize that the blessings of divine outpourings are indispensable. However, we must not fail to prayerfully
and thoughtfully consider the dangers of accompanying mighty
movements of the Spirit of God."[1]

THE BLESSINGS BROUGHT BY REVIVAL

J.I. Packer has called Jonathan Edwards's "most original contribution to theology" not his philosophical work on the nature of the
human will but rather "his pioneer elucidation of biblical teaching
on the subject of revival."[2] Though his thoughts on revival were written in a piecemeal fashion, with five specific works published over
a period of some years, the value of what he wrote on revival is

inestimable for modern students. All but one of these works were originally written to vindicate the two revivals that Edwards had been a vital part of between 1734-42. Edwards had seen revival bring blessing and excess.

Packer concludes that "this immediate aim [i.e., to explain and defend two great seasons of revival] might seem to limit their interest for later generations of readers. . . ." Yet he concludes, "Embedded in them, however, is a fairly complete account of revival as a work of God—in other words, a theology of revival. . . ."[3]

To understand revival blessings we need a healthy theology of revival that can adequately respond to these blessings. Edwards was and is an excellent guide.

On the following pages I have listed five principal blessings that fall upon the church during revival showers. I draw each of these, in various ways, from Jonathan Edwards and his magnificent works on revival. (I would be gratified, and richly rewarded, if you were able to take some time to read Edwards for yourself after you read this chapter!)

Blessing #1:
The Reinvigorating of True Piety

The principal blessing of a revival of true Christianity among believers is the reinvigorating of true piety. J.I. Packer notes, "Though it is through the knowledge of Bible truth that the Spirit effects His reviving work, revival is not merely, nor even primarily, a restoring of orthodoxy."[4] Reformation, as we shall see in chapter sixteen, may come as a result of revival or it may be a precursor to it. Revival differs from reformation in that it is more directly focused upon the experiential aspects of Christianity. Revival reinvigorates the heart by the agency of the Spirit; it leads men and women to a hearty personal dealing with God in the gospel message. Revival removes the sleepiness and barrenness that existed in prerevival times. On the personal level, revival causes a believer to enter into a more vital experience of Christ. Seen through a wider lens, it does the same for the church at large. That is precisely why Edwards titled one of his books *Distinguishing Marks of a Work of the Spirit of God*. Revival, simply put, *deepens experiential piety.*

Jonathan Edwards believed that the substance of a true and vital relationship with Christ is to be seen in conscious heart communion with God. Religion is not a matter of notion, nor of rational insight gained through study. True religion, given by the Spirit in the gospel, moves and touches a person's entire being. It illuminates the mind with light, it fuels the emotions with love for Christ, and it alters the will by the work of the Spirit. In Edwards's classic, *A Narrative of Surprising Conversions*, we encounter story after story of how this paradigm describes the stories of those who were wonderfully converted during the revival. These converts included both young children (there was one who was five years of age) and aged men and women.

The surest sign that God's Spirit is truly at work in revival is to be seen in this blessing of genuine heart piety. Now, this piety is not some vague emotional feeling of religion. It is not a vaporous puff of excitement, here today and gone tomorrow. What this blessing does among the truly revived is raise their esteem for the Lord Jesus Christ. Revival is not merely talk about the Holy Spirit, nor is it merely the display of the gifts of the Holy Spirit. Revival brings multitudes into deeper love for Jesus. We know this is so because of what the apostle John tells us in 1 John 4:2: "This is how you can recognize the Spirit of God: Every spirit that acknowledges that Jesus Christ has come in the flesh is from God."

Revival causes multitudes to look to the one born of a virgin, crucified outside the gates of Jerusalem, raised on the third day, and ascended into heaven. Revival restores the church's true focus, its proper gaze. It gets our eyes off us, our programs, and our efforts, and gets them back on the living Christ.

Edwards concluded that if people are truly convinced of their need for Christ as well as of their sin against Christ, they will appreciate Him profoundly and love Him more deeply. The Spirit will always bear witness to Christ, not to Himself. And the Jesus He bears witness to is the true Jesus revealed in Scripture, not the Christ of ancient gnosticism, revived mysticism, or bankrupt liberalism. Simply put, the Spirit of God leads men and women to Jesus, not to antichrists. Revival showers will always result in this supreme blessing.

Blessing #2: A Direct Attack Upon Satan's Kingdom

Edwards referred to revival showers as a season in which Satan's kingdom is attacked most directly. During seasons when the church slumbers and cherishes worldly goals the enemy has little to fear. When revival comes, however, the Spirit leads the people of God to attack the citadels of Satan.

It's important to keep in mind that this attack is waged with the weapons of God—namely prayer and Scripture. We do not need the "techniques" of modern charismatic revelations to conduct this battle. We need the Word of God, earnest prayer and the power of the Spirit. People who look in Scripture for looking for some special method for fighting this battle.

So how does revival cause the slumbering church to awaken to the battle? Edwards notes that the primary difference between Christ and the enemy, at least at this point, can be seen in Jesus' statement, "My kingdom is not of this world" (John 18:36). Satan, who is called "the god of this world" (meaning the god of this world's system of thought, or what we call its philosophy), is, correspondingly, set in sharpest contrast to Christ and His kingdom. Clearly when the apostle John tells us "Do not love the world or anything in the world" (1 John 2:15) he has in mind the love of those things that belong to the enemy and his system of thought. By this John refers to everything that belongs to sin and the satisfaction that this world offers without reference to God. Edwards, following this line of reasoning, says we may safely conclude that in revival the following blessings will flow from a true work of God's Spirit:

1. Christians will have a diminishing love for worldly pleasure, profits, and honor.

2. Christians will be increasingly weaned from pursuing the material.

3. A deep concern about eternity and the eternal happiness that comes solely through the gospel of Christ will abound.

4. People will earnestly and profoundly seek God's kingdom and righteousness above all else (Matthew 6:33).

5. Those revived will be deeply aware of the awfulness and guilt of sin, as well as the misery which it brings.

It is apparent that Satan does not convict people of sin, righteousness, and the judgment to come (John 16:8-11). Satan will not awaken the human conscience or bring about the awareness of sin. Would the devil open eyes to sin? Would he bring men to realize that they are condemned without Christ? Would he cause them to hate sin, forsake it, and turn in repentance toward God and His Word?

There are those who pose the question, "But couldn't Satan awaken the conscience in order to deceive men?" Edwards argues that to think this way is futile. He reasons that this would be like suggesting that Christ made a mistake when He said to the Pharisees (in effect), "Satan cannot drive out Satan" (Matthew 12:25-26). Edwards reasons:

> . . . if we see persons made sensible of the dreadful nature of sin, and of the displeasure of God against it, and of their own miserable condition as they are in themselves, by reason of sin, and earnestly concerned for their eternal salvation, and sensible of their need of God's pity and help, and engaged to seek it in the use of the means that God has appointed, we may certainly conclude that it is from the Spirit of God, whatever effects this concern has on their bodies. . . .[5]

When the conscience is awakened and revival mercies are flowing into the lives of people, things such as the ugliness of sin, the anger of God against sin, the need of eternal salvation, and the cry to God for divine mercy all fill the minds and hearts of both believers and unbelievers who are pressing into the kingdom of Christ by faith.

Blessing #3: Highest Esteem for the Scriptures

True revival will result in a third significant blessing: high esteem for the Scriptures as the Word of God. When revival has occurred, pastors no longer find it necessary to plead for people to attend worship services. It will be all they can do to pray and prepare for their hungry flocks, who will want more than they can physically provide. Making sure the people of God are fed the truth will be a priority but the preacher will also labor to "get unction" for his preaching, as we've seen. Time will seem as nothing. Sermons will come to human hearts desiring to hear the voice of God. When the Spirit is poured out in revival, the Word of God will be exalted and honored as most people have never experienced. The devil does not cause men to revere the fullness and truthfulness of Holy Scripture. Unholy spirits will never lead men to declare and to believe: "To the law and to the testimony!" (Isaiah 8:20).

In revival, issues of biblical authority and the trustworthiness of Scripture will be established by the immediate working of the Spirit. Sometimes skeptics will instantly drop their long-standing opposition and embrace the Bible openly!

Jonathan Edwards appeals to 1 John 4:6 when he establishes this particular emphasis in his classic work *Distinguishing Marks*: "We are from God, and whoever knows God listens to us. This is how we recognize the Spirit of truth and the spirit of falsehood." Edwards argues that this plainly demonstrates that those apostles and prophets God used to give us the Scriptures were "from God" and thus their word was from God. God has made them the *foundation* of the church.

A movement of God can always be positively measured by the evidence of holy blessing. Further, a work of authentic awakening will result in the Spirit leading men and women to "listen to him" (Luke 9:5). Christ will be heard, in and by the Word of God. This will surely be one of the greatest blessings when the Spirit is poured out upon the church in heaven-sent revival.

The Word of God will always be the singular weapon for true spiritual battle, and revival unleashes that sword! Every minister, true to his calling in grace, must labor night and day over the Word. In a "day of small things" he may only see some fruit as "mercy drops round us are falling." But in revival times his labors will have a happy and amazing effect. Sermons once preached with seemingly little effect will strike down hearers as veritable thunderbolts from on high. Every text will seem alive. Every sermon will be soaked in fervent prayer and find hearers who have never seen or heard such a message.

Jonathan Edwards wisely concludes his remarks regarding this great blessing by adding:

> Every text is a dart to torment the old serpent: he felt the stinging smart thousands of times; therefore we may be sure that he never will go about to raise people's esteem of it, or affection to it. And accordingly we see it to be common in enthusiasts, that they depreciate this written rule, and set up the light within, or some other rule above it.[6]

Blessing #4: Revival Leads People into Truth

The Spirit of God, operating graciously in true revival, is the Spirit of truth. Jonathan Edwards illustrates this point by showing us how the Spirit of God makes people sensible to the God of Scripture. He shows, in particular, that Jehovah is a great God, a sin-hating God. Edwards adds:

> . . . [The Holy Spirit] makes them more to realize [that God
> hates sin] . . . that they must die, and that life is short, and very
> uncertain; and confirms persons in it that there is another
> world, that they have immortal souls, and that they must give
> account of themselves to God; and convinces them that they
> are exceedingly sinful by nature and practice; and that they are
> helpless in themselves; and confirms them in other things that
> are agreeable to sound doctrine: the spirit that works thus,
> operates as the spirit of truth: He represents things as they are
> indeed: He brings men to light; for whatever makes truth
> manifest, is light.[7]

Don't miss the key point here. Revival, as I have labored to
demonstrate, is not about *new* truth! It does not bring blessings that
are *different* from the great blessings the Spirit has brought in earlier
ages. Revival brings greater *degrees of awareness* to the same truths, not
new truths. New revelations, new techniques, new methodologies—
these are not needed and they are never the real issue in authentic
revival. God will take us, by the Spirit's sovereign work, into deeper
experiences of the same essential truths previously revealed in the
Scripture and confessed by all true Christians. What happens is that
He powerfully illuminates our hearts by the activity of the Spirit.
This has been true of every revival since Pentecost.

Indeed, here is another important way we can know whether or
not a revival is of God or not. Does it "confirm them [i.e., those
involved] in things that are agreeable to sound doctrine"? The Spirit
will always "represent things as they are indeed." We can be sure of
this much. Revival never causes people to put their Bibles aside to
"listen to God," but rather causes them to pick their Bibles up as if
they had never read them before. As we shall soon see, when we consider present-day claims about great revivals presently taking place,
we come to realize that much of what is happening isn't leading
people into truth.

Blessing #5: An Increase in
Love for God and People

When the Holy Spirit does any work in a person, whether great or small, He always gives to that individual a deeper love for the triune God and a deeper love for people, especially the people of God. The apostle John supports this when he writes:

> Dear friends, let us love one another, for love comes from God. Everyone who loves has been born of God and knows God. Whoever does not love does not know God, because God is love. . . . Dear friends, since God so loved us, we also ought to love one another (1 John 4:7-8,11).

In his epistle, John speaks of two opposite spirits now at work, displaying the sharp contrast between them. Love is the evidence of the true and right spirit. The apostle speaks of both love and God the Spirit as if they are virtually one and the same. His conclusion is that if God's love is in us, the Holy Spirit is also in us (see also 3:22-23; 4:16). There can be no doubt about this: Love is the *principal mark* of the Spirit's work.

Now, if this is true, revival brings with it yet another great blessing: an outpouring of God's love upon the church. This love will cause believers to love one another, and this great display of grace will spill over into the watching world. Historian Gerald McDermott sounds this particular note when he writes:

> Revivals usually resulted in concern for the poor and unfortunate. Zinzendorf's Moravians cared for the sick, established schools and provided for the aged, widows, and orphans. Edwards taught the Christian's duty to be charitable to the poor—the pre-eminent test of true religion, as important as prayer or church attendance. No commandment, he said, was laid down in the Bible in stronger terms. A time of revival was

the time when this duty ought especially to be preached. He recommended that every church keep a large fund for this purpose. On his deathbed he ordered that any money that would have been used for his funeral be channeled instead to the poor.[8]

Revivals have had a staggering effect upon the social life of the nations in which they have taken place—especially in Great Britain and America. Revivals gave England a social conscience in the midst of the Industrial Revolution, helped to put an end to slavery, and brought women and children out of the mines. Concern for the care and reform of prisoners, compassion for the mentally ill, and care for the living situations of the poor all spilled over into society at large as a result of the love and concern of a revived Christian church in Great Britain and beyond. In America, the mid-nineteenth-century prayer revival deeply affected the ethical and social patterns of people, and this just before the start of the war between the States.

The love that spills over in true revival helps to prompt the reconciliation of estranged people groups. It brings the restoration of families. Brian Edwards has well said that "one of the sad marks of the church in its normal life is that it is often found uniting with those from whom it should separate, and separating from those with whom it should unite."[9]

Revival is the glory of true evangelicalism. It unites people in the gospel without surrendering the truth. It puts the focus squarely upon Christ and His love for those who know Him.

Further, true revival brings believers to love one another with a Christlike love. This is so pronounced a blessing that the unbelieving world cannot help but take notice. Bishop Festo Kivengere of Uganda wrote of how the love of Christ was a powerful witness to unbelievers in his war-ravaged nation, saying:

I have seen many methods devised in attempting to produce a love-fellowship. But the only known power for keeping together

a group of believers—intact in love, fruitful and not ingrown—is
the presence of the Author in the midst who is listened to and
obeyed. It is not the product of man's desire for socializing. It
is a fruit of Christ's self-giving love, which always draws us
together and creates a community wherever people have
opened their hearts to Him. When the Lord is in the midst,
the Holy Spirit makes us alert and sensitive to each other's
needs. This is what the prophet calls "the heart of the flesh" in
place of a cold, stony heart. The Spirit is the One who sets us
"free to serve one another in love." This serving is done in
practical ways which are visible to onlookers. There were many
in Uganda, and eventually in all East Africa, who echoed the
words of the pagan Romans which Tertullian tells us about:
"Behold these Christians, how they love one another!" A
widow whose house is in disrepair may find the believers
together building a new one for her. A hungry family may find
a bag of grain at the door in the morning. A young person may
find that his school fees have been paid. . . .[10]

But can't love, and even profound displays of genuine concern
for others, be manufactured by false prophets and even *appear* as the
blessing of true revival? How do we know, when we see this mark of
revival, whether it is truly *the love of God*? Jonathan Edwards is both
practically and theologically satisfying when he says:

> There is a counterfeit of love that often appears amongst those
> that are led by a spirit of delusion. There is commonly in the
> wildest enthusiasts a kind of union and affection that appears
> in them one towards another, arising from self-love, occasioned
> by their agreeing one with another in those things wherein
> they greatly differ from all others, and for which they are the
> objects of ridicule of all the rest of mankind; which naturally
> will cause them to prize the esteem they observe in each other,
> of those peculiarities that make them the objects of others'

contempt: so the ancient Gnostics, and the wild fanatics that appear at the beginning of the Reformation, boasted of their great love one to another: one sect of them in particular, calling themselves the Family of Love. But this is quite another thing than that Christian love that I have just described; 'tis only the working of natural self-love, and no true benevolence, any more than the union and friendship which may be among a company of pirates that are at war with all the rest of the world. There is sufficient said [in First John] . . . to distinguish it from all such counterfeits. . . . The surest character of true divine supernatural love, distinguishing it from counterfeits that do arise from a natural self-love, is that Christian virtue shines in it, that does above all others renounce and abase and annihilate self, viz. *humility.* Christian love, or true charity, is an humble love. . . . When therefore we see love in persons attended with a sense of their own littleness, vileness, weakness, and utter insufficiency; and so with self-diffidence, self-emptiness, self-renunciation, and a poverty of spirit, there are the manifest tokens of the Spirit of God. . . . The love the Apostle speaks of as a great evidence of the true spirit, is God's love or Christ's love. . . . What kind of love that is, we may see best in what appeared in Christ, in the example He set us, when He was here upon earth. The love that appeared in that Lamb of God, was not only love to friends, but to enemies, and a love attended with a meek and humble spirit.[11]

True love comes from our understanding of (by the work of the Spirit) the profound riches of God's free and sovereign grace given to us in Christ alone. It always humbles us. True revival will never cause us to become "puffed up" or rude toward others. Rather, it will make manifest in us the blessed fruit of holy love. This is always the evidence of a profitable work of the Holy Spirit.

REMAINING FAITHFUL IN ANTICIPATION

We must once again realize that real revival is God's work. He will bless us as He pleases, when He pleases, and how He pleases. To recognize that we need the blessing of God is always a step in the right direction. We can and must sow seed. We can and must plow the ground. We can and must pray for showers. But we must teach believers that all the significant blessings of revival come only from God. And we must obey God in every way possible. To do less is to prove we have no real interest in true revival, personally or corporately. At the same time, we cannot dictate to God what He must do either in our lives or our time in history.

Theodore Cuyler, a nineteenth-century minister in Brooklyn, New York, provides for us a fitting conclusion:

> After a long pastoral experience and frequent labors in revivals I confess that there is much that is utterly mysterious in regard to them. Our God is sovereign. He often seems to withhold His converting power at the very time when, according to our calculations, we ought to expect it. I have had many disappointments of this kind. On the other hand, copious showers of heavenly blessings have descended when we were not expecting them.[12]

Eleven

PROBLEMS AND EXCESSES
IN REVIVAL

Let it never be forgotten that a time of great blessing is a time of great peril.

—Henry C. Fish

You may be assured that the cause of revivals is far more likely to suffer an attempt on the part of its friends to pass off everything for gold, than by giving to that which is really dross its proper name.

—William B. Sprague

Though some should wish it to the contrary, if we put all the recorded revivals together, we shall find that these "phenomena," or unusual things, make up a very small part of the whole. Revival itself is unusual, and the great work of conviction, conversion and the creation of a holy life put all other things into the shade.

—Brian H. Edwards

JONATHAN EDWARDS WROTE hundreds of pages advocating the idea of special seasons when the Holy Spirit is extraordinarily poured out upon believers. He was acutely aware of the multiplied dangers and excesses often associated with these unique occasions. In fact, Edwards observed that a work of grace might well be genuine and at the same time there could be "a considerable degree of remaining corruption and also many errors in judgment in matters of religion, and in matters of practice."[1]

157

No serious reflection upon God moving in revival can ignore the excesses and abuses. Often these become *the* celebrated issue in revival. In some cases, as in much written today, these excesses are actually treated as if they were the genuine marks of a great work of the Spirit. Whether the "mark" is said to be tingling in the hands or warmth in one's physical extremities, many people believe, often in some vaguely defined way, that these marks are *the* proof that God is indeed doing a marvelous thing.

"Let the Fire Fall"

Young and old, men and women, leaders and people alike are getting drunk. Thousands across the churches are laughing, crying, praying, praising, being healed, falling asleep, going into trances and seeing visions of God. People are experiencing fire in their hands, their stomachs and on their lips, some with such intensity that they cry to God to stop. These things are happening in congregations worldwide. It is refreshing. It is festive—the cry is "Drink, drink, drink!" and everyone is getting drunk.[2]

So writes Bryn Jones, an apostle in the British Restoration Movement, in his enthusiastic endorsement of the newest revival movement now sweeping the world.

January 20, 1994, marks the beginning of one of the best-known revival movements in our generation. Leaders of the Toronto Airport Christian Fellowship claim that on the evening of January 20 large numbers of people were "zapped by the Spirit" as "fire fell" upon the congregation. What happened is now well documented. Hundreds of people began to laugh, in some cases hysterically and uncontrollably. Animal noises and roaring like that of lions soon became an added part of the Toronto experience. The story of the rise and growth of this movement has been chronicled in a dozen or more full-length books, both favorable and unfavorable in their conclusions.

It is estimated that several million people have attended the more recent revivals taking place at the Brownsville Assembly of God Church in Pensacola, Florida. This movement began on June 18, 1995. "Some observers say [this church] is the epicenter of a larger American reawakening they compare with the Great Awakenings in the eighteenth and nineteenth centuries." This movement began under the ministry of evangelist Stephen Hill. The pastor, John Kilpatrick, believes that he heard "a sound like a rush of wind" and that he "felt a sensation like flowing water." People began to fall and shake around the building. Kilpatrick was himself laid out for four hours. When he finally stood up he said, "I felt like somebody had stretched my bones." The service lasted six hours. When the people came back in the evening they had a seven-hour service. Hill stayed in Florida for six weeks. Word spread as thousands of people began to come from all over the world. Hill eventually sold his home in Texas and moved to Florida, believing the whole thing to be "divinely directed."

Michael Brown, adjunct professor of Old Testament at Pat Robertson's Regent University, views these events as part of a growing worldwide awakening which includes the Toronto "holy laughter" movement and the 1995 campus revivals which began in Texas and spread widely. Gary Stratton, dean of chapel at Gordon College, Wenham, Massachusetts, believes that as many as 140,000 people (worldwide) are committing their lives to Christ every day. He adds, "It's a significant moment in church history and Western history."

In Pensacola, evangelist Stephen Hill will typically cry to a full house, "The glory of the Lord is here. Just do what you feel!" Hill quite often rails against his critics, on one occasion shouting that "a critical spirit will damn your soul. It'll keep you from revival." But what is the "critical spirit" that leaders like Hill speak against? Hill answers, "A critical spirit is one who analyzes everything. . . . It's a miracle you're alive because you're a stench in God's nostrils."[3]

One Brownsville member who has attended many of the meetings was quoted in *Charisma* magazine:

The best way to explain it is, God is pouring out His Spirit
upon all flesh as it says in Joel in the Old Testament. It started
slowly, and then the Holy Spirit started flowing and coming
upon the people. By word of mouth, the word is spreading
about the manifestations of the Holy Spirit.[4]

One basic thread seems to run through almost all the accounts
of these meetings: Holy Ghost fire and power is being poured out
upon people regularly and the evidence can be seen in physical and
emotional manifestations.[5] When an explanation is offered for the
phenomena, it is generally explained in these ways: "I felt more love
for Jesus while I lay quietly on the floor for a half an hour," or "The
burning I felt in my hands led me to give to my brother in need," or
"God dealt with my mind and showed me the need for cleansing as
I fell back into the waiting arms of another." John Kilpatrick's testimony, noted above, is typical: "I felt like somebody had stretched my
bones."

While we can appreciate these expressions of deepening love for
Christ, and even wish that the issues raised by these kinds of revival
movements were so simple, there is much more going on here than
initially meets the eye. In writing about why we need the Puritans
and their biblical balance in our time, J.I. Packer wisely notes that
modern evangelicals are often

> . . . *restless existentialists* . . . [with an] outlook . . . of casual hap-
> hazardness and fretful impatience, of grasping after novelties,
> entertainments, and "highs," and of valuing strong feelings
> above deep thoughts. . . . They conceive the Christian life is
> one of exciting extraordinary experiences rather than of res-
> olute relational righteousness. . . . The reason why the restless
> experientialists are lopsided is that they have fallen victim to a
> form of worldliness, a man-centred, anti-rational individualism
> (emphasis in original).[6]

As we have seen, true revival must always be measured by the accompanying blessings and whether or not these conform to the Word of God. Mere outward physical and emotional phenomena, as powerful as they appear to be, are *not* the evidence of true revival. Some of the people present in these supposed outpourings have tried to point this out, but often with little or no effect upon the masses of people who believe they are actually partaking in historic, biblical revival. If this is part of the greatest revival since Pentecost, as some claim, who needs to listen to the critics anyway? (Indeed, many of the people in such movements believe we're headed toward a great worldwide revival that will precede the end of this age!)

IS UNUSUAL PHENOMENA PROOF OF REVIVAL?

Critics of revival often find plenty of material for their criticisms when they observe unusual happenings, especially those which cause people to do strange things. What's more, many of us are suspicious of anything that profoundly affects the physical and emotional nature of people, making it somewhat difficult to ascertain exactly what is happening because revivals really do touch people very deeply.

We cannot deny the fact that eyewitnesses have affirmed the presence of unusual phenomena at almost every major movement of God's Spirit in history. Critics have often made much of these excesses as indications that God is *not* at work. On the other hand, friends of revival often claim these phenomena to be living proof for a mighty movement of God. In actuality, neither group is entirely correct, for unusual phenomena are just what they are: phenomena. Yet the excesses we see in revivals—especially some of the newer ones in our own time—do mar revivals, even real ones. We need to have a clearer understanding of unusual phenomena if we want to know what role they have in genuine outpourings of the Spirit.

One contemporary student of revivals sums up my concern well:

> Modern writers often make sweeping statements about physical manifestations in past revivals and about the attitudes of the revival leaders to the phenomena. Those who are unsympathetic to the whole idea of revival often use such phenomena to discredit the genuineness of the movements. . . . On the other hand, some modern Charismatic writers make broad generalizations about such phenomena in past revivals and the attitudes of leaders at the time, together with comparisons with the present, which need to be severely qualified. For example, to state that the phenomena of "being drunk in the Spirit" or "being slain in the Spirit" (phrases with little, if any, biblical precedent) were common in past revivals and were welcomed by the leaders in those revivals makes a number of unwarranted assumptions and begs a number of important questions.[7]

Since revival is a time of intense spiritual activity, as we have seen, it will inevitably include the counterfeit with the real. If God is at work, the enemy cannot be delighted. His tactic will always be to sow confusion and disruption. As Brian Edwards helpfully points out, "It is impossible to read of revival without, sooner or later, stumbling across some unusual, perhaps bizarre, or even frightening events." He notes that these have included "everything from visions to faintings, from 'prophesying' to shrieking. . . ."[8] The presence of these phenomena has caused some people to reject revival altogether. It has led others to allow the emotional elements associated with these phenomena to overtake their minds and the discerning guidance offered by God's Word.

Leaders of past revivals have responded differently to the presence of such phenomena. It is a mistake to think there is a seamless argument here. John Wesley, for example, was initially quite open to these things. His brother Charles, as well as the great itinerant preacher George Whitefield, were both more cautious. When people began to faint or writhe on the ground during sermons, John Wesley said this was evidence of deep conviction. Later he changed this view and even suggested that Satan pushed people to display this "extravagance."

Without a doubt, many authentic revival movements have, unfortunately, been sidetracked or viewed with suspicion simply because of unusual phenomena. No one has more thoroughly dealt with this than Jonathan Edwards. Under his own preaching ministry, as well as that of George Whitefield and Gilbert Tennent, he witnessed excesses and commented upon them extensively. Edwards's views, often cited and frequently misused, are worth careful consideration. The place to begin is to hear his general wisdom on the subject:

> If we look back into the history of the Church of God in past ages, we may observe that it has been a common device of the devil to overset a revival of religion; when he finds he can keep men quiet and secure no longer, then he drives them to excesses and extravagances. He holds them back as long as he can; but when he can do it no longer, then he will push them on, and, if possible, run them upon their heads. And it has been by this means chiefly that he has been successful, in several instances, to overthrow most hopeful and promising beginnings. Yea, the principal means by which the devil was successful, by degrees, to overset the grand religious revival of the world, in the Primitive Ages of Christianity, and in a manner to overthrow the Christian Church through the earth, and to make way for the great antichristian apostasy, that masterpiece of all the devil's works, was to improve the indiscrete zeal of Christians, to drive them into those three extremes of enthusiasm, superstition, and severity towards opposers; which should be enough for an everlasting warning to the Christian Church.

> Though the devil will do all his diligence to stir up the open enemies of religion, yet he knows what is for his interest so well, that in a time of revival of religion, his main strength shall be tried with the friends of it; and he will chiefly exert himself in his attempts to mislead them. One truly zealous person, in the time of such an event, that seems to have a great hand in the affair, and draws the eyes of many upon him, may do more

(through Satan's being too subtle for him) to hinder the work, than a hundred great and strong opposers. In the time of the great work of Christ, His hands, with which He works, are often wounded in the house of His friends, and His work hindered chiefly by them: so that if any one inquires, as in Zechariah XIII.6, "What are these wounds in Thine hands?" He may answer, "Those with which I was wounded in the house of My friends."

The errors of the friends of the work of God, and especially of the great promoters of it, give vast advantages to enemies of such a work.[9]

In defending the revivals of his time against critics, Edwards did an unusually wise thing in regard to the issue of excesses. He argued that there were several things that did not prove, one way or the other, whether or not the movement was of God: 1) unusual things happening; 2) unusual effects upon the bodies of people; 3) increased talk about religious matters; 4) unusual effects upon people's imaginations; 5) many people influenced by the examples of other people; 6) unwise and irregular conduct in people; 7) errors of judgment, even satanic delusions; 8) some people in the movement, even perhaps leaders, falling into heresy or sin; and 9) much preaching about the horrors of hell.

Edwards further observed that some people in his day argued the New Testament says nothing about people weeping, groaning, or sighing—whether in fear of hell or in response to God's anger. He cited the account of the Philippian jailer falling down under the weight of sin and crying out, "What must I do to be saved?" (Acts 16:29-30) as an incident that parallels what might well happen in true revival (Edwards also cites Scripture texts such as Psalm 32:3-4, where we read of the agony exhibited by David when he came before the Lord in repentance).

We know Edwards's observations are trustworthy because he was so careful in concentrating his attention upon the message preached during revivals. He kept God and His Word at the center of all he did. Modern proponents of revival cannot do better than Jonathan Edwards in terms of judging both the blessings and the excesses associated with a move of God. Any assessment of the results of a revival needs to be done with an emphasis on the spiritual impact (see the "blessings" noted in chapter 10).

Asahel Nettleton, the great American itinerant evangelist who had a part in the early stages of the Second Great Awakening, saw some people whom he said had a "horror of mind" so severe as to require that they be taken out of his meetings until they found peace with God. What caused this unusual response? The powerful preaching of solemn themes such as the holiness of God, the strictness of the law, the certainty of hell, and the need for true repentance. When those so agitated were removed, a strange quietness would usually result as the preacher went on speaking. Nettleton once commented to his listeners, "It may perhaps be new to some of you, that there should be such distress for sin." He added, "But there was great distress on the day of Pentecost, when thousands were pricked in the heart, and cried out, 'Men and brethren, what shall we do?'"[10] Thus Nettleton, like many revival preachers, pointed to Pentecost as a precedent for these deeply felt responses. What's more, notice how such "interruptions" then differed from what we see happening today. In the early revivals, anguish was spontaneously expressed by listeners without outside prompting. Today, speakers often make wildly emotional and hypnotic appeals encouraging excessive behavior through "constant suggestions" night after night during a revival campaign.

The experiences we are speaking of have been common in real revivals. In Ulster (1859) the story is told of what were called "strikings-down." At one Presbyterian church a strong man stood up, in a loud voice cried out under conviction, and then fell down. He never, however, became unconscious. In fact, as he was taken from the meeting and asked if he was conscious. He answered, "Yes, *awfully* conscious!" The sheer horror of the felt awareness of sin had thrown him to the ground.[11] He didn't fall because a speaker was waving his hands over a crowd and "causing" rows and rows of people to fall down like dominoes.

MIRACLES AND GIFTS OF THE SPIRIT?

The question of whether miracles and unusual sign gifts continued after the age of the apostles has been a source of frequent debate. This has been especially true in the twentieth century. I raise the issue now not to discuss the various theological arguments for and against the continuation of certain gifts, but rather to consider the presence and relationship of such gifts or manifestations to times of revival.

That there have been unusual displays of the sovereignty of the Spirit during times of revival is a simple matter of fact. Yet the evidence for such displays being widespread is sparse. While dramatic healings, for example, have sometimes happened during revivals, they have never been a *distinct* mark or an evidence of the Spirit's outpouring. Thus the mere presence of seemingly miraculous activity should never be taken to mean a revival movement is of God.

Another "proof" people sometimes cite as a sign of authentic revival is the utterance of prophecies. The proclamations of the "French Prophets" of the Evangelical Revival in eighteenth-century England are a case in point. Even children claimed visions and prophecies in France and became known as "the Little Prophets of the Cervennes." Initially some leaders in England were sympathetic to these claims of prophecy, but when many of the prophecies failed to come true, the claims were rejected by most. Even a young George Whitefield gave a great amount of attention to impressions (i.e., impulses in his mind) which he took to be a means of *secondary* revelation. Jonathan Edwards graciously endeavored to correct Whitefield. After the death of Whitefield's only child, a son of whom Whitefield had made a striking prophetic utterance with regard to his future ministry, the evangelist ceased the practice abruptly with a humble, open admission of his error.

Another sad case is that of Humphrey Jones in the 1859 revival in Wales. Jones was a greatly used evangelist who eventually suffered from sheer exhaustion due to the revival. During this time of mental anguish he began to claim the gift of prophecy, even proclaiming that he had a divine revelation that the Holy Spirit would descend in bodily form at Aberystwyth on a stated day and at a certain time. Jones said this would happen for the purpose of inaugurating the millennium. As historian Eifion Evans has correctly noted, Jones eventually came to his senses but as a result of his foolishness his previously good ministry was permanently damaged.[12]

Jonathan Edwards is frequently cited by those who wish to defend physical phenomena in their meetings as well as displays of prophecies and miracles. This, however, is a rather ludicrous citation. Why? First, Edwards was clearly a cessationist in his view of the apostolic sign gifts. There is no debate about that. Second, following the Protestant view of Christian ministry, Edwards held the office and role of the pastor in highest esteem. He saw anything that undermined the minister and his normative role of preaching/teaching as harmful. Third, Edwards frequently testified to profound experiences of intimate relationship with God. He openly preferred these joyful experiences to any "immediate revelations." And finally, even though Edwards looked for a coming millennial age in which revival would have a worldwide impact, he did not believe the apostolic gifts or "signs and wonders" would have anything to do with this great age. He wrote:

> Some of the true friends of the work of God's Spirit have
> erred in giving too much heed to impulses and strong impres-
> sions on their minds, as though they were immediate significa-
> tions from heaven to them of something that should come to
> pass, or something that it was the mind and will of God that
> they should do, which was not signified or revealed anywhere

in the Bible without these impulses. . . . I don't expect a
restoration of these spiritual gifts in the approaching glorious
times of the church, nor do I desire it . . . it appears to me that
it would add nothing to the glory of those times, but rather
diminish from it. For my part, I had rather enjoy the sweet
influences of the Spirit, shewing Christ's spiritual divine
beauty, and infinite grace, and dying love, drawing forth the
holy exercises of faith, and divine love, and sweet compla-
cence, and humble joy in God, one quarter of an hour, than
to have prophetical visions and revelations for a whole
year. . . . I would therefore entreat the people of God to be
very cautious how they give heed to such things. I have seen
'em fail in very many instances; and know by experience that
impressions being made with great power, and upon the
minds of true saints, yea, eminent saints; and presently after,
yea, in the midst of, extraordinary exercises of grace and sweet
communion with God, and attended with texts of Scripture
strongly impressed on the mind, are no sure signs of their
being revelations from heaven. . . . no wonder therefore that
sometimes [those who follow these impressions, revelations,
etc.] are led . . . into woeful extravagances.[13]

Regarding the controversial matters related to signs and wonders, I doubt if we could find better and wiser counsel than that
offered by Edwards. Even if some of the present-day claims to miraculous gifts prove to be true, we are still faced with the inherent dangers of placing too much emphasis on these aspects of revival. When
miracles *appear* to be taking place in connection with revival, we
need to ask: Are the miracles contributing to the work of the gospel?
How? Why? Could they distract from the more important spiritual
work of the Spirit? Is Christ glorified by these claims and the attendant events? What kind of spiritual fruit does all of this produce in
those affected by them?

WHEN REVIVALS GO WRONG

Richard Lovelace, in his massive book *Dynamics of Spiritual Life: An Evangelical Theology of Renewal*, has a very helpful chapter titled, "How Revivals Go Wrong." In it Lovelace concludes, "Almost every major revival recorded . . . has been surrounded by an aura of irregular religious activity and has also been centrally affected by elements of weakness and sin." This is exactly the point I am seeking to make, and it is the same point made earlier in the extensive quote cited from Jonathan Edwards.

Lovelace refers to "the pathology of awakenings" and suggests that we need a better understanding of the world, the flesh, and the devil. All three are capable of diverting the good fruit of a true awakening.

The World

The world will attack revival from the outside. When the church is alive, wide awake to her calling, and engaging the philosophies and sinful patterns of the world with fresh power and zeal, opposition is to be expected. This is especially true when increasing numbers of people become believers and are added to a revived church. (Conversely, one of the evidences that the church is not revived is that the world, generally speaking, could care less about most of what it does or why it does it, except when elections come along and they see the church as a "power bloc.")

The world will zero in on any faults it can find in Christians, especially in leaders. Rejection of the church's message will be accompanied by various forms of attack and persecution upon those who believe our message. In an increasingly pluralistic environment a church with an uncompromising message—and the power to proclaim it as well—will be hated by many people. This is to be expected (see John 15:18). We can only imagine how the media would respond to a genuine outpouring of the Spirit in our time. (For that matter, we wonder how the church would distort things in our media-conscious environment if a true revival were to happen.)

Opposition *will* come—not only from the world, but also from those within the church who have worldly hearts. In the past, some of the most articulate antirevival forces have come from within the church. This was especially true during the First Great Awakening, when the famous Charles Chauncy of First Congregational Church in Boston wrote his well-known attack entitled *Seasonable Thoughts on the State of Religion in New England* (1743).

What's more, revived Christians sometimes add to the problem. Ron Davies notes:

> Over-reaction against such opposition or caricature on the part of those experiencing revival has its own potential for distortion. Revived Christians can develop a ghetto mentality or a persecution complex when faced with opposition from the outside world or from the "world in the church." They can also develop a sense of superiority and pride, and manifest a critical spirit towards those who attack them. Being convinced of the rightness of what they are doing, and believing that God is on their side, they may doggedly persevere in their chosen patterns of behaviour, and unwittingly go to extremes. They may also separate overhastily from those in the church who are attacking them, rather than remaining in the church group or denomination, seeking humbly to learn from the criticisms and seeking to maintain testimony to what they believe God is doing in and through them.[14]

It is also true that the world can have an adverse effect upon revived Christians in terms of how it attracts them. This is done through the allurement of methods and techniques. (Charles Finney actually encouraged the adoption of "sufficient measures" that would win the attention of the world to the cause of Christ!) As we shall see later, this is especially true when a movement is highly influenced by the theology and practice of revivalism.

The Flesh

Every believer is sufficiently influenced by his own fallenness and remaining corruption to do all manner of harm, even in the name of Christ. During revival, both new converts and "strict" older believers can become a source of problems. Lovelace notes:

> New Christians may envy the spiritual gifts of others and covet them. They may become preoccupied with the emotional side effects of Christian experience and lapse into spiritual gluttony, lusting after joy and ignoring its giver and the responsibility of an obedient walk of faith. Wrath may find its counterpart in censorious judgment.[15]

Revival is God's work. Yet He uses mortal men as His instruments. One of the more interesting aspects of studying revivals is to look at the unusual human instruments that God has been pleased to use. At the same time, there's always the danger that we might give too much attention to those human instruments. One wise student of revival instruments remarked, "The purpose of revival is to make God, not men, famous; to focus the eyes of the people not upon human leaders, but upon the Divine leader; to give glory not to great men but to a great Savior."[16]

Another danger of the flesh is the desire to duplicate revival evidences through human effort. (This again is closely associated with the revivalism we will consider.) This often leads to a kind of manipulation which seems to suppose "that by duplicating methods used elsewhere you can also duplicate results."[17]

Revived believers often act as if they have arrived, the battle is done, and the victory belongs to them. Too much is made out of personal opinion, and people who oppose them are treated as if they are "unrevived" or, worse yet, unregenerate. This kind of spiritual pride can provide a significant foothold for the enemy. Jonathan Edwards cautioned:

The first, and the worst cause of errors that prevail in such a state of things [i.e., in revival] is spiritual pride. This is the main door, by which the Devil comes into the hearts of those that are zealous for the advancement of religion. 'Tis the chief inlet of smoke from the bottomless pit, to darken the mind, and mislead the judgment: this is the main handle by which the Devil has hold of religious persons, and the chief source of all the mischief that he introduces, to clog and hinder the work of God. This cause of error is the mainspring, or at least the main support of all the rest. Till this disease is cured, medicines are in vain applied to heal other diseases. 'Tis by this that the mind defends itself in other errors, and guards itself against light by which it might be corrected and reclaimed.[18]

Personally I have found Edwards's counsel proven true time and again. Those who have experienced even the least moving of God in revival are often the most difficult to correct. The devil does not need to inflate irreligious or carnal people. By contrast, he will work overtime to get those who are filled with zeal for the Lord to become overly interested in themselves and their opinions.

One further effect of the flesh is what has been called "the law of spiritual entropy, which causes the decay of spiritual experience and its hardening into a new formalism."[19] Oddly enough, revival often points out the shallowness and powerlessness of old forms of church life, which only end up being replaced with new forms of church life that are just as shallow.

The Devil

Finally, Jonathan Edwards notes that excesses and errors in revival are prompted through the extremely active agenda of the devil. "Yea," he writes, "the same persons may be subjects of much of the influences of the Spirit of God, and yet in some things be led away by the delusions of the Devil. . . ."[20]

Richard Lovelace suggests, from his own extensive study of revival movements, that Satan usually takes one or more of three lines of attack:

1. He seeks the destruction of the work of revival either by persecution or by the kind of accusation which will discredit it and limit its growth.

2. He infiltrates the work and reinforces its defects in order to provide more evidence for accusation.

3. He inspires counterfeit revival which may deceive the elect and further confuse and alienate the onlooking world.[21]

The enemy stirs up "false fire" in order to draw attention away from the real. While true revival brings about a genuine, unforced, and unplanned unity in the gospel, Satan is active to divide brethren over things that are not central to the awakening God has sent.

PRINCIPLES THAT HARM REVIVAL

Jonathan Edwards devotes considerable attention to one final area of excess and error that we need to mention in association with revival: "wrong principles." Edwards lists several of these wrong principles and notes that ultimately their foundation is bad theology. Some of the wrong principles he lists include: 1) claims to inspiration or revelation; 2) the adopting of new methods to arouse people's interest and concern without thought of the long-term consequences; 3) arguing that the blessing of God on a particular revival minister proves, on the basis of divine providence, that everything he does is now right and thus there is no need for biblical correction; 4) the neglect of external order and of using the *means of grace* (i.e., preaching, prayer, and the sacraments).

The practice of people building their direction upon "impressions and immediate revelations" is quite common in revival. This practice is also extremely common today, an era in which revivalism has dominated. What does Edwards mean by "impressions and immediate revelations"? He answers:

> [People] lay themselves open to a delusion by expecting direc-
> tion from heaven in this way, and waiting for it: in such a case
> it is easy for persons to imagine that they have it. They are per-
> haps at a loss concerning something, undetermined what they
> shall do, or what course they should take in some affair, and
> they pray to God to direct them, and make known to them His
> mind and will; and then, instead of expecting to be directed, by
> being assisted in consideration of the rules of God's Word and
> their circumstances, and God's providence, and enabled to look
> on things in a true light, and justly to weigh them, they are
> waiting for some secret immediate influence on their minds,
> unaccountably swaying their minds and turning their thought
> or inclinations that way that God would have them go, and are
> observing their own minds to see what arises there. . . .[22]

Edwards suggests that a minister should not introduce things
that are "new and strange." He argues that divine providence must
never be our ultimate guide in matters related to human deci-
sion-making during a movement experiencing a great outpouring
work of the Spirit. He says, ". . . providence may, to our dark minds
and weak faith, confirm the Word of God as it fulfills it."
Providence, Edwards soundly reasons, can and must be studied.
There is a very real sense in which that is exactly what we have done
in this chapter—we have looked at the Word of God and considered
the history of God's dealings in seasons of revival. This, Edwards
would insist, is a valid use of providence.

Having said this, we desperately need to heed Jonathan Edwards's
sound counsel:

> There is a good use to be made of providence, of our own
> observation and experience, and human histories, and the
> opinion of the Fathers and other eminent men; but finally all
> must be brought to one rule, viz. the Word of God, and that
> *must be regarded as our only rule* (emphasis added).[23]

If revival, as we've seen, is a time of great blessing, then it is imperative for us to understand that it is also a time, potentially, of great peril. The enemy does not sleep during seasons of blessing. And the flesh does not lose its power either. Believers who long for God to move in reviving mercies need to prepare themselves to be "as wise as serpents and harmless as doves" (see Matthew 10:16).

Part Four

HISTORICAL AND CONTEMPORARY ISSUES

Twelve

REVIVAL AND REVIVALISM: THE BIRTH OF THE MODERN MOVEMENT

The whole story of revivals is involved in these two facts; viz., that the influence of the Holy Spirit is concerned in every instance of sound conversion, and that this influence is granted in more copious measure and in greater power at some times than at others. When these factors concur, there is a revival of religion.

—Joel Hawes

By 1854, a correspondent of the Independent *could write jovially, "Brethren, if you will follow the above directions for two months, and do not enjoy a revival of religion of the old stamp, you may tell me and the public, I am no prophet."* . . . *If salvation was available for the asking, then a revival was a matter of getting the greatest possible number to ask—a matter of salesmanship. As theology grew simpler, technique became predominant.*

—Bernard Weisberger

THE LATE ALEXANDER Whyte noted that "there is a mystery about revivals. God's sovereignty is in them." The student of revival and revival history will not consider this subject for long without coming to the same conclusion. Revival is the *sovereign intervention* of God. When asked to identify the author of revival, the late historian J. Edwin Orr noted, without the slightest hesitation, that in every case revival must be traced to God's sovereign purpose.

Typically, serious treatments of this subject will acknowledge that God is the author of revival. One example can be seen in the standard multivolume reference work of an earlier time, edited by the famous team of John McClintock and James Strong. In an entry accurately titled "Revivals of Religion" this old source notes that revival "is the work of God. He only can forgive sins, or renew the heart."[1]

That true revival is a work of divine grace is beyond serious question. But if revival is a work of God's grace, then from man's perspective it must be something *uncaused* by human will. We must understand this basic truth: We never *cause* God to bless us. We cannot earn or merit His blessing, even through obedience to His precepts. Furthermore, we dare not try to tell God what to do. We are entirely dependent upon Him for life and godliness. If any message stands out consistently in the Bible it is this: God cannot be helped or hindered by mortal flesh.

The frequently used illustration of the Christian being God's arms, God's legs, and God's mouth may make a point regarding the *how* of God's using us as His channels, but we must never think of God as sitting in a kind of celestial wheelchair waiting for us to do His work. This notion of God, all too common, is actually destructive of true religion. It will never promote the biblical doctrine of revival.

We are so utterly dependent upon God that our only hope is in Him alone. Only this understanding humbles us. And if we are humbled we may be prompted, by the Spirit of God, to look to God alone to rescue us. This will end all feverish attempts we make to program and develop human resources in order to bring about a revival. It will also underscore the simple fact that any blessing we receive comes from God alone. Further, if our trust is in the Lord, the means that God has appointed for us to receive His blessing—namely, prayer and preaching His Word—will be used exclusively. There is no room for human flesh to glory in the presence of the Almighty—absolutely none!

The late Arthur Wallis, himself a charismatic, was surely correct when he wrote:

> While acknowledging that Scripture gives some place to man's responsibility in the matter of a spiritual outpouring, it would surely be erroneous to suggest that the blessing inevitably follows when God's people fulfill certain conditions. That would be taking the initiative out of God's hands and placing it in the hands of men. It would mean that man could release the power of revival as and when he chose, just as one of the great powers could release on the world a holocaust of nuclear power at the touch of a button. History shows that revival does not come in such a mechanical way. When, in trying to explain it, we have taken all the known factors into account, we are still left with the element of mystery. We can only exclaim with Paul, "How unsearchable are His judgments and how inscrutable His ways!"[2]

Yet as we have already seen (chapter 4), there are widely divergent views about revival within modern evangelicalism. As we noted, these views can ultimately be reduced to two: Revival is given either because we meet conditions, or it is given because God is pleased to grant it. In this chapter we will attempt to gain a better historical understanding of how these two views arose within evangelical Christianity. The older view, that God "pours out His Spirit" as He pleases, we call *revival.* The newer view, that we meet conditions and thereby promote or cause (in some sense) revival, we call *revivalism.*

A SHIFT IN THINKING

Several definitions are in order at the outset. Solomon Stoddard, the grandfather of Jonathan Edwards, reflecting the old school thought about revivals, referred to them as "some special seasons wherein God doth in a remarkable manner revive religion among his people." This was the common usage of the term until the 1820s, nearly a century later than Stoddard. Another phrase frequently used by theologians and ministers was "a surprising work of God." The very expression underscores their view of revival.

After the Civil War (1861-65) a new view of revival had clearly emerged within evangelicalism. Iain H. Murray notes:

> Although the ideas for it were born earlier, it was not until the last forty years of the nineteenth century that a new view of revival came generally to replace the old, and a distinctly different phase in the understanding of the subject began. A shift in vocabulary was a pointer to the nature of the change. Seasons of revival became "revival meetings." Instead of being "surprising" they might now even be announced in advance, and whereas no one in the previous century had known ways to secure a revival, a system was now popularized by "revivalists" which came near to guaranteeing results.[3]

The effects the eventual adoption of this new view actually had upon the church were remarkable, and they are still with us today. I am convinced that much of the present confusion regarding revival resulted from this alteration.

Admittedly this chapter thrusts us into the stream of historical controversy. We must tread very carefully; I do not wish to deny that God used men who made mistakes. In addition, it is all too easy to adopt a certain view of things and then read that view back into the people and events of another era. At the same time, certain events and people did profoundly stamp what we now consider revival. It is important, therefore, that we know how we got to this present understanding of revival, which I am calling, for historical reasons, *revivalism*.

If evangelicalism took a wrong turn in the nineteenth century, then it is vitally important that we understand how and why. I will try to demonstrate that wrong views of revival are a major hindrance to right views of conversion, Christian living, sound doctrine, and ultimately, even real revival. Almost every widespread revival since the Great Awakening has included several errors that stem directly from this time period.

I know this sounds intolerant to our age, but I humbly submit that these errors have dishonored God and brought discredit upon the name of Christ. It might well be that real revival is actually so rare in our time precisely because God will not grant another great outpouring of His Spirit until His people are better prepared to respond properly to the gift itself. It could be, if I am correct, that revivalism actually hinders revival!

THE CATALYST TO CHANGE

Mention the name Charles G. Finney (1792-1875), and most people immediately think of the greatest revival preacher in American history. He clearly was the prominent leader in the later stages of the Second Great Awakening. His success, if measured by both numbers and public interest, was undoubtedly phenomenal.

A converted lawyer with no formal theological training, Finney quickly became the best-known preacher in North America during the 1820s and 30s. He was born in Connecticut, but his parents moved to New York when he was only two. At 16 he was already a teacher, but after four years of teaching he returned to Litchfield, Connecticut, to attend an academy. He thought seriously about matriculating at Yale, but his tutor talked him out of it and urged him to privately study law. After several years of teaching, Finney returned to New York in 1816, where he entered the law office of a judge in Adams, near Lake Ontario. He passed the bar exam and became an assistant in a firm.

Finney's religious background was minimal. He described himself to be "as lost and ignorant of religion as a heathen." Through the prayers of his fiancée and the invitations of several friends he decided to settle the matter of personal relationship with God. In late 1821 he went through three long days of seeking peace. In his now-famous *Memoirs* he writes that "a strange feeling came over me as if I was about to die. I knew that if I did I should sink down to hell." Soon after this, on October 10, while praying, Finney had his dramatic experience. He writes that while he was alone in the law office his heart suddenly "seemed to be liquid" and that his feelings appeared to "rise and flow out" of him. "I wanted to pour my whole soul out to God," he added. He fled the office and sought a private place of prayer. He said the room appeared to be filled with brilliant light as he fell upon his knees seeking God. He wrote that at this point "it seemed as if I met the Lord Jesus Christ face to face" and what seemed to him like waves of electricity flowed through his body like "liquid love . . . the very breath of God."[4]

Almost from the moment of his conversion Finney felt an urge to preach. He was only 29 at the time, and left his legal career to devote all his energy to winning souls. Interestingly, he was also involved in a lawsuit but broke off the case, telling his client that he had a "retainer from the Lord Jesus Christ to plead his cause."

Finney was tall and handsome, had eyes that penetrated right through people, and was marvelously endowed with speaking ability. People were captivated by his presence. Finney was tutored for two years by his pastor, Rev. George Gale of the Presbyterian Church, before seeking a license to preach. The St. Lawrence Presbytery licensed him to preach on December 30, 1823, and six months after that he passed his ordination requirements.

In the examination that preceded his ordination, things happened that should have given significant insight into what might follow. He was required to preach an extemporaneous sermon. Finney refused to enter the high pulpit, choosing rather the floor of the center aisle. The examiners were annoyed but approved him anyway. The ordination exam also required candidates to take vows that affirmed the Westminster Confession. Although Finney had not seriously studied this document, he was not entirely ignorant of its contents. He had heard the teachings about man's total depravity, the imputation of Adam's sin, the need for divine satisfaction in the atonement of Christ, and the efficacious work of the Holy Spirit in regenerating sinners dead in their transgressions. From the very first he rejected these teachings as "contrary to reason." He especially disliked the doctrine of *human inability*, insisting that it was completely unacceptable to hold men responsible for faith in Christ if they were somehow not capable of having faith through their own *human* ability.

So serious were Finney's theological departures from the orthodoxy of Protestant evangelicalism that this is a story in itself. Suffice it to say that he rejected the Protestant doctrine of a sinful human nature as well as the doctrine of the imputation of the believer's sin to Christ and of Christ's righteousness to the believer. In his struggle with the dominant Edwardsian theological content of the early 1800s he parted not only with the Calvinists but even from the more traditional Arminian theology of men such as John Wesley. Amazingly, Finney argued, "I insist that our reason was given us for the very purpose of enabling us to justify the ways of God; and that no such fiction of imputation could by any possibility be true." The publication of Finney's writings in coming years demonstrated, beyond any reasonable doubt, that he considered not only the doctrine of original sin to be "anti-scriptural and nonsensical dogma" but he also believed that the new birth was not a divine gift of God. Finney wrote that:

> . . . regeneration consists in the sinner changing his ultimate choice, intention, preference. . . . when mankind becomes truly religious, they are not enabled to put forth exertions which they were unable before to put forth. They only exert powers which they had before, in a different way, and use them for the glory of God.[5]

John Thornbury sums up Finney's doctrinal views well when he writes:

> Finney found the commonly accepted doctrines of grace not only intellectually unacceptable but also functionally intolerable.

If these views were irrational, they were false, and if false, delete-
rious. He believed that a vibrant and thriving Christianity could
not co-exist with such concepts as inherited depravity and "con-
stitutional" regeneration. Those beliefs, though hoary with age
and loved by thousands, were, according to Finney, inimical to
godliness and damaging to evangelism. Successful preaching, he
maintained, must be based on the proposition that men have
the full ability to convert themselves.[6]

In his *Memoirs*, which until quite recently were available only in
a severely edited edition, Finney states that his personal efforts were
to consist of two major battles: the first was to defeat sinners by his
campaigns for Christ, and the second was to destroy Calvinism.
Initially his pastor, George Gale, withstood him. Finally, under
Finney's adept persuasion, Gale came to embrace Finney's ideas in
1825.

Finney proceeded to go from place to place preaching as an itinerant evangelist. He drew large crowds instantly and was a convinc-
ing polemical orator. Sinners were told, in no uncertain terms, that
they needed no divine agency but had to summon power from
within themselves to be converted. Thousands responded. Pastors
and laymen who had held to orthodox positions resisted for a time,
but the impressions he made upon them were so great and the numbers so large that many eventually succumbed and embraced him.
Also, prominent figures supported Finney early in his career. By the
end of 1826 Finney was a celebrity in the West and his revivals were
spreading rapidly.

The first formal opposition to Finney probably came from The
Oneida Association, a group of Congregational ministers in western
New York who condemned his revivals. His preaching caused such
agitation in the Presbyterian church in Auburn, New York, that
many people withdrew and formed a new church. The initial concern had to do not so much with doctrine but methodology since

Finney's clearest expression of his divergent theological views would not come until later. What offended ministers in the early days of his ministry was his style—he was considered harsh, crude, and even abusive. (Most evangelicals who read Finney today consider this part of his strength, saying that he was singularly a *revival minister*.)

The New Measures

In time, a controversy arose that came to be called "The New Measures Controversy." What exactly were these New Measures? They included such things as public praying for people by name, which embarrassed those who opposed Finney but impressed others, who perceived Finney as being bold. (He also allowed women to pray in public meetings, which was not done at the time.) Finney used informal speech rather than measured and reverential language. New converts were very quickly given leadership roles in his meetings (this had not been done in revivals in the past), and those who didn't go along with the meetings were publicly denounced. Finney was especially noted for calling sinners to profess their repentance publicly. This eventually led to what was referred to as the *anxious bench*, where special seats were provided for those who wanted to be saved. This practice evolved into the "invitation system" of modern evangelism, where, in effect, sinners are told that by coming forward (raising a hand, signing a card, and so on) they will most assuredly be saved on the spot. All of this led to the practice of admitting people into the church almost *immediately* upon profession of faith in Christ, regardless of their understanding of biblical truth.

During 1825-26, Finney met with Asahel Nettleton, the greatest itinerant evangelist of the eastern states, on two different occasions. Nettleton was the last itinerant evangelist of the "older" way. His life and highly effective ministry have been all but forgotten because of the historical changes that came through Finney's success.[7]

Following the two private visits with Finney, Asahel Nettleton wrote a letter to a minister in Utica in which he outlined serious disagreements over the New Measures. He added, with reference to Finney's present labors, that "there is, doubtless, a work of grace in Troy." His further observations are important to the story:

> We do not call into question the genuineness of those revivals, or the purity of the motives of those who have been most active in them. . . . But the evils to which I allude are felt by the churches abroad; members which have gone out to catch the spirit, and have returned, some grieved, others soured, and denouncing ministers, colleges, theological seminaries, and have set whole churches by the ears, and kept them in turmoil for months together. Some students of divinity have done more mischief in this way than they can ever repair. . . .

> The evil is running in all directions. A number of churches have experienced a revival of anger, wrath, malice, envy, and evil-speaking (without the knowledge of a single conversion) merely in consequence of a desperate attempt to introduce these measures. Those ministers and Christians who have heretofore been most and longest acquainted with revivals are most alarmed at the spirit which has grown out of the revivals of the west. . . . The friends of brother Finney are certainly doing him and the cause of Christ great mischief. They seem more anxious to convert minister and Christians to the peculiarities, than to convert souls to Christ.[8]

Nettleton resisted becoming involved in this controversy for many months. But many friends of revival pled with him, and finally he felt he could not remain on the sideline any longer. His thoughts on what was happening in Oneida County convey the reasons for his entry into the controversy:

> Irregularities are prevailing so fast, and assuming such a character, in our churches, as infinitely to overbalance the good that

is left. These evils, sooner or later, must be corrected. Somebody must speak, or silence will prove our ruin. Fire is an
excellent thing in its place, and I am not afraid to see it blaze
among the briers and thorns; but when I see it kindling where
it will ruin fences, and gardens, and houses, and burn up my
friends, I cannot be silent.[9]

The Meeting at New Lebanon

On July 18, 1826 a historic meeting was held between Finney and
several of his friends, and Nettleton with several of his supporters. This
meeting, held in New Lebanon, New York, became the turning point
in the Second Great Awakening in America. For all intents and purposes, revival work would never look the same again. This, we might
say, was the place where the "old way" finally lost and the "new way" of
revivalism as popularized through Finney's success, triumphed.

Before this meeting Finney printed a sermon titled, "How Can
Two Walk Together Unless They Be Agreed?" In it he said that opponents of his New Measures disagreed with him because of "their
frosty hearts." Finney further stated, "Now, while their hearts remain
wrong, they will of course, cavil; and the nearer right any thing is,
the more spiritual and holy, so much the more it must displease
them, while their affections grovel." This sermon, printed in Philadelphia in March of 1826, drew considerable attention.

Nettleton wrote to a well-known Presbyterian pastor in New
York, Gardiner Spring, saying that Finney showed some serious misunderstanding of the most basic elements of true religion. Nettleton
suggested that Finney exalted false zeal, pride, and self-righteousness
in opposition to meekness and humility. When Nettleton went into
New York he found what he described to be "a civil war in Zion...a
domestic broil in the household of faith." Nettleton's letter to
Gardiner Spring was published in *The New York Observer*, thus many
people knew the concerns of these two protagonists even before they
ever met in New Lebanon in July.

Nettleton's letter stated the exact concerns he planned to express at New Lebanon. He said that for Finney to dismiss all evaluation as "unchristian" was a serious mistake. "Without great care and close examination, the preacher will unwittingly justify all the quarrels and divisions in our churches." He noted that the apostle Paul would not even allow men to be teachers unless they were "of full age, who by reason of use have their senses exercised to discern both good and evil." The apostle also would never allow a young convert to teach and lead "lest he fall into condemnation, reproach, and the snare of the devil." Nettleton concluded his letter by sharing about the dangers of spiritual pride, quoting from the works of Jonathan Edwards on revival.

The conference in New Lebanon ended without any kind of agreements. Both sides departed more divided than ever. Finney felt vindicated when, in the months following, large churches in the East invited him to speak in their pulpits. He was allowed to continue pursuing his long-held goal to "reform the Presbyterian Church" by attacking even more openly the cherished Westminster Confession of Faith.

OTHER INFLUENCES TOWARD CHANGE

Initially the theological roots of the churches in the East were more strongly attached to the confessions and doctrinal standards of historic Reformed theology. Eventually, however, this changed as both the nation and the church became more and more defined by democratic individualism. A theologian named Nathaniel W. Taylor had a major role in influencing this change. He was pastor of the First Congregational Church in New Haven for many years, and eventually became professor of Didactic Theology at Yale. While at Yale he began to teach views that troubled churches near and far.

Taylor, who studied at Yale, did a dissertation that included new views of the doctrines of the divine decrees and the free agency of man. He practically denied the idea of divine decrees (or the eternal plan of God) and openly taught the freedom of the will.

Nathaniel Taylor, a charming and exceedingly bright man, quickly attained great fame. He was known in his early days as "the pride of all Yale college." What Taylor did theologically was to refine and change much of the theology developed by Jonathan Edwards. The way for these changes had been prepared by a transitional theologian, Samuel Hopkins, who taught that there was no sin except *actual* transgression. In other words, he denied the doctrine of the imputation of Adam's sin to the human race (see Romans 5). Hopkins thus attacked the idea that a corrupt nature was passed down to all humans through Adam. In spite of this, Hopkins held strong views on the decrees and insisted that sin had a part in God's plan. Taylor, in turn, took up these ideas and further developed them. He not only rejected the idea of inherited and imputed sin but also taught that the human will is absolute and cannot be *influenced* by any external power. This logically led to the deduction that regeneration (i.e., the new birth) takes place through moral persuasion rather than by inward renovation of the human nature by the Holy Spirit.

In ways that may not have been intended by Nathaniel Taylor and his youthful Yale followers, his views were, in certain respects, remarkably similar (at several points) to those of the evangelist Charles G. Finney. There was no personal relationship between Taylor, the educated and urbane Yale theologian, and Finney, the individualistic, legally trained western evangelist, but it didn't take long for the impact of Taylor's views, combined with Finney's revivalism, to produce a synthesis of thought and practice in the church of both the East and the West. This "New Haven Theology" became part of the larger American theological drift away from the orthodoxy of Edwards and the Protestant Reformers. It is significant, I believe, that when Taylor's views were proclaimed, those who most wholeheartedly embraced them were Methodists. Wilbur Fisk, who at that time was president of Wesleyan University, said to one of the New Haven proponents that "your Calvinism is my Arminianism."

The famous Presbyterian clergyman Lyman Beecher sought to be a mediating influence by trying to end opposition to the western revivals and the New Measures. He later came to Taylor's defense. Lyman's daughter, the renowned Harriett Beecher Stowe, said that her father had "an unbounded and romantic attachment" to Nathaniel Taylor. A Beecher biographer wrote that Taylor was "his first friend and dearest idol." They had first met in Timothy Dwight's study at Yale and had discussed the theology of Jonathan Edwards ever since. By the 1830s Beecher was an open advocate of the Finney-Taylor theological coalition. In time, Beecher's influence opened the door for Finney to speak in pulpits that previously would have never been open. When Finney was urged to preach in Boston, he told Catherine Beecher, another of Lyman's daughters, "Your father vowed solemnly at the New Lebanon Convention he would fight me if I came to Boston, and I shall never go there till he asks me." In August of 1831 Finney went to preach in Boston at Beecher's invitation. By this time, the old era of evangelism was virtually dead, and the revival theology and practice of earlier days was fading into historical oblivion.

ASSESSING FINNEY'S IMPACT

It would appear that Finney was used to introduce many men and women to Christ all across America during the 1820s and 1830s. It would also appear that even Finney eventually came to doubt the number of true converts produced by his meetings. What we know with certainty is this: Finney's theological and method-ological innovations brought great change to the American church.

But what exactly did Finney believe? What were his actual prac-tices in promoting the cause of revival? Did this man, so beloved and quoted by modern evangelicals, actually deny the historic orthodoxy of Protestantism? Let the reader judge by what follows.

As we noted earlier, contemporary research by Barna and Gallup clearly shows that in our generation there has been an erosion of understanding regarding the doctrines of sin and grace. This has led, as it always will, to an insufficient doctrine of grace. The results of this understanding can be seen all around us. "If one feels utterly condemned and helpless, a gospel that proclaims divine grace as

forgiveness is the undoubted answer, but if one feels merely way-
ward, unhappy, unfulfilled and weak, a gospel that offers infused
assistance is quite sufficient."[10]

But how we arrived at this present position is the issue before us.
It was not liberalism that prepared the way for our present theological confusion—at least not among evangelicals. It was Finneyism. It
was Charles G. Finney who wrote:

> There is nothing in religion beyond the ordinary powers of
> nature. It consists entirely in the right exercise of the powers of
> nature. It is just that and nothing else. When mankind be-
> comes religious, they are not enabled to put exertions which
> they were unable before to put forth. They only exert powers
> which they had before, in a different way, and use them for the
> glory of God.[11]

But what happens to the doctrine of divine sovereignty in revival
if conversion is merely using "the ordinary powers of nature"? Finney
concluded that "revival is not a miracle, nor dependent on a miracle,
in any sense. It is a purely philosophical result of the right use of the
constituted means—as much so as any other effect produced by the
application of means." The word "means," used here, is synonymous
with "measures," used earlier. Revivals will succeed then, argues
Finney, by using "powerful excitements."[12]

Were Finney's Converts for Real?

Finney's clear aim was to create "excitements" of religion. This
was what he meant by "revival." He used various "means" to accomplish his goal. Finney often used personal denunciation—praying
publicly for people present in his audience, whom he identified by
name, and told to repent of specific sins, which he often named. His
goal was "an excited state of feelings." Normal church life was can-
celed in order to promote excitements. In Finney meetings, emotional pressure was common. Said one eyewitness, "Force was a

factor, and 'breaking down' his process." Josephus Brockway, an eye-witness of the 1826-27 revival in Troy, New York, said this revival was "a machine put in motion by violence, and carried by power."[13]

These "revivals" had many weaknesses, not the least of which was the large number of spurious converts produced. A.B. Bod wrote in 1835, "It is now generally understood that the numerous converts of the new measures have been, in most cases, like the morning cloud and the early dew. In some places, not a fifth, or even a tenth part of them remain."[14] Even Finney's friends generally came to the same conclusion. Asa Mahan, a fellow revival laborer with Finney for many years, wrote, "I cannot recall a single man, brother Finney and father Nash excepted, who did not after a few years lose his unction and become equally disqualified for the office of evangelist and pastor."[15] Several further quotes from Finney's friends make this same assertion. One wrote:

> Let us look over the fields where you and others and myself have labored as revival ministers, and what is now their moral state? What was their state within three months after we left them? I have visited and revisited many of these fields and groaned in spirit to see the sad, frigid, carnal, contentious state into which the churches had fallen—and fallen very soon after our first departure from among them.[16]

And Joseph P. Ives, a Presbyterian minister, wrote in 1838:

> During ten years, hundreds, and perhaps thousands, were annually reported to be converted on all hands; but now it is admitted, that his [Finney's] real converts are comparatively few. It is declared even by himself, that "the great body of them are a disgrace to religion."[17]

The only conclusion we can draw from these observations is that Finney's impact for good was not nearly so great as many accounts have told us. "Converts" often fell away, resulting in what were called "burnt over" districts in upstate New York. In these areas many people, hardened by the process of religious conversion, became cynical, apathetic, and cold. Pastors repeatedly refused to invite Finney back into their area when they surveyed the damage he had done.

In telling Finney's story, we have mentioned the "anxious bench" as the forerunner of the modern invitation to come forward in response to the gospel. This method of calling upon sinners is now received by evangelicals almost universally the world over, as if it had come directly from Christ and the apostles themselves. The historical fact is this: The invitation is a relatively recent innovation and was introduced in the Rochester revival in 1830. Here is Finney's own word of explanation and defense of this "new measure":

> I had found...that something was needed, to make an impression on them that they were expected at once to give up their hearts; something that would call them to act, and act publicly before the world, as they had in their sins; something that would commit them publicly to the service of Christ.[18]

Protracted meetings have a history of their own, dating from the days of frontier revivals. With campaigns lasting for several days, and involving cooperating ministers, the effects were astounding. The events would include preaching, prayer, and inquiry meetings. Those elements were not new. But individuals zealous for converts saw that the protracted setting was conducive to building emotions and expectations to a feverish level. At the right time "decisions" were then called for by the minister.

Were Finney's Beliefs Heretical?

Whether or not one applauds Finney's innovations, the errors of his theological beliefs create an even greater problem. You need not be a theological scholar to understand that Finney's errors transformed the church's thinking within a few decades. Multitudes eventually accepted many of Finney's ideas, and most of those ideas have gone virtually unchallenged since the 1860s.

It is not too strong a claim to say that Finney actually hated the doctrine of original sin and the corresponding truth of imputation. He wrote, "There is no proof that mankind ever lost their ability to obey, either by the first sin of Adam, or by their own sin." And later, in the same section of his *Systematic Theology*, he concludes, "The Bible everywhere, and in every way, assumes the freedom of the will."[19]

Finney further taught, based upon his view of "moral government," that regeneration was a moral suasion by which the Holy Spirit caused a person to be willing to obey much the same way a parent causes his or her child to be willing to obey. The Holy Spirit works so as to bring obstinate wills to surrender. In this thinking the Holy Spirit overcomes the human unwillingness to repent. The final authority in all of this is human reason:

> If the doctrine in question [natural man's inability to obey the law of God] be true, it is from that moment absurd and unjust to require the performance of any duty of him. . . . It is nonsense to affirm that [acting contrary to the law of God] can be sinful in the sense of blameworthy. To affirm that it can is to contradict a first truth of reason.[20]

Finney approached the Bible through the means of rationalism, or from the context of his own human reasoning power. This resulted in an entire theology subjected to human rationality and caused him to oppose virtually every traditional Protestant position regarding sin, grace, and salvation. Nowhere does his serious departure from historic evangelical Christianity appear more obvious than when he speaks of justification and salvation.

Regarding substitutionary atonement, a central truth of the gospel, Finney concluded, "If He [Christ] obeyed the law as our substitute, then why should our own return to personal obedience be insisted upon as a *sine qua non* of our salvation? . . . Example is the highest moral influence that can be exerted." He then went on to deny the historic doctrine "that the atonement was a literal payment of a debt."[21]

When Finney discussed the new birth, he insisted:

> Original or constitutional sinfulness, physical regeneration, and all their kindred and resulting dogmas, are alike subversive of the gospel, and repulsive to the human intelligence; and should be laid aside as relics of a most unreasonable and confused philosophy.[22]

Even more startling is Finney's view of justification, the central doctrinal concern of the Protestant Reformation. He wrote, unabashedly:

> [F]or sinners to be forensically pronounced just, is impossible and absurd. . . . As we shall see, there are many conditions, while there is but one ground, of the justification of sinners. . . . As has been already said, there can be no justification in a legal forensic sense, but upon the ground of universal, perfect, and uninterrupted obedience to lawe . . . The doctrine of an imputed righteousness, or that Christ's obedience, is founded on a most false and nonsensical assumption [namely substitutionary atonement].[23]

The great theologian B.B. Warfield was not far from the truth when he made this observation about Finney's theology: "God might be eliminated from it entirely without essentially changing its character."[24]

REVIVALISM'S IMPRINT ON TODAY'S CHURCH

Finney's methods and theology, thankfully, were not adopted by all evangelicals. But the changes he initiated established a new direction

for the church. Many evangelicals progressively adopted the revivalism of Charles G. Finney and thereby lost both the older understanding of revival and the theology behind that understanding. The
shift, already in evidence as early as 1861, prompted John Angell
James, a noted minister in England, to say, "I do not desire, I do not
advise a bustling, artificial effort to get up a revival, nor the construction of any man-devised machinery. . . . I want God's work, not
man's. . . . I want no revivalist preachers."[25]

In the last 40 years of the nineteenth century Finney's influence
upon revivals began to dominate the thoughts and patterns of the
church. Revivalism—i.e., the idea that men could *promote* revivals and
cause them to commence through meeting specific *conditions*—took
hold of the evangelical mind and heart. A shift in vocabulary, which
signaled the changes in belief and practice, has been noted by Iain
Murray:

> Seasons of revival became "revival meetings," instead of being
> "surprising" they might even now be announced in advance,
> and whereas no one in the previous century had known ways
> to secure a revival, a system was now popularized by "revival-
> ists" which came near to guaranteeing results.[26]

Because of this shift in meaning and emphasis, many Christians
from the end of the nineteenth century onward began to reject the
idea of revival altogether. This may have been because they were concerned about the errors and excesses they saw at the "new" revivals.
Only recently has there been significant scholarly work done which
shows the shift I have outlined in this chapter. This work bodes well
for the recovery of a proper definition of revival.

Several recent historians have demonstrated that the character of
revivalism was directly linked with the revivalist methodology of
"calling people to the altar." This public invitation "to receive
Christ" was designed:

> . . . to separate the penitents—those actively seeking salvation—
> from the rest of the congregation so that they could be made
> more easily and intensely subject to the psychological and
> social pressures of the minister and of the community of the
> converted.[27]

Thus revivalism sought *external* evidences for the work of the Holy Spirit. It associated various excitements with conviction, repentance, and the new birth. This ultimately created an environment that made it possible for our modern "counterfeit" revivals to be considered acceptable by large numbers of people.[28]

The shift to revivalism which began in the mid-nineteenth century can now be seen in almost every segment of modern evangelicalism. In 1996, an ad promoting the National Day of Prayer included this statement: "It's time we tapped into our most powerful *natural* resource" (emphasis added). One critic responded to this ad, saying, "Nowhere in the copy is God viewed as the supernatural giver of all blessings in Christ; rather, prayer is a human technique that secures natural ends through natural means." This same ad actually goes on to demonstrate this critic's point: "Now more than ever," we read, "our nation needs to be united. Prayer pulls us together." This strange appeal is then followed by this exhortation: "It's essential that we use this vital resource and take time to 'Honor God.' The returns are worth the investment. Prayer: We've always had it. It's time we used it."[29]

At first glance this may appear to be nothing more than an innocent misuse of language, or perhaps an ad copyist's overstatement. But based on what we have seen in this chapter, we know that we're looking at the fruit of revivalism—the "new way" in which *man* does something to generate results. If we want to understand true revival and pray biblically for God to grant such again, it is vital that we understand the critical difference between the old way—revival, and the new way—revivalism.

Thirteen

REVIVAL: IT'S IN THE AIR!

There is nothing he (i.e., Satan) is so much afraid of as the power of the Holy Ghost. Where he cannot arrest the showers of blessing; it has ever been one of his devices to dilute or poison the streams. . . . With the obvious signs of the times in view, who does not see that this artful foe would enjoy his malignant triumph, if could prejudice the minds of good men against all revivals of religion? This he does, not so much by opposing them, as by counterfeiting the genuine coin, and by getting up revivals that are spurious and to his liking. Revivals are always spurious when they are got up by man's devices, and not brought down by the Spirit of God.
—Gardiner Spring

I WILL NEVER forget how utterly amazed I was by it all. I was watching television on the evening of December 31, 1995. In a few more hours, 1996 would begin. I expected the Christian talk-show hosts to be discussing the events of the past year and pointing us to the imminent coming of the Lord. After all, most of them had, at one time or another, cited material from newspapers and magazines that appeared, at least to them, to line up with the prophetic texts in Daniel and Revelation. In years past, I had become accustomed to hearing, on New Year's Eve, discussions about the Lord's return. Some popular evangelical teachers had been saying—at least since I was a freshman in college back in the 1960s—that we must be the terminal generation. Everything seemed ready for the second coming, at least according to their way of interpreting signs.

But I was in for a real surprise this evening. The topic on every program I surfed was not the coming of the Lord but the coming of revival—the coming great awakening. That was it. And I was truly amazed as I listened to what people were saying. This awakening, they insisted, would not be like any previously witnessed in American history. Indeed, this awakening was either now beginning or already here. The evidence for this revival was all around us, said the television speakers. "The greatest revival since Pentecost has begun," said one confident preacher. If we wanted to experience this new move of God, we needed to "step in" counseled another. The river of God was flowing; only those who "quenched the Spirit" would miss out on this new worldwide move of the Holy Spirit.

IS GOD UP TO SOMETHING?

I have been studying revival, biblically and historically, for quite some time. My interest in revival grew out of the brief shower of blessing I experienced while in college in 1970. As I watched the television that New Year's Eve, I confess I could not understand why these people were so sure revival was taking place. I wanted to believe them, but there was no real evidence for the extravagant claims they made. Had I missed something? My fear was simple. If revival was *not* in the air, then people who heard all this talk about revival would become skeptical and confused when they didn't see the evidence. I pray this will not be the case.

Several days later I traveled to speak in Los Angeles. While I was there, I was given an article taken from the *Los Angeles Times* dated December 31, 1995. The caption read: "God Is Up to Something, and It's Big." In the article, religion writer Larry Stammer described exactly what I had just witnessed on religious television: "For growing numbers of Christians, especially evangelicals and Pentecostals, there is a palpable sense that the kingdom of God is near, that God is up to something big—and that it is going to happen soon."[1] Stammer showed how interest in the "literal return of the cosmic Christ" had often fostered wrong predictions. In spite of this recent history a growing number of evangelicals believe that these times are different. Bill Bright said, "Through the years we've seen the harvest. We've see all these tens of millions of people respond to the Gospel. But . . . *what's happening today has been unprecedented, I'm sure, in all of history. I doubt there has ever been a time like this*" (emphasis added).

What were the signs of this great revival these evangelical leaders were talking about? Stammer offered answers from the evangelicals themselves: thousands attending Promise Keeper rallies and the 1997 march at Washington, D.C.; college campuses where large numbers of students were then making public confessions; the fall of atheistic communism; racial reconciliation; growing movements of prayer and fasting worldwide; and reports of unprecedented num bers of conversions in Africa, Asia, and Latin America. Stammer added: "And the approach of the year 2001—the third millenium—only serves to heighten expectations among believers that God will soon show himself in dramatic ways." Further, Pat Robertson, speaking at Pray & Fast '95 in November, openly stated the vision of most by saying: "We've all expected that God is getting ready to send a mighty move of His Spirit upon the earth."

Many individuals are inclined to write off such claims and accounts as the next wave of an ever-changing charismatic movement—a movement that as of late has been characterized by the radical fringe of the "signs and wonders" movement and the "word of faith" teachers. Those who dismiss all this talk of revival say that the real need of the church is for reformation.

Others seem equally certain that this new "move of God" is different. This one is the real deal, they assure us. This one will be true to Scripture. This one will refresh the church and cause us to "experience God" in new ways. This one is more widely evangelical and genuinely ecumenical, not simply charismatic. Some even argue that this move of God is just the beginning of something bigger than the Great Awakening (as evidenced in Dr. Bright's comments) witnessed during the days of Whitefield and Edwards. Dr. Billy Graham also seems to be of this latter persuasion when he says:

Seldom has the soil of the human heart and mind been better
prepared than today. . . . I've never seen so many people come
to salvation in such a short period of time. . . . Historians will
look back, if we live that long, and say this has been a great
period of revival. Wouldn't it be awful if you slept through it.
We're here because of the urgency of the hour. All that we see
happening in the world is a preparation for the gospel.[2]

Most evangelicals, when they discuss this revival, admit they see
elements of the false and the genuine in this new move. Still, they
encourage us to be filled with hope, since every move in the past has
had both true and false elements. They further remind us that we
must be ever so cautious in analyzing this new revival lest we
"quench the Holy Spirit." Because of such dire warnings the average
believer enters into any discussion of this matter with a measure of
fear and trembling. Who, after all, wants to quench the Spirit?
Unless you have adopted a theological position that is antirevival, or
your heart is stone cold towards the possibility of a present move of
the Spirit, you must not write off things too quickly, so the argument
goes.

On the other hand if you don't endorse these claims of revival
(which now come from almost every quarter of evangelicalism) and
get behind the movement you may be viewed as a critic. If you find
that a measure of honest skepticism remains in your mind what are
you to do? Write off interest in revival altogether? As I listen to pastors and laypeople all across North America, I hear all of these concerns and many more.

It would appear, on the surface, that some people have concluded that the one thing the church does not need right now is
another revival. Theologian David Wells, who has given us some of
the most important theological analyses of our time, actually wrote:

. . . we need reformation rather than revival. The habits of the
modern world, now so ubiquitous in the evangelical world,

need to be put to death, not given new life. *They need to be rooted out, not simply papered over with fresh religious enthusiasm.* And they are by this point so invincible that nothing less than the intrusion of God in His grace, nothing less than a full recovery of His truth, will suffice (emphasis added).[3]

Wells writes these sobering words for a very good reason. If revival is still understood, as it is by the overwhelming majority of evangelicals, as "fresh religious enthusiasm" (i.e., more of what we are doing now with some kind of added blessing or excitement), then we definitely *do not* need another revival. (Even the respected A.W. Tozer once noted that if revival is more of what we are already doing he didn't want it either!) But, as I attempted to demonstrate in the previous chapter, the problem with revival as we presently understand it is that we possess a deficient view of revival itself. The reality of our current situation is clear: We live with a continually evolving Americanized version of revivalism which we can adjust to the next movement and the newest excitement with only minimal attempt to define what is actually happening. And we keep calling each one of these new movements *revival.* We seemed to have stopped using the word *revival* with reference to huge evangelistic rallies and "God Bless America" campaigns. This is an improvement, but now we have adopted the term for almost any spontaneous movement of prayer or confession that pops up. (I am sometimes tempted to call for a five-year moratorium on describing any new movement as a revival until *friendly* critics and supporters have both had serious time to assess what is really going on!)

Calls to Coming Revival

Perhaps the most significant contemporary call to revival, understood in this sense of revivalism, comes from Dr. Bill Bright, the founder of Campus Crusade for Christ. Bright's book, *The Coming Revival,* is one of the clearest calls to revival(ism) available today. He tells the reader how God has assured him that revival will *definitely* come. His testimony is clear and his view all too common:

Early one morning after three weeks of fasting, I received the assurance from God that He would visit America in transforming, revival power. I found myself overcome with tears of gratitude. There are those who say God does not speak to you except from His written Word. Of course, the Word is the primary means by which He speaks. But He also talks to us by His Spirit within us (John 14:26; 16:13). His divine impressions are always consistent with His holy, inspired Word. God has never spoken to me audibly, and I am not given to prophecy. But that morning His message to me was unmistakably clear.[4]

Typical of the material which claims revival is coming soon or is already here, Bright's book defines revival as "a sovereign act of God." Almost every attempt to define revival today begins with this kind of disclaimer regarding our role in causing God to move. But from that point onward, there is little significant similarity to what I have called revival. How can I make such a sweeping claim? Read the following comments from Dr. Bright, which come just a few paragraphs after he wrote that revival was "a sovereign act of God."

In America today, we need not wait for a sovereign act of God to bring revival. We do not have to wait for a general outpouring of the Holy Spirit on the church and the nation. Our task is to surrender to the Lordship of Christ and the control of the Holy Spirit, fast and pray, and obey God's Word. *Meeting these conditions, we can expect the Holy Spirit to transform our lives* (emphasis added).[5]

Among modern evangelicals we probably wouldn't find a more striking confirmation of how our modern-day perspective parallels the theology and thought of Charles G. Finney.

The very next chapter in Bright's book is titled "Causing the Fire to Fall." How do we "cause" the fire to fall? Bright answers confidently, over and over, "By prayer and fasting." This technique ("measure") becomes the tool by which we cause or prompt God to pour out the blessing of revival upon the waiting church. Our problem, Dr. Bright reminds us, is unbelief and disobedience.

In another chapter, "America at the Crossroads," Bright concludes that "God wants revival." He goes on to quote several leaders who share his vision, including Pat Robertson:

> We have come to an unprecedented moment in our history—a time when the potential for positive change has never been greater. In the midst of political turmoil and discontent, we are seeing a renewal—a reawakening of the personal values and beliefs that have sustained this nation throughout its history.[6]

Robertson is further quoted from an address he gave at Bill Bright's first national prayer and fasting convocation (1994), in which 600 Christian leaders participated. Robertson said: "God is visiting the earth. I have never seen such response to the gospel as I see these days. This is an unbelievable time of [spiritual] hunger in the world."[7] Bright adds that David McKenna, author of *The Coming Great Awakening*, "sees certain stirrings on college campuses that he believes will result in a revival by the year 2000."[8]

Dr. Bright concludes his remarkable claims with a statement that must be considered, if his words are taken at face value, as a God-given prophetic word for the church:

> During my forty-day fast, the Holy Spirit assured me again and again that God will send a great revival to America and the world when His people heed His call to turn to Him, according to 2 Chronicles 7:14. I am confident that this awakening will result in the greatest spiritual harvest in history, and the Great Commission will be fulfilled in our generation.[9]

Pastors' Prayer Summits

Calls for revival, and expressions of hope regarding the beginnings of great revival, abound. One of the more prominent but generally less publicized movements began in 1989. Initially 45 pastors met for prayer in what was called a Prayer Summit. Similar summits have since been held all across North America. Originally sponsored by what was then called Northwest Renewal Ministries, the movement has grown rapidly. The name was changed in 1994 to International Renewal Ministries to reflect the involvement of church leaders in Japan, South Africa, Australia, and India.

These summit gatherings have drawn pastors together from various denominational backgrounds to spend several days together in prayer. In my travels across the country the past several years I have met scores of pastors who testify how these meetings greatly benefited them personally.

This summit, now a "prolonged, four-day worship experience attended...by a diversity of Christian leaders from specific, targeted communities," touches leaders from almost every background. The ministry sponsors tell us that the purpose of these meetings is "to seek God, His kingdom, and His righteousness with the expectation that He will create and guide them through a humbling, healing, uniting process which will lead them to *a unity of heart, mind, and mission*, and *will qualify them for the blessing of God*" (emphasis added).[10]

Pastors regularly express that "a hunger and power drives the movement beyond a four-day Summit." The *Newsline* of this ministry reports that "God is moving." How? Through prayer retreats for pastors and church board members, pastors' wives Prayer Summits, and special days of prayer for various groups. Even larger prayer rallies and "citywide celebrations of unity" have been held. The ministry reports that pastors and laypeople "are persevering in prayer until heaven-sent revival comes." Terry Dirks, vice president of the ministry, writes, "To God be the glory. We are watching a movement of the Spirit of God!" Dirks, expressing what large numbers of people are reporting, adds, "We stand on the threshold of a modern-day spiritual awakening."[11]

The Summit meetings are "without preaching" and provide various opportunities to confess sin and seek unity with one's brethren. An informational sheet produced by the ministry several years ago includes the following excerpts from notes and letters:

> It was like a dream come true to have brothers from so many different denominations praying, crying, singing, and celebrating together. The unity we experienced during the prayer summit was an experience we will never forget.
>
> —Covenant Church minister

> I could use so many adjectives to describe the effects of this conference, but none would do it justice. To say it was answered prayer, the cry of God's heart, the cry of my heart for many years, would be the understatement in the extreme. If the pattern established by this conference is followed, if the momentum set in motion can be sustained, it cannot but be the beginning of true revival that quite likely will spread worldwide.
>
> —Youth With A Mission leader

> I feel like I have been on a Spiritual Mount of Transfiguration. . . . I highly recommend this experience to anyone and would urgently urge you to be a part at any cost.
>
> —Church of God minister

> While we were told there was no "agenda," I soon discerned an outline that was very gently moving us along with the obvious concurrence of the Holy Spirit. . . . I enjoyed the conference and I was greatly blessed. Furthermore, I want to commit myself to the "Covenant of Continuing" and to make plans now to attend this conference next year!
>
> —Episcopalian minister

As revival fires swept through the upper room, I was touched and cleansed. I discovered what prayer was all about! It was a life-changing renewal experience, and a spark that ignited a revival fire in my heart.

—Baptist minister

I lost a few things during the four days. Some preconceived ideas about other ministries, a fear of associating with men from other expressions, a hesitancy to discuss our common beliefs, etc. . . . we have embarked on an exploratory trip back to wholeness.

—Church of Christ minister

As a person from the "liberal" tradition of the United Church of Christ, this event was very different from what is familiar to me. It has stretched me to see the ways of extensive prayer life and has allowed me to know personally more ministers of the evangelical, charismatic, and Pentecostal traditions than I have ever known.

—United Church of Christ minister

I cannot help but believe that what we are now experiencing is a modern "Great Awakening." Let's keep it up!

—Assembly of God minister

We can hope that much good does come from these gatherings. The idea of prayer between ministers of differing denominations is good and the intention appears sound on the surface of things. No doubt many pastors are greatly helped. However, profound concerns remain if we are to properly relate this to true revival.

Terry Dirks does actually warn about the misuse of the term *revival*. In regard to claims about revival in Portland just a few years ago, he said, "This is not man-produced. It is not a program. We're seeing lives changed. That's something only God can do." Portland evangelist Bob Cryder, a leader involved in this movement, adds, "If revival is in the sanctuary, we are still in the foyer. How close are we to the door? No one can say. *But we are definitely headed in the right direction*" (emphasis added).[12]

This last statement by Bob Cryder seems open to different interpretations. The conclusion that "we are definitely headed in the right direction" is plainly based upon certain theological presuppositions that I wish to humbly challenge in the spirit of Christian charity. It's obvious that these sincere and earnest men desire for God to do a marvelous work in them and their churches. There can't be much doubt about that. At the same time I believe that based on what we're seeing, there is legitimate reason to doubt their understanding of what true revival is. A measure of theological correction is called for based upon the language they're using and the concepts they're communicating. We could say, tentatively at least, that theology is clearly not in the driver's seat in these new waves of prayer and confession.

When theology isn't kept in its proper place, as truth which flows from God through His Word, then the results will be mixed at best. Sometimes they will even be seriously flawed. The emphasis on "qualifying for the blessing of God," a phrase which appears in a statement from this movement, is an illustration of my concern here. So long as we think in these terms we will never understand law and grace as we ought. To speak of "qualifying for the blessing of God" distorts the simple fact that the very basis of grace is this: Only Christ "qualifies" for God's blessings since He alone obeyed God and perfectly kept His holy laws. It is this understanding of law and gospel which is foundational for building a church that prays for God to pour out His Spirit in real revival blessing.

Another element of this nationwide prayer movement—as well as the Promise Keepers movement—is the idea that "for the Lord to do a powerful work of revival in a community, believers need to rediscover Jesus' heartbeat as expressed in His 'High Priestly' prayer in John 17. In a word they need to work together. . . ." This statement, taken from the cover of Joseph Aldrich's definitive book, *Prayer Summits: Seeking God's Agenda for Your Community*, aptly explains what drives many of these movements. Aldrich writes:

> Believers from the Presbyterians and Baptists, the Methodists and Assemblies of God, all true builders, are being joined together by God into a dwelling place of God. We are the means through which God reveals His glory . . . if we keep the walls up, the gates in good repair, and don't fall from within.

> The goal of the church, the Body of Christ in action, is to build up the house of the Lord through evangelism and edification. If the true dwelling place of God breaks forth in our cities, great revival will break out.[13]

Notice where the emphasis lies in these words—we see reference to *conditions being met* so that "great revival can break out." *Revivalism* (as opposed to *revival*) is very apparent both above and beneath the surface in the literature put out by this movement. It is odd, at least to me, that Aldrich goes on to suggest that the apostle Paul's warnings about dividing the church into carnal factions relate to the *local* church. Yet several paragraphs later Aldrich returns to his *big picture model* of the church and quotes approvingly the charismatic Francis Frangipane, who claims, "It will take a citywide church to win a citywide war." Aldrich adds, "In other words, where disunity reigns, don't expect the Lord to build His house or guard the city."[14]

There can be little doubt that behind such calls to revival is a goal (spoken or not) of building a new wide-angle type of Christianity in America. This goal assures us that denominations and associations of churches, built upon ethnic and even doctrinal differences, are no longer desirable. To seek revival, according to this model, we must make every effort to "tear down the walls" and restore our John 17 unity. The proponents of this model usually define unity with an extremely minimal test of faith containing five or ten short statements. Things such as sacraments, church discipline, and the nature of divine revelation are never addressed out of a fear that efforts to create unity might falter. This minimalizing effect has always been characteristic of revivalism. Some of the more outspoken leaders in this new call for revival actually insist that by breaking down the old ways we may be able to usher in the great awakening now at hand.

Denominational Movements for Revival

A number of denominations have made prayer for revival a major priority in the past five years, including the mainline United Methodist Church. This could be a good sign. No one should take offense at an increase of prayer if those involved retain even a modicum of concern for vital Christianity. Yet again we need to note the large-scale confusion of revival with revivalism, which threatens to bring very mixed blessings.

There are many leaders and groups we could study, but they are simply too numerous to consider in a single chapter. One example must suffice. A prominent leader in denominational prayer efforts is Henry Blackaby of the Southern Baptist Convention. The largest Protestant denomination in America, the Southern Baptist Convention, now has a Prayer and Spiritual Awakening Office led by Blackaby. Before taking this role, Blackaby was a pastor/leader in the early 1970s revival in Saskatchewan, Canada. He communicates the hopeful spirit of evangelicals everywhere regarding what is happening across our land. Says Blackaby, "I don't know when there's been such an explosive sense that God is about to do something."[15]

Thousands of Southern Baptist churches have made prayer a top goal for their denomination for the 1990s. One of the more encouraging aspects of this movement is how prayer has been more soundly connected to the denomination's goals for evangelism through what is called "Bold Mission Thrust." Another encouraging aspect is that this emphasis, centered within a group that has a more definite doctrinal framework, tends to retain a more healthy view of the doctrine of the church. In this setting the revival prayer effort is not so much to focus on uniting everybody *without distinction,* but rather to protect an understanding of the marks of a Bible-teaching church, such as the preached Word and the ordinances. In some cases even church discipline is being restored as a result of this increase in prayer for revival. This is all to be heartily commended.

This emphasis has resulted in several books, workbooks, video series, and the bestselling *Experiencing God Annotated Study Bible.* A closer look at these resources reveal much of the theology and methodology of revivalism, which seems to remain at the heart of it all. The strength of the book *Experiencing God* is that it seeks to unite Christian experience with the Bible in a helpful manner. But there are definite deficiencies in the approach taken. There is a good deal of unhelpful mysticism within Blackaby's book, and the doctrine of sanctification is presented in a manner consistent with the views taught in revivalism (i.e., the "Deeper Life" idea). The book is filled with imprecise and even dangerous theological conclusions. An example can be seen in the following statement: "Whenever God gets ready to do something, He always reveals to a person or His people what He is going to do."[16] What does this actually mean? What proof for it is found in Scripture? The text the authors cite is Amos 3:7, which refers to God speaking *uniquely* through His prophets.

This underscores a consistent pattern in modern revivalism—continual appeals to ideas and practices that are rooted in texts used without any theological framework or confessional position. This "grab-bag" approach ultimately uses the Bible in a manner that detracts from God-centeredness and sound doctrine.

Concerts of Prayer

One of the most important ministries which has been used to stir modern interest in revival is Concerts of Prayer, founded by David Bryant. Bryant, formerly of InterVarsity Christian Fellowship, is a man of great energy and tremendous vision. His spirit is filled with hope and he communicates with the kind of genuine passion so deeply needed in this sleepy time. This ministry is actually named after Jonathan Edwards's appeal for transdenominational meetings for prayer aimed at God giving revival to the church. Thousands of such "Concerts of Prayer" are held monthly across the United States.

David Bryant has an intense interest in spiritual awakening and as a result has become a prominent teacher on the subject of prayer and revival. Having prayed in a group with David on one occasion, I was personally impressed with his genuine love for Christ and his deep desire for revival. His book, *The Hope At Hand: National and World Revival for the Twenty-First Century* (Baker, 1995), has undoubtedly had a good effect upon thousands. A recent book by Bryant, *Stand in the Gap: How to Prepare for the Coming World Revival* (a major revision of Bryant's groundbreaking earlier book, *In the Gap*) reveals even more of his view. David believes that a world revival, like none witnessed before, is now beginning and the fuller effects are soon to come. He says, forthrightly, "We are on the threshold of the greatest revival in the history of the church." He quotes, with approval, J. Christy Wilson, who once said, "I believe we've entered the fourth Great Awakening. It has already started—and it may be the last one. Because in this awakening God can complete His plan for the nations."[17]

Bryant clearly draws upon some of the better theologians of revival. He is also a marvelous storyteller. He has used extensive sources in his research, and often very well. Yet he also tends to make some of the same mistakes as other revivalist spokespersons. For example, prayer, which has become the virtual *sine qua non* of this current revival interest, becomes for David Bryant a virtual third sacrament. Preaching and communion have little or no place in the picture, as in most other aspects of the present revival movement. We are told that if we can only mobilize enough prayer warriors and "stand in the gap," revival *must* come. The working assumption throughout seems to be this: If so many people are mobilizing to pray, it must be an indication that God will soon send revival.

Though we should be glad that increasing numbers of believers are praying, this is not, in itself, proof that revival is close at hand. It may well be that we shall pray for the length of an entire generation and never see powerful answers to our pleas. The timing of revival is securely in God's hands. We must pray because God has told us to pray, not in order to prompt revival. Massive movements of prayer will not impress God, per se. Brokenness and deep repentance are also needed, and these elements will only become manifest when the Spirit uses God's Word to bring about true contrition.

Books on Revival

The increasing number of books which have appeared on the subject of revival over the past ten years are yet another indication of a growing interest in the subject. For this interest we should give thanks. One editor of a major publishing house has noted that books on prayer and spirituality are quickly replacing those on "recovery."

There can be little doubt that spirituality has been "in" during the last decade. Several years ago, *Newsweek* observed, "Astonishingly the current edition of *Books in Print* lists nearly 2,000 titles on prayer, meditation, and techniques for spiritual growth—more than three times the number devoted to sexual intimacy and how to achieve it." That number has continued to grow rapidly since that article was written in 1993. Werner Mark Linz of Crossroad Publishing, a Roman Catholic publisher, noted, "Books on prayer are our biggest sellers."

This rising emphasis on prayer and spirituality is apparent not only in Christian bookstores but also within the general Christian community. C. Peter Wagner, the well-known church growth advocate, typifies this change of direction. *Christianity Today* stated:

> [Wagner, who] became known in the 1970s for trademark terms like "body evangelism" and "felt-need events" . . . realized in the eighties that something was missing. Now Wagner says he has a new "assignment" from the Lord to articulate the connection between evangelism and prayer. Phrases like "strategic-level

intercession" and "warfare prayer" have begun peppering his books and Fuller Seminary lectures.[18]

The main emphasis in this movement, as I have written elsewhere, is this: "Believers can be so affected by demons that a particular kind of technique or method is needed to stop them. The techniques needed for this battle must be learned."[19]

As we consider the rising interest in spirituality, it's important for us to understand how people are actually defining spirituality. Martin Marty, a theologian and historian who has been a frequent critic of revivalism from within the mainstream of liberal tradition, tells us that in the 1960s the word *spiritual* had lost its meaning to most. Now, concludes Dr. Marty, ". . . spirituality is back, almost with a vengeance. . . . I find myself treating concern for spirituality as an event of our era." Timothy Jones adds, " baby boomers are shopping around. Some delve into shamanism or Zen meditation. Others talk of 'creation spirituality' and even pray to a politically correct 'goddess.'"[20]

Let's face it—prayer and meditation are genuinely hot these days. *Newsweek* ran an amazing cover story several years ago entitled "Talking to God." More and more Americans were found to be talking to God. *Newsweek* noted, "This week, if you believe at all in opinion surveys, more of us will pray than will go to work, or exercise, or have sexual relations."[21] Interest in spirituality is up all across America. And, it is clear that interest in revival parallels much of this same interest in spirituality in the culture at large.

This trend is particularly fueled, among evangelicals, by authors like Richard Foster, a Quaker, and Henri Nouwen, a Roman Catholic. Evangelical churches, many leading seminaries, and even major denominations have all focused on spirituality for the last few decades. This interest seems to have reached a peak in the last few years. It is hard to tell where this trend might lead, but combined with people's interest in revival, it plainly makes for a new type of individualized evangelicalism. This "new model evangelicalism" is one that is far less rooted in the doctrinal confessional life and practice of the Protestant Reformation and its heirs.[22]

Promise Keepers

In less than eight years Promise Keepers (PK) has grown from an idea in the heart of Coach Bill McCartney to a nationwide men's movement touching millions of Christian men and thousands of local churches. (It has recently begun to develop an international strategy.) The amazing growth of PK clearly stems from both spiritual hunger within the hearts of men as well as the need to recover some measure of commitment to the priorities of marriage and family. The movement has the endorsement of a growing number of evangelical leaders as well as mainline denominational leaders. At the same time, it is opposed by what appears to be a very small handful of critics.

I have tracked this movement's growth from its inception, and have read a good bit of its material. I've also attended several of its meetings. I have personally known Coach McCartney since the 1970s, and have prayed for him and those who work around him. There are things within the PK movement that have clearly helped large numbers of men. Who would not rejoice to see men loving their wives more and praying for a friend's salvation and the nation's well-being?

Clearly the harshest critics of this movement have been the radical feminists and those bent on destroying any remaining moral values within our society. This alone should make us defend our brethren and their efforts. Yet not all the criticism of PK is in this same vein. There are some Christians who, with sincere hearts, have wondered about certain claims made by PK that their meetings are the greatest evidence that real revival is taking place in our generation. My comments along this line will be intentionally brief, since I wish to address only one question: *Is* this movement evidence of true revival in our time? (Much could be said about *both* the strengths and the weaknesses of this movement.)[23]

In a time when people are searching for spiritual reality, and churches and leaders have high expectations of coming revival, the simple observable fact is this: Promise Keepers is another fast-growing revivalistic movement. What is happening in this movement is nothing like revival as we have seen it biblically and historically. The great danger, here again, is that multitudes are coming to believe that these stadium events and the "March to Washington" rally are *real* revival. When we conclude that all of this is revival, we will surely settle for something less than what we so desperately and genuinely need. The idea that these events are part and parcel of revival is being continually implied, if not actually said, on a very frequent basis. Let me illustrate.

New Man, the official magazine of the PK movement, has devoted several articles over the past few years to the subject of revival. In late 1995 an issue appeared with these words on the cover: "Men in Revival: Snapshots from Promise Keepers 1995." The lead article, written by David Halbrook, is titled: "Is This Revival?"[24] The article is well written and accurate in its handling of both biblical and historical information. Halbrook quotes almost the same sources I have used in this book and concludes that both PK and college confession movements ". . . are, logically, a type or precursor to revival. Yet *logic* and *revival* are contrary terms." I hope he means that revival is beyond human planning and methodology. God is never illogical, though God's ways are sometimes "beyond tracing out," and thus mysterious, or hidden, to us. Revivals actually demonstrate to us, in wonderful ways, the mystery of providence. God's purposes in this present world order are not always the same as ours. Revival demonstrates this clearly.

Halbrook goes on to quote noted evangelical historian Bruce Shelley, who wisely writes regarding present revival that "the jury is still out" since only lasting fruit can measure the reality. Shelley adds, "The supreme biblical test is a lasting change of behavior. It has nothing to do with the joy, hand-clapping, shouts, professions of faith, or even being saved. It's whether lives are being changed behaviorally and permanently. It's too early, even with Promise Keepers, to see lasting signs of revival, though I'd like to give them the benefit of the doubt." Halbrook asks, "So, which is it? Is the church riding a crashing wave of revival, or simply watching from shore as a mighty storm gathers in the distance?"

The author goes on to define and contrast revival with revivalism. He does a wonderful job, concluding that:

> The second path, known as revivalism, arose from the remarkable evangelistic career of Charles Finney. It is a purely American phenomenon that, in Finney's own words, depends less upon God's sovereign grace and more on the tools of human enterprise.

> The accepted model for verifiable, large-scale revival in the United States is the Great Awakening of the 1730s-40s. Unplanned, unprompted, it began unexpectedly in the pulpit of an unknown pastor named Jonathan Edwards.

> This was true revival, Shelley contends, because "it was spontaneous, unorganized and seemed to happen without planning."

Halbrook also quotes Richard Owen Roberts, a contemporary writer and historian of revival: "When Finney was present something happened, but when he was absent those following him lost all power to produce revival. The fruit was less stable and the fall-away rate shot up considerably."

This is precisely my point about what is happening today. If revivalism is the adopted pattern in all these new movements, as we have seen, then we ought to be a bit more cautious regarding the claims that revival is taking place. Halbrook, quoting Richard Owen Roberts again, adds, "If revival were to occur at present, with so many sleepy clergy, its life would be automatically shortened."

This excellent article makes some very astute observations, yet in the same magazine we read repeated references to PK's plans and programs, which demonstrate an entirely different understanding of revival than that communicated by Halbrook. For example, in an advertisement for the 1996 PK Clergy Conference in Atlanta, the copy says the conference offers "follow up that will help all gathered *to bring revival* to our churches and spiritual awakening to our communities." The inference is obvious: revival will be present if you come to Atlanta, where we will train you how to take it home and multiply it in your church and community.

Coach McCartney is much more reserved in his recent public comments. In a widely circulated July 28, 1997 letter inviting a million men to attend the Washington Sacred Assembly, held in October 1997, McCartney wrote: "God has revived the church in America at three important times in our country's history. But there hasn't been a national revival in America for 140 years. It is clear that we are long overdue." He adds, "I now see that the favor God has bestowed on Promise Keepers was for this—to call all Christian men to seek God with a whole heart, and to ask for His mercy on behalf of the church."[25] I am not sure most people will see the irony here: God has raised up a movement of men *outside* the church to call upon God to be merciful to the church. It is a massive understatement to call this a biblically bankrupt—or at best, naïve—theology of the church.

After the Atlanta Pastors' Rally at the Georgia Dome in 1996, tapes and excerpts of the messages were circulated. The themes that ran throughout this meeting were repentance, revival, and reconciliation. It was often alluded, and sometimes said, that racial reconciliation would precede the coming revival. One popular speaker, Wellington Boone, proclaimed, "We are on the verge of the greatest revolution in the history of the church, and you are called to be a part of it."[26] McCartney stated, "The church is in bondage to the giant of denominational restrictions and another giant of racial and ethnic boundaries. PK is dedicated to uniting men through vital relationships." Later he added, "If the church ever stood together, almighty God would have His way."[27] Consistently, Coach McCartney refers to our *letting* almighty God have His way. I have heard this and similar comments over and over. They originate from an absence of good theology and from perspectives that are rooted in revivalism.

James Ryle, McCartney's controversial Vineyard pastor, stated in his Atlanta address that "we are today a part of history in the making." He urged the pastors to go and have citywide meetings where "denominational distinctives are set aside. Unity is based on our love for Jesus. It is like the Trinity—organic unity."[28]

Perhaps the most striking call to unity came from the bestselling author Max Lucado when he said, "That is why the world will not believe [i.e., our disunity with each other as believers] . . . our prayers will not be answered. The sin of disunity causes people to go to hell." We are told that when such calls for unity (which were often connected to the coming of revival) are heeded, then the power of the Holy Spirit will come. The question that a discerning listener should ask is this: "What *type* of unity? What denominational distinctives must I put aside to enter into this unity that you keep speaking about?" McCartney responded to this in his address and said, "I am not saying that we should dismantle our denominations and ignore our distinctives, but we should concentrate on the 95 percent where we agree."[29]

This sounds very appealing at first glance. Unity is surely an important theme in John 17. All of us who love the Lord must earnestly desire unity. What is troubling to me, however, is that these new revival movements generally don't limit this call for unity to the 95 percent of what we agree upon. When we listen to the nonessential matters they are quite often large in number. The essential elements (which are supposed to be the 95 percent) appear to come down to only two specifics when you listen to the speakers carefully: 1) love for Jesus, and 2) an experience of the new birth. Max Lucado added, in the same Atlanta gathering, "Would it not be wonderful not to be known as either Protestant or Catholic? This is a God-sized dream and no one in our generation has ever seen the church united."[30]

Never do we hear about other essentials that are clearly taught in God's Word, such as human depravity and bondage to sin, the efficacy of Christ's atonement for all who believe, the necessity of the imputation of Christ's righteousness as our only hope of salvation, and the necessity of practical holiness as evidence of saving faith. In addition, classical doctrines such as Christ's two natures, the Trinity, and the ascension are either assumed, misspoken, or ignored altogether. And, there is no serious doctrine of the church to be found anywhere.

Another major emphasis that appears in this new wave of revivalism is "small groups." PK says that the man who is a Promise Keeper will be committed "to pursuing vital relationships with a few other men, understanding that he needs brothers to help him keep his promises."[31] While it is true that we all need help along the journey of life, especially in keeping our word, and small groups such as Bible studies or Sunday school classes can be beneficial, we need to be careful about placing an inordinate amount of importance on small groups. That today's revival movements stress small groups is not accidental; the connection between small groups and spirituality is a part of modern revivalist thinking. It has its roots in a combination of revival history and modern psychological insights. The Methodist portions of the Evangelical Awakening stressed groups of ten people or so who would meet to pray and offer spiritual help. This emphasis has been joined, in our generation, with a large measure of modern psychological insight linked to studies about group socialization. The dynamic of the small group is a major part of the ongoing strategy of today's revivalism. But where is the *necessity* of this as a key to growth actually to be found in the New Testament? It appears that the New Testament's emphasis is upon God's provision of elders in the local church who watch over the flock (see Acts 20). Small groups may be useful, but they are not *necessary*. The problem with the PK claims, and others like it, is that nowhere in Scripture are men commissioned to simply take this task upon themselves and do it with "a few other men."[32]

Again, the issue in all of this is not wrong motives but poor theology. Add to this an inconsistent understanding of what revival truly is—which always lurks beneath the surface of what is written and spoken—and you have the modern mix. The result of all of this may well be "burned over" churches caught up in yet another movement that will run its course and eventually give birth to a newer movement that will also run its course and leave people wondering what is going on. This is part and parcel of the fabric of American revivalism, the very thing so clearly defined and warned about in the excellent article David Halbrook wrote for *New Man* magazine.

PK seems to have made a positive difference in the lives of many men across America. I thank God for this and encourage the men involved to remember that Jesus Christ is the only true Promise Keeper who ever walked the earth. We can hope that the men involved with PK will become better promise makers and better husbands and fathers as a result of this movement. In regard to some of the present claims for real revival we can pray that it will genuinely come in the days ahead. At the same time, let us be hesitant to proclaim that we *know* it is coming, or that it is *definitely* here.

THE CHURCH'S NEED TODAY

We began this chapter by showing that there is growing interest in revival within our land. We questioned if this present interest is truly healthy. We demonstrated the close association with Finney, in terms of the general paradigm for awakening held by most who promote revival. We conclude by urging fellow evangelicals to recover a God-centered perspective on His work in the world today.

Ultimately, the remedy for the distressed condition of the American church will not come by way of human inventions, which are the heritage of historic revivalism. Revival may well come soon, but it won't be because of methods, but God's graciousness and kindness. This much seems apparent: The greater need at the present time is for a new Reformation—a return to the institutions of Christ stated in the Word of God—and the restoration of sound scriptural discipline in the church, both formative and corrective.[33]

Fourteen
_____

HOW SHALL I RESPOND?

The greatest work that is going on in the world is that of the conversion of sinners, and the edification of saints. Sometimes this work proceeds slowly and silently under the stated ministry of the Word, one after another being secretly impressed with the power of divine truth, and taken under the teaching of God's Spirit....At other times, it is accomplished in a more extraordinary and remarkable way, vast numbers being brought suddenly under the power of divine truth, and exhibiting in a striking manner the effects of divine grace.

—James Buchanan

IN *THE COMING REVIVAL* Bill Bright states forthrightly his view that the modern church has an alternative that has not been adequately tried yet—at least not by multitudes of Christians. He tells us the church in our time does not have to be like the Ephesian church, which had "lost their first love" (see Revelation 2:4). We can escape this mediocrity and supine condition if we will be "filled with the Spirit." In Dr. Bright's view this is actually not all that difficult to attain. It is ultimately a matter of using the right means for the desired end. He writes:

> I am often reminded of something I have tried to teach our Campus Crusade staff and others. All we really have to do as believers, from the time we get up in the morning until we go to bed at night, is love God with all of our heart and soul and

225

mind and strength, obey His commands, and trust His promises. That is all. Everything else flows from that.[1]

If I didn't know better I would not believe Dr. Bright really means what he writes here. Yet this is precisely what he does mean, as he has taught millions of people this concept for decades. Quite honestly, in view of what I see in my own wicked heart, even after years of personal prayer, intense Bible study, repeated attempts to love God with my whole heart, and honest efforts to witness for Christ to the lost in public and private, Dr. Bright's statement takes my breath away. Only a view of sin that is far too small and a view of self that is far too big could come up with a theological idea such as this.

How different is Dr. Bright's widely popular view of the life of sanctification from that of historic Protestant theology, where we read statements like this: "The corruption of [human] nature, during this life, doth remain in those that are regenerated. . . . both itself, and all the motions thereof, are truly and properly sin." The same statement goes on to say, "This sanctification is throughout, in the whole man; yet imperfect in this life, there abiding still some remnants of corruption in every part. . . ."[2]

THE ABSENCE OF THE GOSPEL MESSAGE

Nothing, quite frankly, could be more disturbing about the present revival emphasis than the sheer absence of the objective gospel message of the apostles. These men did not turn their world upside down by telling people about the wonderful discovery of the "Spirit-filled life." They did not preach *experience* at all. Their message was something infinitely bigger and better than any sinner's experience. These apostles and ordinary folk were in the midst of real revival, which is clearly evident to us in the book of Acts. What they talked about was "Jesus, and him crucified" (1 Corinthians 2:2). Their glory was always in Him alone.

unbelievers. Their testimony is not, 'God says,' but, 'I think.'" In the modern church people are seeking new excitement, a new experience. "They want to find a richer experience than faith in the gospel because they fail to see the glory of the gospel. . . ."[5] As a consequence we are a generation of Christians who have turned our eyes inward seeking to "live by the Spirit." We fail, in looking in this direction, to recognize that the operation of the Holy Spirit is always to turn our eyes outward to Jesus and His truth revealed in Holy Scripture.

We see something of Jesus' own response to a similar thrill-seeking age when a woman who saw a display of His power cried out from the crowd, "Blessed is the mother who gave you birth and nursed you." Jesus' stark reply is witness against most of the revivalism of our time when He replied, "Blessed rather are those who hear the word of God and obey it" (Luke 11:28). Revival then, with a proper understanding, is a fresh hearing of the Word of God and a fresh obedience to it. It is not meeting a set of conditions (seven or otherwise), or keeping a set of promises that we make in a stadium or small group.

IS THERE A PLACE FOR EXPERIENCE?

But what about *experience*? Am I suggesting that experience is unimportant in the Christian life? Well, if revival is a fresh outpouring of the Holy Spirit, as we have consistently called it, then will not revival result in fresh, vital Christian experience? Absolutely! But consider the gospel once again: The message of Christ is the source of all true power (Romans 1:16), not the work of the Spirit *independent* of the message of Christ. Let me explain this further.

The *realization* that God has forgiven me in Christ alone, by grace alone, is a supernatural work. This *realization* comes only by the power of the Spirit. To know that my sins are truly forgiven and that I have a true hope of eternal life is a glorious assurance. This assurance comes only by the Spirit.

Revivalism, by contrast, has developed its own unique brand of assurance indicators. For decades people were told their assurance rested in going to the altar and "breaking through." Then it was "accepting Jesus into your heart" and "appropriating the Holy Spirit" so you could enjoy victory. All of this continually took the spotlight off Jesus and His gospel and put it back on the individual and what he or she could do or experience. In the most recent revival movements, the evidence of the Spirit's sovereign work has been reduced to "holy laughter." The sad parade simply goes on and on.

But true biblical conversion is always a lifelong process. The biblical command, literally, is "be [being] converted. . . . " This work does begin at some point; in seasons of true revival that point is often decisive for multitudes of newly born believers, and in nonrevival times it is not always as decisive. The problem is that many people have made a whole theology out of the "new birth" experience that stresses the date, time, and place of an event more than Holy Spirit-given assurance grounded in the gospel itself (see Romans 8).

Furthermore, true conversion actually never ceases in this life. We are "being saved" every day according to the New Testament. To live under the Lordship of Jesus Christ by the power of the Spirit is to experience dramatic operations of the Spirit within our life, whether we fully recognize such at our level of experience or not. To face afflictions, defeats, and even death itself is profound experience for me as a believer. However, none of these experiences grants to me the actual *power* of salvation. "The experience which saves us is that which Christ experienced when He died on our behalf and then rose from death to be our Mediator and Sovereign King. We can never experience anything even close to this. But we can believe it."[6]

MISTAKING REVIVAL FOR REVIVALISM

Any concept of revival that is separated from the gospel and the person of Christ is not real revival. It may have in it elements of God at work, for which we should give thanks. It will be used to bring some to faith, almost in spite of its method and content. But at the end of the day *it is still revivalism*. It's people attempting to bring about a work of God. It will produce clouds without rain. It will feed the church with cotton candy, when only real food can bring life and lasting godliness. Without a doubt, true revival is both desirable and beneficial. But if we keep associating revival with revivalism we will end up being content in all the wrong ways. And we will rob God of the glory that we are required to give Him.

Consider for a moment the two greatest revivals ever: 1) the revival following Pentecost and the ministry of the apostles, and 2) the reformation and revival of the sixteenth century given by the Spirit through the human agency of the Protestant Reformers. Both revivals changed the course of human history. What was the central concern during these times?

> The basic question people were asking was, "How can a man be just with God?" "How can I be acceptable and pleasing before a righteous and holy God?" The question was *theocentric*. Men's earnest inquiry grew out of an overwhelming sense of God's holiness and their own guilty standing and corrupt state.[7]

Revivalism, by contrast, has not raised this question in our time. There is little, if any, dealing with the law of God in present movements. There are oblique references made to certain sins, but often without any reference to the holiness of God's character. We are not confronted with Luther's question, "How can I find a gracious God?" Rather, we already assume that God is gracious. What we want is happiness, fulfillment, and satisfaction. We want to find the new and exciting adventure that will challenge us as "Spirit-filled" Christians.

To some extent this explains one of the most amazing phenomenon in recent years—the "laughing revival." If the law of God is rejected, or generally ignored, then the gospel ultimately becomes inconsequential. The gospel message becomes a way to get into the Christian life when you are ready to "sign up" or "make a commitment to Jesus." And supposedly the real blessings come when you get to the experience of the "wonderful things God has for you" as a spiritual person. Those who defend "holy laughter" (and some individuals have done a good amount of serious writing trying to do exactly that) will always appeal to history, even to Jonathan Edwards, as mentioned earlier. They also appeal to Scripture. "Doesn't Psalm 126:2 indicate that laughter is sometimes the move of God? Doesn't that verse say, 'Our mouths were filled with laughter, our tongues with songs of joy'?" Well, yes, there certainly are times when laughter is appropriate, even desirable. But there is a huge leap here from the joy expressed in this verse to a major revival that is said to be evidenced by uncontrollable laughter. It seems to me that James has the better counsel for our generation when he writes to the church in his age, which was only a few decades removed from the greatest revival period ever:

> You adulterous people, don't you know that friendship with the world is hatred toward God? Anyone who chooses to be a friend of the world becomes an enemy of God. Or do you think Scripture says without reason that the spirit he caused to live in us envies intensely? But he gives us more grace. That is why Scripture says: "God opposes the proud but gives grace to the humble." Submit yourselves, then, to God. Resist the devil, and he will flee from you. Come near to God and he will come near to you. Wash your hands, you sinners, and purify your hearts, you double-minded. Grieve, mourn and wail. Change your laughter to mourning and your joy to gloom. Humble yourselves before the Lord, and he will lift you up (James 4:4-10).

Rather than a revival of laughter, we are in need of a revival of weeping that comes through the clear preaching of the law and the gospel. May God grant it, even in this day when the shadows of judgment are slowly but surely lengthening across the church in America.

Part Five

WHERE DO WE GO FROM HERE?

WHAT TO DO
UNTIL REVIVAL COMES

The only true reformation is that which emanates from the Word of God.

—J.H. Merle d'Aubigne

No religion is pleasing to God unless founded on truth.

—John Calvin

I do not desire, I do not advise bustling, artificial efforts to get up a revival, nor the construction of any man-devised machinery. . . . I want God's work, not man's. . . . I want no revivalist preachers.

—John Angell James

UNDOUBTEDLY THERE IS a rapidly growing interest today in the idea of revival. Thousands of evangelicals are not only aware that something needs to happen to their nation, but more particularly, to their churches. The need to be corporately renewed is genuinely great. It seems that thousands of earnest believers are asking God to send revival. This asking is itself a positive indication of an awareness, even if it is modest, of the magnitude of our need. This awareness needs to grow into a flame of earnest intercession.

But revival, as we have seen, is not something we can do to solve our great problems. We can neither cause real revival nor promote it. Revival is an extraordinary and unique act of God the Holy Spirit. It is a shower of mercy sent from the hand of the Lord. It is God dealing with us in mercy rather than in judgment. According to Luke it is a season of refreshing from the presence of the Lord (see Acts 3:19) during which believers are deeply humbled before the Lord and lifted up by God Himself through the gifts of fresh life and power. Through such a visitation unbelievers are converted and added to the church—quickly, powerfully, and in great numbers. This last observation cannot be overstated.

We see this illustrated in Paul's initial visit to Thessalonica. When Paul left this city there was a growing and healthy new church. The quality of the congregation's life can be observed in 1 Thessalonians 1–3. What's amazing about the great things that were taking place in the church at Thessalonica is that Paul had ministered to these people for only two or three weeks! In 2 Thessalonians 3:1, Paul asks these new believers to pray "that the message of the Lord may spread rapidly and be honored, just as it was with you." That's what had happened in Thessalonica: "the message of the Lord . . . spread rapidly." That is an apt description of how the preaching of God's Word works during revival. In these marvelous seasons of refreshing, truth spreads rapidly. People are born from above in extraordinary numbers and generally with immediate effect.

When this effusion of the Spirit floods upon dry ground, God enters into the affairs of human history in such a direct way that He *openly* turns back godlessness. In revival even those who do not believe the gospel often receive the general benefits of the showers since very often social problems are profoundly addressed with new zeal. These effects occur because the Spirit is working out God-centered fruit in believers that touches everything around them.

Further, in revival, God visits a people, a church, scores of churches, a nation, or even a continent in such a manner that multitudes of people are brought to a sharp awareness of the felt presence of God. God becomes the topic of conversation. Conversions are the news. Overnight, eternity seems to be the interest of multitudes. Backsliding Christians are restored while those who have made false professions of faith are soundly converted. This all begins within the visible church. Prayer becomes the joy of revived believers.

God-centered, bold, and powerful preaching leaves a pronounced impact upon the church. The desire for deep personal holiness increases among both the young and the old. These God-given results overflow so much that inevitably they will spill over into society in general.

That has always been the pattern in true revivals. We have observed this in a number of accounts already cited. The exact pattern is never identical but the general direction is consistent. There is mystery to God's timing and God's ways. He is God! Yet the general characteristics are clear for us to see: 1) an awareness of God's presence; 2) responsiveness to God's Word; 3) sensitivity to sin; 4) liveliness in the community; and 5) fruitfulness in testimony.[1] It's when we see this kind of fruit that we know we're witnessing genuine showers of mercy from God.

BUT WHAT SHOULD WE DO?

Through our study together I've endeavored to demonstrate that biblical, historic, God-centered, and healthy views of revival maintain that God is completely sovereign in all that takes place during an awakening. We can never extort this blessing from God. We dare not demand it. And we certainly do not deserve it. Since there are no conditions we can meet (as in a contractual relationship) in order to bring about this desired renewing of the Holy Spirit, what then should we do? Wait passively? Pray with a fatalistic frame of mind? Wring our hands and blame God when we don't see revival? The wise counsel of J.I. Packer, a theologian who understands revival, points us in the right direction.

> To look to human ingenuity, however, for that which only God in His grace can give is arrogant, inept, and in the outcome barren. And that is how it is in the matter of renewal. When Christians, by the Laodicean character of their lives and their ecclesiastical systems, have quenched the fire of God's Spirit, and so brought about a withdrawal of God's presence and

glory, it is beyond their power to kindle the fire again, much as they might wish to do so; only God himself, by His own quickening visitation, can renew, and for this we have to wait on Him in patient, persistent, penitent prayer until He is pleased to act. Charles Finney, who for a decade after his conversion was used by God in a continuous revival ministry, came to think, evidently generalizing from that experience, that self-examination and earnest prayer on a congregation's part would always secure a divine visitation and fresh outpouring of the Spirit immediately. But the experience of many who have sought to implement this formula, and indeed the different and disappointing experience of Finney himself in later years, shows that this is not so. In no situation can revival be infallibly predicted or precipitated; there are no natural laws of renewal for man the manager to discover or exploit.[2]

Arguably the greatest theologian of revival in American history is Jonathan Edwards. In *A Treatise on the Religious Affections*, Edwards described the cyclical nature of divine awakenings. He demonstrated that throughout history revivals have crested and fallen much like the waves of the ocean, one after another, impacting the church uniquely in each special season of grace. The timing of these great waves can never be predicted, and their occurrence must be attributed entirely to God's wider purposes and sovereign plan.

D. Martyn Lloyd-Jones observed that this explains, to some extent at least, the bigger picture of Christian history, which has never been a straight line:

> The history of the church has been a history of ups and downs. It is there to be seen on the very surface. When you read the history of the past you find that there have been periods in the history of the church when she has been full of life, and vigour, and power. The statistics prove that people crowded to the house of God, whole numbers of people who were anxious

and eager to belong to the Christian church. Then the church was filled with life, and she had great power; the gospel was preached with authority, large numbers of Christian people delighted in prayer. You did not have to whip them up to prayer meetings, you could not keep them away. . . . The whole church was alive and full of power, and of vigour, and of might. And men and women were able to tell of rich experiences of the grace of God, visitations of His Spirit, a knowledge of the love of God that thrilled them, and moved them, and made them feel that it was more precious than the whole world. And as a consequence of all that, the whole life of the country was affected and changed.[3]

But is such revival *really* the *great* need of our time? Considering the magnitude of the problems in this dark hour in church history, how could we answer in any way but the affirmative? When "truth [has so evidently] stumbled in the streets" (Isaiah 59:14), how can anything but the recovery of truth be the greatest need of the day?

Cultivate a Passion for Reformation

Concern for biblical truth is inevitably an expression of our concern for God Himself. To love God is to be concerned for His glory. To be concerned for His glory is to truly love Christ and His church—all of these are biblically related to love for God, which results in the pursuit of divine truth. To know Christ is to know and love Him who is "the way and *the truth* and the life" (John 14:6 emphasis added).

Biblical reformation is always founded on a recovery of reverence for God's Word. The pattern for reformation can be seen in the books of Ezra and Nehemiah, where steps are taken by Israel's leaders to bring about the recovery of God's Word in the lives of God's people. Ezra notes that first the Lord "moved the heart of Cyrus king of Persia to make a proclamation throughout his realm" (Ezra 1:1). Here is where the work of God, in bringing about reformation, begins.

A similar concern should be seen in the cry of the psalmist who said: "Revive me, O LORD, according to Thy word" (Psalm 119:107 NASB). This pattern can be repeatedly seen throughout Psalm 119. (The Hebrew word translated "revive," "renew," "preserve," or "quicken" was used frequently in Psalm 119 and appears in four other Psalms: 71, 80, 85, 143. It is the Hebrew verb that comes very close to our historical idea of revival.) In Psalm 119, the word is used 11 times! What's especially interesting is that the context of the entire psalm is the supreme importance of truth as revealed in and by the Word of God. This is why historian J.H. Merle d'Augbigne, in his work *The Reformation in England*, concludes that "the only true reformation is that which emanates from the Word of God."[4]

The entire Bible demonstrates that reformation and revival should always be linked together. Roland Lamb, in a lecture given to the Conference of the British Evangelical Council in 1967, correctly observed:

> . . . the biblical truth is that God acts in judgment on His own as at other times He acts in mercy. He is active both in revival and retribution. He acts in judgment against His backslidden and rebellious people to bring them to cry out to Him for revival, "We are afflicted very much; quicken us O Lord, according to thy word." Such is the testimony of both Scripture and subsequent church history. . . . Indeed, in one sense, "revival and reformation" is really the complete history of the true people of God. Certainly it was the biblical history of Israel![5]

But which comes first? The order of Psalm 119 puts revival first. This underscores the absolute sovereignty of God in any recovery, personal or corporate. The psalmist asks God to do what he understands only God can do—revive the work of His grace. People need to understand that God alone is the giver of life. Paul states the purpose of this when he exults:

Oh, the depth of the riches of the wisdom and knowledge
    of God!
How unsearchable his judgments,
    and his paths beyond tracing out!
Who has known the mind of the Lord?
    Or who has been his counselor?
Who has ever given to God,
    that God should repay him?
For from him and through him and to him are all things.
    To him be the glory forever! Amen (Romans 11:33-36).

The Bible makes it clear that God acts in judgment at certain times. Often He actually grants us very little explanation as to what He is doing and why. At other times He stirs up earnest pleas in His people's hearts, relents from judging them in divine chastisement, and sends copious showers of mercy through real revival. To insist that the church can advance *only* by or through such awakenings is as much a mistake as to insist that revivals are nothing more than emotional disturbances and bothersome interruptions in the flow of Christian history.

Both the Bible and church history indicate that revival and reformation should both be kept before the church when she languishes and endures seasons of judgment. Sometimes revival mercies have directly prompted biblical reformation; other times, reformation was clearly the precursor of true revival showers. I suggest that our times are in desperate need of both reformation and revival, but it seems to me that reformation must be pursued *immediately*. This is because we have fallen so far from the great doctrinal truths which humble man *and* exalt God; e.g., human depravity, holiness, providence, and divine sovereignty in grace. The church has established her life and practice upon "what works" more than upon "what's right." Until truth is restored by those who actually pray for revival are we not persisting in the problem and only adding prayer to our disobedience?

We can and must continue to pray and earnestly beseech God to pour out the blessings of revival. At the same time, every leader and concerned believer must deliberately pursue reformation. We cannot wait. Continual calls for concerts of prayer and extraordinary efforts to bring many people together to pursue God and ask Him for revival are commendable and encouraging. Yet we should at least recognize that the person who gave us the idea of "concerts of prayer" (Jonathan Edwards) plainly understood that the recovery of God-centered doctrine was essential as well. Edwards urged people to participate in "concerts of prayer" in a definite doctrinal context that sought, above all else, the glorification of God. Can we do less than labor for such a context within the modern church? How can we pray for revival if we are not passionate about God's truth? (At the same time, we have to realize that a passion for God's truth will grow and be helped by true revival!)

Commit to Loving God's Truth

The wise man tells us in Proverbs 23:23 that we must spend whatever resources we have to gain truth. If we care about God deeply, we must love truth deeply. "What is not true is not of God. What is false is anti-God. Indifference to the truth is indifference to the mind of God."[6]

Truth is crucial because God is truth (see Ephesians 4:20-21; John 15:6; 16:13). Jonathan Edwards defined truth as "the consistency and agreement of our ideas with the ideas of God." To not love the truth has eternal consequences (see 2 Thessalonians 2:8-12). Finally, the simple fact is this: Without a love for the truth there is no real salvation (see 2 Thessalonians 2:13; James 5:19-20).

Tragically, this generation has severed truth from life in almost every imaginable way. The preference of a therapeutic model over a truth model is evident. The church of our time is far more interested in "how it makes us feel" than whether or not it is true. (Paul, the apostle, made much more of truth than even the messenger—i.e., his tone, manner, communication style, or how people felt when they were exposed to his ministry; see Galatians 1:8; Philippians 1:15-18. Paul's ministry was passionately driven by fidelity to truth; see 2 Corinthians 4:2; 6:6; 13:8.) Theologian David Wells addresses the problem I am discussing when he writes:

> As the nostrums of the therapeutic age supplant confession, and as preaching is psychologized, the meaning of Christian faith becomes privatized. At a single stroke, confession is eviscerated and reflection reduced mainly to thought about one's self. . . . Thus it is that the pastor seeks to embody what modernity admires and to redefine what pastoral ministry now means in light of this culture's two most admired types, the manager and the psychologist.[7]

We must understand these times. What is under siege in modern evangelicalism is not piety, but truth. Many people are praying and talking about revival, but truth, at best, is only assumed. At worst it is openly assaulted. Many Christians no longer look to truth to define *who* they are and *what* they do. One writer comments on today's pressures upon seminaries to adjust their focus away from truth to "what works":

> . . . some nationally recognized leaders conduct seminars around the country asserting, "If you want to hire someone who knows theology, then look for a seminary graduate. But if you need someone who can actually do ministry, don't hire a seminary grad. Look for someone from within the church."

> Unfortunately, this naive and overly simplistic belief is growing in acceptance. And sadly for the church, a shallow and doctrinally vulnerable membership could characterize its constituency a few generations down the road.[8]

A number of pressures are squeezing the church into a pattern of lowering the bar of what is true and ignoring whether truth really matters. This ends up "dumbing down" the thinking of ministers and members, and the result is more and more mindless practice. Ultimately we're left with worldliness as described in the Epistle of James. David Wells has properly sounded the trumpet in this regard:

> The stream of historic orthodoxy that once watered the evangelical soul is now dammed by a worldliness that many fail to recognize as worldliness because of the cultural innocence with which it presents itself. . . . The older orthodoxy was driven by a passion for truth, and that was why it could express itself only in theological terms. The newer evangelicalism is not driven by the same passion for truth, and that is why it is often empty of theological interest . . . We now have less biblical fidelity, less interest in truth, less seriousness, less depth, and less capacity to speak the Word of God to our own generation in a way that offers an alternative to what it already thinks.[9]

Os Guinness, a Christian sociologist, has noted that Americans, "under the pressures of modernity . . . have rejected 'content for style, truth and meaning for impressions, beliefs for games, ethical rules for social roleplaying.'"[10] How true. And how tragic. The church has followed the pied piper of the world into this arena. What matters in many evangelical churches is "impression," not "truth and meaning." In many churches, if someone raises a good question about the lack of content in the worship music he will encounter a passionate defense about style. If he dares to suggest that the worship has departed from the New Testament pattern, he is told that he is expressing deep cultural biases. Yet a reformation grounded in concern for truth must always address the issue of conforming the church to the Bible, not to the times.

Nearly 75 years ago J. Gresham Machen, a great defender of orthodox Christianity in the midst of growing liberalism in the Presbyterian denomination, observed that the main reason for the loss of the gospel in his church was the decline of zealous love for the truth. He made the point that truth is imperiled not only when language is used to make false statements but also when true statements are made only because they are useful and not because they are true. This problem, rooted in what philosophers call *epistemology* (or the way of knowing something), now shows itself in evangelical books and articles that appear to be studies in the art of intentional ambiguity. Machen stated the problem this way:

> It makes little difference how much or how little of the creeds of the church the Modernist preacher [read: "evangelical" in many cases today!] affirms, or how much or how little of the biblical teaching from which the creeds are derived. He might affirm every jot and tittle of the Westminster Confession, for example, and yet be separated by a great gulf from the Reformed faith. It is not that part is denied and the rest affirmed; but all is denied, because all is affirmed merely as useful or symbolic and not as true.[11]

Machen went on to describe "a temper of mind" that existed in the church of the 1920s. It was hostile to "precise definitions." He said, "Indeed nothing makes a man more unpopular in the controversies of the present day than an *insistence upon definition of terms* (emphasis added)." He concluded, "Men discourse very eloquently today upon such subjects as God, religion, Christianity, atonement, redemption, faith; but are greatly incensed when they are asked to tell in simple language what they mean by these terms."[12]

Pressure from various interest groups, now within our evangelical churches and institutions, prompt many believers to feel "victimized." This kind of pressure makes the work of truth-based ministry extremely difficult for a reformation-minded leader. Further, a hypersensitive concern for being slandered as bigots makes many Christian leaders unwilling to speak the truth in regard to a whole host of issues ranging from abortion to homosexuality to divorce. Even respected Christian institutions, once solidly conservative and trustworthy, now show a fear towards media pressure that seems to make speaking the truth in love an impossibility, at least on certain issues that might offend their cultivated constituency. The "donor" often seems to reign, not the truth!

What can we do? We have no choice: We must seek reformation, bit by bit. We understand that such work will be incremental, and never complete. But we must begin. We must seek to restore the truth, and we must begin with the most obvious and vital areas. Let me illustrate this with actual examples from the history of reformation and revival.

LEARNING FROM PAST EXAMPLES

The Sixteenth-Century Protestant Reformation

When Martin Luther nailed his famous *Ninety-Five Theses* to the door of the University Church in Wittenberg at approximately noon, October 31, 1517, he had no idea that he was being used by God to launch the greatest recovery of the gospel in history. What Luther was doing, in his own mind, was issuing a challenge for debate. The issue was to be the sale and abuse of indulgences.[13] Luther himself wrote years later that when he drafted his theses in 1517 he was still a "mad papist." Only later, after taking a first small step in the direction of church reformation, did the light of the glorious gospel actually shine profoundly and clearly into the heart of the German monk. He would come to see the truth of grace alone, faith alone, and Christ alone over the next several years.

The action of one man seeking the reformation of the church at a very practical level of life and devotion was the spark that began the most widespread and thorough recovery in 1,500 years of church history. This effort, begun unself-consciously by a determined and courageous monk, was eventually attended by spiritual showers all across Europe that brought many conversions and great spiritual renewal that can only be understood as true revival.

The first glimmer of dawn actually came several centuries before, when God ignited a recovery movement among the Waldensians of the twelfth century. The papacy steadfastly opposed this movement, but in time their light spread into virtually every part of spiritually darkened Europe. In the fourteenth century, John Wycliffe, called "the morningstar of the Reformation," challenged the church to center its life and practice around the Bible alone. Converted at age 19 in 1348, Wycliffe was early led to see that the Bible alone should be the rule of all faith and practice. Every doctrine and practice that did not rest clearly upon Scripture was to be rejected if the reformation was to succeed. Wycliffe correctly perceived that the ground of faith and practice in the fourteenth century was the papacy and the church. His efforts at reformation resulted in his sending out "poor priests" (Lollards) to preach the Bible to the common people. These enlightened and empowered (revived!) preachers were the first heralds of the coming day of full light in the sixteenth century.

As we progress through this story, we need to keep in mind that reformation is always called for in every generation. But why? Don't we ever "get it right" and remain faithful for long periods of time? Not usually. The tendency of the church—given its struggle with the world, the flesh, and the devil—is to compromise, initially in subtle and small ways. This compromise eventually causes people to turn away from the clear teaching of the Word of God. This happens step by step, over decades of time—much like a small drip from a bad faucet eventually causes the loss of hundreds of gallons of water. This steady drip increases in intensity and volume until a flood of infidelity and apostasy replaces the flood of the previous recovery and revival. And unfortunately, most believers pay little attention to the drops when they first appear.

In the "fullness of [God's] time" the Lord calls a man, a woman, a handful of people here and there to stand against the slide, to call for reformation according to the Scriptures alone. In some cases, when reformation does not take place, whole areas of the world where once the gospel thrived are left without light. (Consider the Middle East, where the early church once thrived!) In other cases, the church is wonderfully restored through reformation and revival.

Contrary to what many people may think, we can never anticipate God's ultimate plan for particular nations and peoples.

A century from now, if Christ tarries, America might well be enshrouded in total pagan darkness while Latin America and Africa are the continents on which true Christianity thrives. Just a little over 100 years ago Great Britain was covered with marvelous gospel light, though the forces of modernism were rapidly spreading within the visible church even then. Today, Christianity has a very small presence in a sea of liberal religion and paganism which now blankets the entire United Kingdom. Church buildings have become monuments to a past era, and the true church in Britain faces a century in which its task looks much more like that of the church in the first century than that of the church in the nineteenth century.

Pastor and author Alistair Begg once said to me that many of America's megachurches may soon be vast "carpet showrooms" if we continue down the path we are presently on. Revival alone will *not* halt this slide. We need reformation and revival together. Reformation efforts must be undertaken by pastors and church leaders in every region and community of this nation. This must be done church by church; there is no other pattern. Some will, no doubt, lose their pastoral positions. Others will be driven out into a wilderness of uncertainty, both emotionally and financially. All, however, who stand for the truth of God's Word will know the presence of their Lord as they obey Him. Though the consequences may be great, reformation is no longer an option for those who know their Bibles and care for the flock of God.

The three marks of the church, as noted by John Calvin (a right preaching of the gospel, the two sacraments, and church discipline), must all be recovered if we are to begin the process of reformation. This effort will no doubt be slow, arduous, and painful unless the showers soon fall. But the effort must be made whether the rains come or not. The timid will need encouragement and the faint-hearted may not make it, but true reforming pastors must make every effort, "counting it all joy." They must accept the challenge without hesitation because they know that God is calling them to the work of biblical reformation.

The Irish Revival of 1859

There is much we can gain from reading the accounts of those who participated in the 1859 awakening that touched six of the nine counties in northern Ireland. Like other revivals in the nineteenth century, this one was birthed in a season of reformation that preceded the outpouring of the Holy Spirit.

The 1859 revival had its origins in the Presbyterian Church. For decades, reaching back into the eighteenth century, the heresies of Arianism and Unitarianism had crippled the witness of the church in Ireland, especially in Ulster. God prepared a man, Henry Cooke, to challenge this compromise. He labored night and day for the purifying of his church by the Word of God. He would have no part in an ecclesiastical peace that allowed serious error. Cooke said:

> If you can convince me from Scripture that Trinitarians, Arians, and Socinians can form a Scriptural church, and cordially unite in licensing and ordaining one another, I shall resign my present views, and unite with you in preserving our present Constitution.[14]

By 1829 Henry Cooke led the party in the General Assembly which defeated the spokesman for Unitarianism, a Dr. Montgomery of Dunmurry. Montgomery had made a three-hour public tirade against Henry Cooke before the assembled presbyters at Synod. Cooke then calmly, patiently, and theologically answered Montgomery's attacks. Cooke's biographer notes that when Cooke finished, the effect was amazing:

> . . . the effect produced upon the Synod and the entire audience surpassed anything they had ever witnessed. As a reply to Montgomery, it was admitted to be not only conclusive, but overwhelming. I have been informed by one who was present

that many of the country people, when their hands became
painful with long clapping, took off their shoes in the heat of
their enthusiasm, and beat them together.[15]

By 1835 Cooke had successfully led the Ulster Synod to enact a
requirement that all ministers subscribe to the Westminster
Confession of Faith. A professor by the name of J.L. Porter wrote:

> The importance of the work he accomplished cannot be over-
> estimated. Presbyterianism in Ireland had fallen asleep long
> before he entered the ministry. The Church, as a whole, was
> satisfied with a cold observance of the routine of worship.
> There was no power in the pulpit; there was no energy in the
> Synod; there was no spiritual life among the people. Mission-
> ary work, whether at home or abroad, was not thought of.
> The Church seemed indifferent to Christ's command and
> commission—"Go ye into all the world, and preach the gospel
> to every creature."[16]

One historian tells us that many people in the 1830s felt Cooke's
efforts would disrupt the church unduly and harm its testimony of
unity before the world. (This is the same response we can expect
today when we endeavor to bring reformation about.)

A Unitarian magazine had this response to Cooke and his efforts
for reform:

> Let the consequences of the present excited state of feeling in
> the Synod of Ulster be what they may, let them be adverse, or
> let them be prosperous, the principal part of the blame, or
> praise, the merit or demerit, will rest on the head of Rev.
> Henry Cooke. He is the man who sounded the earliest note of
> alarm. He it is who blew the first, the loudest, and the longest
> blast—a blast with which the walls of our Church still continue
> to reverberate. So great is his ardour, that he roams, like Peter

the Hermit, from one place to another, preaching a crusade against Arianism.[17]

I relate this historical account in some detail to underscore a not-so-obvious point. Controversy over doctrine, the recovery of truth, and concern for true reformation have often preceded times of great spiritual blessing in the church. Compare this to what we see happening in today's efforts to bring revival. Many are telling us that revival will come when we have unity, not when we struggle for truth. They say, "Let God restore the truth when the revival comes." In Cooke's case, the struggle was *first* for truth. Only then in the 1850s did two different revival movements take place, the later being the famous 1859 awakening.

This same pattern—of putting the truth back in its proper place, and then revival following—also appears in the revival that took place in the church in Scotland. The same is true for a revival in Germany in the 1800s.

Revival in Germany[18]

As the nineteenth century dawned upon Germany, rationalism had eclipsed biblical revelation and true Christianity. Churches were empty, and philosopher Immanuel Kant's cry, "Think for yourself, do not depend on deity" had won the day in most academic circles. The masses of people who had once attended church in the land of the Protestant Reformation had given up on visible Christianity and the Bible. They did not see Scripture as a faithful record and revelation of God and His truth.

Jacob Schmidt, writing in a rationalistic journal of the times, stated well the view of most: "Without reason there is no religion. The Scriptures must stand up to the scrutiny of reason. They are only true when they pass the muster of man's mind." Critics repeatedly said the only Christians left were the pietists in evangelical Lutheranism who had an undue "reliance on emotional experience of God . . . fanaticism, enthusiasm, denial of reason and a pedantic attachment to the letter of the Bible."

So bad was the scene in the German cities that one Englishman recorded in *The Evangelical Magazine and Missionary Chronicle* (1814) that he found only one evangelical clergyman in the entire city of Hamburg. He wrote that the churches were empty. The parish church in Mannheim had 10,000 members, but on a given Sunday less than eight men and 50 women worshiped there. This was fairly typical. Conservative theologian Reinhold Seeberg summed up the times by writing, "Piety exists without a pastor. Piety also survives outside the church. This abandonment of the church is a remnant of rationalism."

Yet a springtime of blessing was about to break out in church after church. The famous August Tholuck, in a speech given in 1825 which was aimed at skepticism, noted: "I can testify that the state of things is continually improving; and evidently by the special blessing of God." A renewing ignited quietly by God found an alliance of fervor in what was happening in England, Scotland, North America, France, and the Netherlands. The revival, which took place between 1815-1830, crossed confessional boundaries and drew together Lutherans and Calvinists.

After 1830 Professor Wayne Detzler notes that the German "revival was pressed into the doctrinal forms of the various churches." He adds, "As theologians had blazed the trail to destruction during the rationalistic catastrophe, so during the revival theologians led the way back to the Bible." In Tubingen professors began a branch of the British and Foreign Bible Society to get the Scriptures out to students. August Niemeyer, the chancellor of Halle University, ordered rare Bibles for the school's library with the idea of winning students to faith in Christ. August Neander, a professor of church history in Berlin, defended biblical doctrines such as the resurrection of Christ, His deity, and the substitutionary atonement—all with the goal of restoring evangelical doctrinal faith. Ernst Hengstenberg, a famous Old Testament teacher, concluded that "a very great increase has been going on in the number and zeal of the friends of evangelical doctrine." Professor Neander's work had a great impact on the churches of Berlin; by 1836, half of the churches were served by evangelical clergy, some of whom had been his students. An English professor of the time toured Germany and observed that there was a widespread return to the "genuine principles of the inspired record."

J.D. Morrell, writing for the *Congregational Magazine* (London, 1841), noted that this move of God, which included both reformation and revival, brought about a whole new class of theologians, whom he dubbed "Bibler theologians." Among such were the aforementioned Hengstenberg, Tholuck, and Neander. (All of whom were great scholars as well.) Wayne Detzler wrote that these theologians "were distinguished by their fidelity to inerrancy, and their rationalistic opponents accused them of slavery to the letter of the Scripture."

This historical vignette from Germany reminds us of the profound relationship that exists between reformation and revival. In the case of the German church of the 1830s, both reformation and revival ran as simultaneous tracks side by side. As God renewed the faith of the laity, who had no true ministers to feed them, He also ignited the recovery of a high view of the sacred Scriptures in order that newly reformed and awakened ministers might go back to the church to lead her through the dark days that followed in Germany's life.

REFORMATION *THROUGH* REVIVAL

Which is most important? That the church be holy and filled with zeal for Christ? Or that she be faithful and continually reformed by the truth of Scripture?

I believe that these questions bring about a potentially false dilemma. I, for one, cannot make a choice between the two, nor can I dictate which must ultimately come first. As we have seen, revival might well bring new reformation, though this generally has not happened in the American era of revivalism since Finney. True reformation, on the other hand, would reestablish interest in truth at the deepest levels. It often does this by restoring historic creeds and confessions to their proper place. At the same time, many believers come to love the creeds of the church and the precision with which they state the truth yet never rediscover a genuine concern for godliness and personal devotion to Christ. That's very tragic.

If reformation is to be truly based upon a return to Holy Scripture as the *source and norm* of all faith and practice, then how can it not care for revived godliness and genuine spirituality? Remember, reformation is the recovery of *biblical truth* that leads to the purifying of theology. It always involves the *rediscovering* of the Bible as the judge and guide of all thought and correspondent action.

If revival is an authentic moving of the Holy Spirit, how can it not create concern for what is truth since the Holy Spirit is the Spirit of truth? Indeed, real revival is always the application of truth to human experience. Thomas J. Nettles shares this observation:

> Revival is the application of Reformation truth to human experience. It occurs one person at a time and may appear in individuals who thereby become somewhat isolated from the more general apathy around them; or it may appear on a relatively massive scale radically altering the spiritual face of an entire church, community, or even nation. Normally, therefore, revival involves three things: the presence of Reformation doctrine either preached, read, or otherwise known; the experiential application of that doctrine accompanied by loving but careful investigation of that experience; and the extension of such an experience to a large number of people.[19]

Reformers and revivalists seem to be separated by a wide gulf; the first often fearful of revival and its excesses, while the latter are afraid, or unconvinced, of the place of truth and theology in the life of a healthy church. What should we do? "We should encourage and practice teaching and preaching that unites reformation and revival," concludes Tom Nettles. He adds, "Likewise, all that tends to erode true reformation or pollute true revival must be resisted and corrected."[20]

Professor Nelson D. Kloosterman also offers wise counsel along this line:

> Some associate reformation with doctrinal purification, and revival with personal transformation. Reformation produces creeds, they say, but revival produces character. If reformation aims at external faith and order, revival deals with internal reality and relationships. Or consider this formulation: reformation emphasizes the objective, whereas revival accents the subjective.
>
> History . . . has a way of propelling us toward one or the other side of the teeter-totter. In fact, our ecclesiastical identity might even be defined by one of these imbalances or another, which we view and transmit as our "peculiar distinctive." One denomination stresses the need for subjective spirituality, another the duties of cultural obedience. One group emphasizes the second commandment, another the fourth, and still another the fifth.[21]

The truly evangelical heirs of the Protestant Reformation have always insisted that the church must be continually willing to deal with change by conforming to the Scriptures. This idea is expressed in the oft-quoted Latin phrase *semper reformanda* (always reforming). This is the position which recognizes that conversion is daily. This change is called for in the New Testament by such ideas as *repentance*, *renewal*, and *return*, all of which point to what we have called revival.

Reformation without revival may well produce a new formalism that produces smugness, triumphalism, and cold orthodoxy. And revival without reformation can produce subjectivism that leads the church very quickly into a whole new set of errors that may cause her to lose the gospel almost as quickly as she rediscovered it during the revival.

What is needed is reformation *through* revival. We must pursue reformation on every level possible, all the time praying for the renewing of the Spirit and for the opening of the heavens with greater blessing upon our efforts. Our goal should be to bring the church back to faithful obedience to the Word of God, and we can undertake this effort through prayer that is filled with hope. All the while, we need to remember that it is God's sovereign good pleasure to give the blessings as He pleases. We do not dictate the measure of His blessing, but we do obey Him in faith.

I've heard it said that while we seek and work for reformation we must pray and wait for revival. In one sense I agree with this, yet in another sense I believe that there is mystery here as well. As we saw with Martin Luther, he never set about to cause a reformation. The initial spark that lit the greatest fire since Pentecost came by God's own timing, as the two centuries *before* the Reformation plainly demonstrate. In the case of Henry Cooke in Ireland, he responded to what was before him in the serious doctrinal aberrations of his time. God surprised everyone with the results and two decades later sent revival. In the case of faithful German church leaders in the early 1800s, the pattern is again different. The clergy was almost entirely bankrupt, yet a few lay leaders were seeking to be faithful to God's Word and pray for recovery. God gave back the truth through four or five prominent biblically centered professors and thinkers, and in time sent revival.

In each case we've examined, the human leaders did what was plainly before them to do. They put their hands to the plow and acted as responsible stewards of the grace of God. They responded in obedience and faith. God was clearly working in and through their determined efforts, whether or not they were fully aware of it. They had no reason to think circumstances would get better in their lifetimes yet they remained faithful and hopeful. They persisted in prayer, asking God to do for them what He alone could do. And in the fullness of His time, He gave abundant showers of revival blessing.

This, then, is the general pattern we should observe. How tragic it would be, in a day when a small and emerging reformation effort is taking place, to have it come to nothing because churches are filled with "sound" people without renewed hearts and minds. It is possible. Orthodoxy does not save souls, Christ does. We need to recognize, in every effort made for doctrinal reformation, the meaning of these words:

> My faith has found a resting place,
> Not in device nor creed;
> I trust the Everliving One,
> His wounds for me shall plead.
>
> I need no other argument,
> I need no other plea,
> It is enough that Jesus died,
> And that He died for me.[22]

Personal renewal is exclusively the work of the Holy Spirit. So is corporate revival. Ministers and church leaders must realize that reformation is always the order of the hour. But they must just as fully recognize that unless the Lord attends their efforts with His power, little of eternal value will be accomplished. Conferences for reformation are important, but prayer for revival should always saturate these efforts.

A DAY OF SMALL THINGS?

In Zechariah 4:10, God asks Zechariah, "Who despises the day of small things?" He said this to address the discouragement that prevailed among the Israelites at this time. The work of rebuilding the temple that the Babylonians had destroyed had begun under Zerubbabel. The foundation was put down but the work was proceeding slowly. The walls were, as yet, not completed. Progress seemed impossible. Worst of all, at least in the eyes of the people, was that the new temple was nowhere nearly as grand as the one that had been destroyed. The people were comparing the present temple with the past one, and had fallen into the trap of "despising the day of small things." As a result, they became easily discouraged and, for a while, neglected the rebuilding of the temple altogether.

There is a lesson here for us. We must be careful as we urge increasing numbers of people to pray for revival and to believe that God might be pleased to yet "revive us again in the midst of the years." On the one hand, as we point out that revivals are rare, we might discourage earnest prayer and vision regarding the future. On the other hand, if we overemphasize the potential for revival and an outpouring of God's Spirit, we could end up with many disappointed people if revival doesn't come.

In Zerubbabel's time the grave danger was that of looking back to the days when the temple was far more glorious. This would cause the devout to despise the present and its own blessings and difficulties. I am convinced that Christians today could very easily look at the great revivals of the past and be wrongly disappointed with the present time. I myself have studied the past outpourings of the Spirit with such interest—and for so long—that sometimes I am inclined to "despise the day of small things." A friend, David Kingdon, who lives in Wales, where many revivals have occurred, has helpfully written:

> The same temptation (i.e., to despise the day of small things) is
> real today. We may look back to past seasons of the outpouring
> of the Holy Spirit . . . make a comparison with the present,
> and settle down to await revival in what amounts to a spirit of
> resigned fatalism. We may read of the mighty revivals of past
> centuries and wistfully say, "If only we had such a revival today,
> things would be different." And so they would, but what is our
> duty in a day of small things?[23]

Interestingly the book of Zechariah has as much to tell us about revival as any Old Testament book. Right here in the middle of the book, we are reminded of the need to remain optimistic and responsible even in "the day of small things." Revivals are rare, as we have seen. We cannot stage them, plan them, or promote them. Whatever the reasons for God's delays, even if we have been asking for decades, we must not lose heart. He knows what He is doing and always does what is right. We must not become cynical. We need hope—the kind of hope that leads us to press on in obedience. This is why serious efforts toward reformation are always in order, especially as we pray earnestly for revival.

Some people have recently suggested that there is very little we can do until revival comes. I greatly disagree. Let me explain.

A few years ago I came to realize that as much as I had prayed for revival and hoped that God might yet send large effusions of the Spirit in my lifetime, I needed to realize that I could live and die and never see any kind of great awakening. I realized that I had to accept this possibility. I can't just wait for a revival to come before I get active in the work of proclaiming the gospel. If revival never came, then what would be my excuse before the Judgment seat of Christ if I failed to witness, to handle the Word accurately and faithfully, and to pray as I ought? How could I answer the Lord of the church for not telling the whole truth and nothing but the truth no matter what consequences followed? Is it not my present duty to obey regardless of the outcome? Will I stand before Christ in that coming day and say, "Lord, I didn't seek to fulfill the great commission, I didn't help with resolving problems in the North American church, and I didn't give sacrificially for the work of Christ because I was eagerly waiting for revival to break out across the nation"?

A WORD OF ENCOURAGEMENT

Some people who are zealous to see revival tend to think that the problem in our age is powerlessness and weakness in the church. They plead with people to pray more, give more, and stand in the gap against the godlessness of our culture. They have associated the need of the hour with all kinds of issues: everything from saving the family, church growth, the pro-life cause, turning America back to God, and therapeutic self-fulfillment are put forward.

It may appear that what the church needs to do is simply work harder. I hope that what I've shared in this book has persuaded you, and hopefully a growing number of other Christians, that this approach is not adequate. It looks to man rather than to God. This is the kind of thinking I have sought to challenge throughout this book.

The power we truly need is not in our actions, but in the gospel message itself (see 1 Corinthians 1:17; 2:5). Ray Ortlund, Jr., expresses my thoughts very well when he says,

> We should not think, "Well, of course we have the gospel. The Reformation recovered it for us." Such complacency will cost us dearly. Every generation of Christians must be retaught afresh the basic truths of our faith. The church is always one generation away from total ignorance of the gospel, and we today are making rapid progress toward that ruinous goal. Rather than carelessly assume the gospel, we must aggressively, deliberately, fully and passionately teach and preach the gospel. All the treasures of wisdom and knowledge are hidden in Christ. If we do not intentionally search out, we will miss them.[24]

May God be pleased to give us back the gospel of Christ. It is clearly under siege in the household of its friends. Until we get this message right, how can we hope for the Spirit to descend with power? Indeed, perhaps getting the message right, joined with earnest cries for revival, will be the very means God uses, as He has in the past, to bring the light of truth back into our dark times.

Will you, dear reader, join me in pursuing doctrinal reformation? Will you join me in praying for real revival, a time when God moves? Use whatever influence God may have given you to stir up others. But above all else, confess your own sin, repent, and fall in love with Christ once again.

Part Six

Appendices

A HUMBLE ATTEMPT TO PROMOTE EXPLICIT PRAYER

God Himself has instituted prayer as a means of grace. Although revival is usually preceded by prayer, we have in all humility to recognize that prayer too is a spiritual gift, something that cannot be created artificially or regimented. Therefore we are not to think that we can organize prayer as though we were in control. Certainly we should do all we can to make our regular prayer meetings informative, interesting and vital, at the same time seeking to stir up participation and zeal. Nevertheless, true intercession cannot be measured in terms of good organization or eloquence. The most powerful prayers have sometimes consisted of the groans of God's suffering, persecuted people. What were desperate cries out of weakness proved to be the most effectual prayers (Psalm 102:17; Exodus 3:7; Daniel 9:17-19; Nehemiah 9:32-37). Our present weakness and discouragements may be turned to our advantage as we pray, remembering the Lord's name is at stake and His cause that is contested by the powers of evil. In our feebleness we must recall that He is strong and full of sympathy.

—Erroll Hulse
Give Him No Rest: A Call to Prayer for Revival (1991)

I HOPE THAT you have rejoiced in the accounts of the revivals mentioned in this book. My hope is that you've come to appreciate the importance of reformation and revival, and that you'll want to make your newfound knowledge a practical part of your everyday life. With that in mind, I've listed some things we can be doing in the days ahead.

First, encourage yourself, and other Christians, to learn more about revival. You can do this in several ways. Begin by reading the biographies of men and women who were mightily used in revival. You'll also want to read historical stories that include revival accounts. Find sermons and other similar materials that speak accurately and helpfully on this subject; a bibliography is included at the end of this book for that purpose.

Second, I encourage you to find others who have a genuine interest in biblical reformation and revival. Join them in discussing this vital subject. Talk about what is happening in our world, but always keep your primary focus upon God and His Word. Believe that He can intervene in history and that if it pleases Him to do so, He can restore the fortunes of Christ's church in our time in a matter of months, or even days, through revival. Feed your hope with God-centered conversation and listening. If you are a minister, invite those who know something about this subject to speak to your flock. Expose your people to the kind of thinking that will fuel their interest.

I would further urge ministers to preach the great doctrines of the Bible clearly and plainly. Preach often on the person and work of Christ. Preach the absolute sovereignty of God, exalting the One who gives eternal life as He pleases. Become a truly earnest man who pleads with your people for real heart change. Do not be satisfied with merely teaching sound doctrine. Get a solid understanding of the Bible's doctrines, pray through that understanding personally, and then preach God's Word as "logic on fire" (Lloyd-Jones) and as a man passionately serious about making the truth plain to everyone. Aim at the conscience. (If you do not personally have a clear conscience, take care of that first, and then aim at the consciences of your hearers!)

Finally, recognize the important connection prayer has to revival. Though you cannot force God's hand, you can and you must beseech God for greater grace for these days.

Jonathan Edwards wrote:

> It is God's will through His wonderful grace, that the prayers
> of His saints should be one great and principal means of carry-
> ing on the designs of Christ's kingdom in the world. When
> God has something very great to accomplish for His church, it
> is His will that there should precede it the extraordinary
> prayers of His people; as is manifest by Ezekiel xxxvi.37, "I will
> yet, for this, be enquired of by the house of Israel, to do it for
> them." And it is revealed that, when God is about to accom-
> plish great things for His church, He will begin by remarkably
> pouring out the spirit of grace and supplications, Zechariah
> xii.10.[1]

This truth regarding "the spirit of grace and supplications"
should compel Christians to have a strong incentive to pray if they
long for an authentic move of God. Edwards actually went so far as
to prove that it was a *positive duty* of Christians to pray for revival. In
1746 a group of Scottish Reformed ministers circulated a memorial
throughout the English-speaking world urging special "extraordinary" prayer on Saturday evenings, Sunday mornings, and the first
Tuesday of each quarter. This continued for seven years! Jonathan
Edwards prepared a treatise, with a typically long and explicit name,
to support this Scottish effort: *A Humble Attempt to Promote Explicit
Agreement and Visible Union of God's People in Extraordinary Prayer for
the Revival of Religion.*

Jonathan Edwards's observations are still worthy of consideration today. He reasoned that the duty of believers was to pray for
worldwide revival because: 1) the Bible contained promises of worldwide extension of the church; 2) the terms of the Lord's Prayer teach
it; 3) the problems of the times showed that revival was greatly
needed.

Edwards reasoned this way:

> If we look through the whole Bible, and observe all the exam-
> ples of prayer that we find there recorded, we shall not find so
> many prayers for any other mercy, as for the deliverance, restora-
> tion, and prosperity of the church, and the advancement of
> God's glory and kingdom of grace in the world . . . the greatest
> part of the book of Psalms is made up of prayers for this mercy,
> prophecies of it, and prophetical praises for it. . . . [2]

Did the Scottish Reformed ministers' efforts for fervent, united
prayer result in true awakening? We do not know. Eternity will reveal
to us the intrinsic place and purpose of their prayers (and ours).
Some years later the Second Great Awakening flourished, and the
conditions which followed for decades may well have flowed out of
this seven-year season of explicit prayer. Packer concludes that whatever may have come from this prayer effort, "here is a task for all
God's people in every age: to pray that God will build up Zion, and
cause His glory to appear in her, by revival blessing." [3]

Is that the concern of your heart as well? If you haven't already,
won't you join me and others in taking up this call to pray earnestly
for true revival?

Appendix Two

REVIVAL AND THE FUTURE

David was not a believer in the theory that the world will grow worse and worse, and that the dispensation will wind up with general darkness, and idolatry. Earth's sun is to go down amid twofold night if some of our prophetic brethren are to be believed. Not so do we expect, but we look for a day when the dwellers in all lands shall learn righteousness, shall trust in the Saviour, shall worship thee alone, O God, "and shall glorify thy name." The modern notion has greatly damped the zeal of the church for missions, and the sooner it is shown to be unscriptural the better for the cause of God. It neither consorts with prophecy, honours God, nor inspires the church with ardour. Far hence be it driven.

—Charles H. Spurgeon
Treasury of David, 1874

ONE OF THE most interesting of all doctrines is Bible prophecy. Christians largely agree on the major elements regarding the Bible's teachings about the end times—for example, that Christ is to return physically at the end of this present age, that the resurrection will take place at His coming, that the judgment will follow His coming, and that eternity in either heaven or hell will be the ultimate destiny of every mortal who has ever lived on this planet.

However, there have also been areas of considerable disagreement regarding details related to the scenario of the end. Will Christ's coming precede or follow the age called the millennium (see Revelation 20:1-6)? Will Christ come to rapture the church before the seven-year tribulation, or will He come during or after this final, tumultuous period? (Or, will there even be a seven-year tribulation?) These issues and more have often divided orthodox Christians unduly, especially in North America. It is important to note that no major historic confession of faith or creed of the Christian church ever makes these frequently debated points a test for orthodoxy. At the same time, various views of prophecy have had a major impact upon the church's interest in revival over the last three centuries. For this reason I want to address several questions related to revival and prophecy.

THREE VIEWS OF THE FUTURE

The three historic views of Revelation 20 are premillennialism, amillennialism, and postmillennialism. Each view is held by representative evangelical Christians in our time and each has held a kind of ascendancy during different eras of church history. Postmillennialism, for example, was the widely held view during the time of the First and Second Great Awakenings in America. Only after the Civil War did this begin to slowly change. The twentieth century has seen the rise of premillennialism as the most widely held view among evangelicals, though the other two views have retained high regard in many conservative circles and institutions. Amillennialism has always had a greater influence upon certain parts of the church (e.g., Lutheran and Reformed) throughout the same time period. Augustine's view of the end, which was amillennialism, can be found in a number of sound evangelical books in our day.

My purpose is not to review the strengths and weaknesses of these three positions but to show how each can and does interact with the subject of revival.

Premillennialism

This position views the book of Revelation in a futurist sense, at least from chapter 4 to the end. The understanding is that the book records events that have yet to happen. Many premillennialists believe that these events will happen soon. There is a strong sense, among most who hold the varying perspectives of this view, that we may be nearing the end of this age, especially as we draw near to the next millennium, which will begin on January 1, 2001. This opinion is stated frequently in sermons, popular bestselling books, and widely distributed tracts.

Some premillennialists tend to think that revival could well precede the end, while others are less sure or simply have little or no interest. Dr. Billy Graham, for example, seems to have taught over the years that we might well see a great revival and that the end would come almost simultaneously with that revival. Others are more bleak in their prospects for the number of people who will respond to the gospel in these days, believing like the earlier dispensational school that this age could only become more and more apostate. These individuals expect, as did the Plymouth Brethren in the last century, that the church will be less and less faithful to the gospel in the days leading up to the Lord's return. Within this view there is no serious expectation of revival, at least in any large sense. (This is often based upon a reading of Revelation 3:14-22, which views the present as the Laodicean Age.)

Many dispensationalists see elect Israel, or the remnant of believing national Israel, saved by a great work of the Holy Spirit in the coming time of Jacob's Trouble (see Jeremiah 30:7). They also believe that there will be some kind of an outpouring of the Holy Spirit, perhaps during the seven-year tribulation period, which will bring some type of universal blessing before the return of Christ. Such a view could believe that there will be a great revival during the seven-year tribulation, but it must be noted that this is not for the *present* age. Historic premillennialists are more sanguine about the certainty of all of this.

A friend, Robert H. Lescelius, himself a dispensational premillennialist, has tried to work this out in the light of subject of revival. Bob has spent a lifetime studying and praying for revival and helpfully observes:

To all of this we say that revival is not basically a subject of prophecy. [I am] speaking as a dispensational premillennialist, yet feeling that the varied convictions on eschatology need not be an issue in this matter. The passages used by a postmillenarian or an amillenarian concerning Israel and interpreting them for the church, the premillennialist can take by application and in principle in prayer for revival. The promise to Israel of Isaiah 44:3 was taken as the fuel of faith in the praying that was answered in the Hebrides Revival of 1950. "For I will pour water upon him that is thirsty, and floods upon the dry ground: I will pour my Spirit upon thy seed, and my blessing upon thine offspring." This is too glorious a promise to suffer the fate of a dispensational knife!

Where the premillennialist will see Isaiah 54:1-2 as a call of Israel to their Messiah to come in deliverance in the future Tribulation Period, why cannot we also use it as a basis to call upon the same Lord to come down by His Spirit to deliver His afflicted church today? . . . Oh, that He would come down and melt and move the mountains of indifference, coldness, bondage, Satanic adversaries, and rebellion of men! He has done so in the past. Even nations have trembled. Why not again?

We believe the church needs no prophecies of revival, for she has ample promise of provision already in the New Testament to accomplish God's purpose for this age. Revival for the church is not a subject of prophecy. The church has the same dispensational provision of the Spirit she had at her beginning. No matter how dark the hour, her potential power is the same. God's purpose will triumph, even in these dark days of apostasy. Prophecies of an ever deepening, ever darkening world condition need not keep us from expecting revitalization. In fact, such times make such revitalization all the more necessary.[1]

I believe Lescelius is correct. One who holds to premillennial views of the end of the age need not be an opponent of revival, or even indifferent to this subject. Rather, premillennialists should be stirred by the very truth they profess and pray that God might do an even greater work of real revival in the coming days, even if it is immediately prior to the Lord's coming. Lescelius concludes his helpful counsel to his fellow dispensationalists by adding this pastoral exhortation: "We need not, and must not, be content with Laodicean lukewarmness in our churches. May we heed our Lord's command to the Laodicean Church" (see Revelation 3:19-20).

Amillennialism

The amillennialist generally believes that Revelation 20 is best interpreted in a manner which sees this present age as that referred to in the text. This view often takes a number of the prophecies which dispensationalists limit to ethnic Israel and applies them to the church. By this method a number of old covenant texts can be related to the present time and to "spiritual Israel."

Amillennialists have almost universally believed that revival is a distinct possibility throughout this age, though some amillennialists are found within traditions that either have no interest in revivals or have become negative about them. Since most individuals within this school of thought do not pretend to know how near the end might be, they maintain that any series of events may yet occur before Christ returns. They say that one of the events which may precede Christ's eminent return could be a worldwide awakening. Certainly local and national revivals are a possibility. Following Augustine, many amillennialists hold tenaciously to the sovereignty of God in all human affairs and thus believe that God might yet send a great revival to the church, even in America. Much like the premillennialism of Billy Graham, this view could easily accommodate the idea of revival and apostasy running side by side until the day of the Lord.

Postmillennialism

The most clearly misunderstood view of Revelation 20 is that held by the postmillennialists. Many conservative Christians cannot understand how anyone who believes in total depravity, the rampant evil which exists in the modern world, the present active work of Satan, and the way in which the twentieth century has witnessed one great war after another could believe in some type of millennial kingdom which will come during the present age. Part of the problem here is that few people have actually bothered to understand the way in which postmillennial interpreters actually read the text of the Bible. Assumptions regarding postmillennialism abound, and seldom do critics of this view take the time to make sure they understand it accurately.

What is particularly striking about such opposition to postmillennialism is that at one time the exact opposite would have been the case among Bible-believing Christians in America. Many of America's greatest Bible preachers and scholars held this view. Should we merely assume that the leading evangelical theologians of the nineteenth century had no biblical basis for their views?

Biblical postmillennialism should not be confused with nineteenth-century liberal ideas of social progress. Evangelical postmillennialism was certainly not "evolutionary optimism." It was not, furthermore, liberal theology. Professor John Jefferson Davis, of Gordon-Conwell Theological Seminary, himself a postmillennialist, writes helpfully:

> The postmillennial vision of the spreading kingdom of Christ
> not only energized the great nineteenth-century efforts in home
> and foreign missions, but also from 1815 onward motivated
> social reforms in the areas of peace, temperance, public educa
> tion, the abolition of slavery, and concern for the poor. There
> was a widespread conviction during this period that the advanc
> ing kingdom of Christ required not only personal regeneration

but also efforts to redeem and transform unrighteous social structures.[2]

It is important to note that no serious postmillennialist believes Christ will *physically* reign on the earth during the age associated with their interpretation of Revelation 20. In fact, it is generally agreed that the 1,000 years mentioned should be taken as *representative* of a long period of time.

But what exactly is the postmillennial view of things, and why does this matter at all to our thinking about revival? John J. Davis writes that the main tenets of postmillennialism are:

1. Through the preaching of the gospel and dramatic outpourings of the Holy Spirit Christian missions and evangelism will attain remarkable success, and the church will enjoy an unprecedented period of numerical expansion and spiritual vitality.

2. This period of spiritual prosperity, the millennium, understood as a long period of time, is to be characterized by conditions of increasing peace and economic well-being in the world as a result of the growing influence of Christian truth.

3. The millenium will also be characterized by the conversion of large numbers of ethnic Jews to the Christian faith (Romans 11:25-26).

4. At the end of the millennial period there will be a brief period of apostasy and sharp conflict between Christian and evil forces.

5. Finally and simultaneously there will occur the visible return of Christ, the resurrection of the righteous and the wicked, the final judgment, and the revelation of the new heavens and the new earth.[3]

This view is termed postmillennial simply because it believes, in distinction from the other two major views of prophecy, that Christ's return will *follow* the period of "millennial blessing."

Why, then, has this understanding often been associated with hope for revival and a definitive theology of revival? The conservative biblical postmillennialist does not believe that world conditions, per se, have a significant role in what the sovereign God might well be pleased to do in revival at any point in history. The darker the moment in history, the more glorious might be the light of reformation and revival. Hope is not placed in increasing better social conditions but in a sovereign God who intervenes in history as He pleases and when He pleases.

The question for most serious postmillennialists who follow Scripture is this: "Is the gospel yet to become a world-transforming power to all the nations?" The answer, they offer, is a resounding *yes*.

Here are a just a few sample quotations from some of those who shared this great hope of an age to come which would be filled with gospel blessing (revival):

> *I had a strong hope that God would "bow the heavens and come down" and do some marvelous work among the Heathen.*
> —David Brainerd
> Missionary to the American Indians (1744)

> *There have been great and glorious days of the gospel in this land; but they have been small in comparison of what shall be.*
> —James Renwick
> A martyr (1688)

> *There will come a time when the generality of mankind, both Jew and Gentile, shall come to Jesus Christ. He hath had but little takings of the world yet, but he will have before he hath done.*
> —Thomas Goodwin
> Puritan theologian (17th century)

> *Strong and certain was the conviction of the Christians that the church would come forth triumphant out of its conflicts, and, as*

it was its destination to be a world-transforming principle, would attain to dominion of the world.

—J.A.W. Neander
German church historian (19th century)

We also rejoice in hope. We have many and express assurances in the Scriptures, which cannot be broken, of the general, the universal spread and reign of Christianity, which are not yet accomplished. Nothing has yet taken place in the history of Divine grace, wide enough in extent, durable enough in continuance, powerful enough in energy, blessed enough in enjoyment, magnificent enough in glory, to do anything like justice to those predictions and promises. Better days, therefore, are before us, notwithstanding the forebodings of many.[4]

—William Jay
Nonconformist minister, 1769-1853

Jonathan Edwards, the greatest revival theologian who ever graced the church, held to these same millennial ideas. This can be seen throughout his writings and prayers for the future mercies of God to fall in true awakenings.

What should we make of all of this? Should we subscribe to post-millennialism if we believe in revival and wish to promote it? Postmillennialism might well rekindle interest in revival but I do not think it does this on its own. Whether or not you are inclined to believe this view of prophecy, you must at least recognize that there are quite a few texts in the Scriptures that lend themselves to a more optimistic understanding of the future prospects for the church in this age. This element of hope is perhaps the greatest contribution postmillennialism can make to those who are open to rethinking things they may have taken for granted. (Again, I am not trying to argue in favor of any one of these three positions; I'm simply pointing out the effect the views can have on our perspective.)

The Puritans categorized a multitude of biblical texts as referring to a "latter-day glory." They built their arguments around the New

Testament passage of Romans 11. Is this chapter referring to a kind of third epoch at the end of this age, a time when Jew and Gentile will be gathered into one through the awakening mercies of God? All three schools of prophetical interpretation include those who argue that the answer must be yes. Indeed, this appears to be the most common conservative view of Romans 11 when the various commentaries are consulted. If this view is correct, then "how much greater riches will their fullness bring" (see Romans 11:12) could well be referring to a wonderful time of revival yet to come.

HOPE FOR A FUTURE REVIVAL

One does not need to adopt any one of the three views to believe that this hope for great revival might well be grounded in the Scripture. No view, as I have shown, should preclude the possibility of real revival, either locally or internationally. Our views of prophecy should never be used to hinder prayer and hope for revival. Furthermore, views that might be used to promote revival praying and discussion must be carefully and biblically expressed or strange things may well be the result (for example, modern prophetic claims that are used to promote counterfeit revivals).

All of this is said to encourage the reader to think more deeply about the subject of revival, especially in relationship to the kinds of issues godly men weighed heavily in past generations.

Appendix Three

SOME QUESTIONS AND ANSWERS

*We have seen some of the general characteristics of revival—
a sense of the majesty of God, of personal sinfulness, of the
wonder of salvation through Jesus Christ and a desire that
others might know it. And we have seen, too, that in a time
of revival people are aware of the presidency of the Holy
Spirit over everything and the life of the whole community.*
        —D. Martyn Lloyd-Jones
        Revival (Crossway, 1987)
        (from a sermon preached in 1959)

FOLLOWING ARE THE kinds of questions that are repeatedly asked when I teach on revival in my travels across North America.

1. Is revival really necessary?

If by *necessary* you mean that we cannot obey God, preach the gospel, pray, and make disciples as our Lord commanded us unless we have revival, the answer is no. The church has clearly known blessing and help without revival. But revival is desirable and should be prayed for by the church because it displays the glory of the gospel with the greatest effects to the watching world. Revival also brings a focus that has usually been lost. Revivals are not God's only means for advancing the church, but they are a wonderful means of blessing that should be desired by His people, especially when they have endured long periods of drought and lifelessness.

2. If revival does not come soon, should the church despair?

Not at all. How can those who know and love Christ as their Lord, who is ever present with them by His Spirit, despair? We must recognize that judgment may well pervade much of what is being done in our time, yet at the same time we may rejoice that our "names are written in the book." This sorrow, experienced by and through chastisement, mixed with joy by the filling of the Spirit, is always the lot of Christians, even in times of revival. We need to realize that revival is never a panacea for the church. It is a sovereign interruption that restores fuller health and greater blessing to the work and ministry of the church.

3. Is revival a cure-all for what plagues the modern church?

I hope I have demonstrated that revival has never been a cure-all for the church. Revival has brought times of great blessing, but with it has come new problems which demand wisdom and biblical assessment. Many people in our dark day speak of revival romantically, as if it would bring a new Golden Age. Authentic revival, however, brings full days and taxing long evenings. As new converts swell the church, the workload for ministers and mature leaders becomes much heavier.

Will revival rescue America and restore the nation? (One wonders if those who promote this type of thinking realize that the supposedly ideal America of the past, as they envision it, never really existed!) If revival is understood as something that will rescue our denomination, our programs, our city, our nation, then we will more than likely be disappointed with real revival.

Revivals have sometimes prepared God's people for dark days that followed. Revival prepared the Southern States for the bitter period of the Civil War and reconstruction, while Eastern Europe experienced revival in some corners before the Communist takeover after World War II. The church in China knew revival before the Communist oppression. During the years that followed the Communist seizure of power, the church in China has been built and sustained by what may be one of the greatest revivals since Pentecost. A revival in North America might well equip the church to live through a dark period as well. Only God knows.

4. If God is the sole author of revival, then what is the point in becoming informed and exercised about the subject?

To say that we cannot *cause* God to bless us is not to say God does not bless us *through* biblically ordained means that may properly be used to accomplish His sovereign purpose. Yes, Scripture clearly teaches that we are utterly dependent upon God for all of life, physical and spiritual. However, we should not take that to mean we are to *passively* wait for God to bless us, but rather, we are to pursue His blessings in complete dependence upon Him as the author and giver of every good and perfect gift (see James 1:17).

We have noted that there are two biblical means God has blessed in beginning and fueling true revival: prayer and preaching. We should use these means *expectantly,* knowing that if God is pleased to do anything, whether in judgment or in mercy, He will use these means to accomplish His purpose. If we acknowledge the sovereignty of God in revival we will not be hindered but humbled. We will realize that there is no room for the flesh to glory in His presence. Indeed, I have tried to demonstrate that a generation with such incredible self-confidence needs this truth more than almost any other biblical doctrine if we want to pray rightly for true revival.

Second Samuel 6 records the story of how well-intentioned people wanted to carry the Ark of the Covenant on an ox cart of their own design. When "the oxen stumbled" (6:6) Uzzah "took hold of the ark of God." The result was instant death in divine judgment. On a spiritual level much of what we do today is the result of our own manufactured ox carts made for helping along the work of God. Our theme is well expressed in the title of a recent religious bestseller, *If It's Going to Be It's Up to Me.*

The fact that God is the sole author of real revival should not discourage us at all. Because He is such a great and awesome God, nothing is too hard for Him (see Genesis 18:14). The times are desperate, the hour is late, judgment clearly hangs over us, but no obstacle is too great for God. Each of us was born again in the midst of the darkest of conditions; darkness presents no problems for our Father. He who can say, "Let light shine out of darkness" (2 Corinthians 4:6) can do with the denizens of earth as he pleases.

5. Is revivalism really a serious problem?

I believe this could be the central problem of evangelicalism in this generation. The chickens of this Finneyesque approach have now come home to roost in abundance! Because we think revivals can somehow be promoted, and that they will come when certain conditions are met by us, we keep trying to develop more machinery to get one started. With each successive "event" that takes place in America we hear more rave reports that we are experiencing revival. Yet if we listen to the sermons, pay careful attention to the prayers, and interact with the participants, the only reasonable conclusion we can draw is that another wave of revivalism has now been stirred up in significant ways.

The ideas taught in revivalism have influenced all of North American Christianity and are now spreading across the world. Why should the evangelical church be really desperate for God to revive her if she can ultimately do something that will *cause* the revival to begin? Why labor and sacrifice for a long-term reformation when we can have a short-term display of revivalism and all these huge numbers of professions?

Whether it is the modern evangelism of "easy believism" or the charismatic emphasis upon "signs and wonders" as the real mark of power, the problem is essentially the same. All of this is grounded in a theological perspective that gives man far too much credit and God far too little. "He must increase" should be our prayerful cry in this hour!

6. But what part does man have in revival?

Divine sovereignty never negates human responsibility. We can and must act in obedience to God. The mystery of the seeming tension between these two biblical truths—of divine sovereignty and human responsibility—cannot be solved by rational syllogisms and logical inferences. We must obey as if everything depended upon us and pray knowing that everything depends entirely upon God.

We must begin by removing all personal hindrances to real revival. Our personal sins grieve the Spirit (Ephesians 4:30) and our collective sin quenches His work among us (1 Thessalonians 5:19). God is not pleased with our sins and we must confess them and forsake them. If deadness and lack of real blessing characterize our assemblies, then we must come to grips with the fact that the reason lies within us (see Psalms 32 and 51).

As was noted in question three, we must also pray. We have biblical examples, as well as biblical and historical precedents, for such prayer. We also have divine commandment for prayer. Some of the most pregnant and encouraging material for revival prayer can be found in Ezekiel 36–37. More specifically, in Ezekiel 36:37, we read these amazing words: "I will yield to the plea of the house of Israel and do this for them." God says He will do His work *because* He is asked and He will yield to the asking of His people. Have we forgotten the two parables of our Lord (the only two parables He told that offer instruction about prayer) which teach us the importance of importunity (Luke 11:1-13; 18:1-8)?

We would do better to spend time, especially as churches, pleading with God to show us the lukewarmness of our condition (Revelation 3:16). Who of us can read Revelation 2–3 and not conclude that our Lord is speaking these penetrating words to the contemporary church? Who would not agree that it is we who have forsaken our first love (Revelation 2:4) and "have a reputation of being alive, but . . . are dead" (Revelation 3:1)?

Often I have pondered Jesus' words to the lukewarm congregation in Laodicea: "I counsel you to buy from me gold refined in the fire, so you can become rich; and white clothes to wear, so you can cover your shameful nakedness; and salve to put on your eyes, so you can see" (3:18). If we would spend time getting a true picture of our need—"wretched, pitiful, poor, blind and naked" (3:17)—we might be more inclined to run to Christ and ask Him to enter the door of the church afresh (Revelation 3:20). The picture of Christ standing outside the church, I fear, is a haunting image of a present reality.

Now, it's possible that we'll get a clear picture of our need and cry out to God, and yet still not see a mighty awakening. Does that mean we should quit? Never. Psalm 44 encourages us to continue, even in the face of divine delays. We have to remember that delays are not necessarily a negative response. We may not see a Great Awakening in America, but the entire church would surely be much healthier for seeking revival and addressing the problems that hinder divine blessing.

7. Are we seeing mighty movements of revival today?

The answer to this is yes and no. In some places, such as China, revival appears to be happening right now. I have also witnessed some evidence of revival in south India. (I am quite sure other parts of the globe are seeing the kind of "outpouring of the Spirit" that I have explained in this book.) But I would say that we are most definitely *not* seeing fresh outpourings of the Spirit, at least in a widespread manner, across North America. To call something revival does not make it revival! We only deceive ourselves and make things worse if we call something revival yet it does not bear the characteristics of true revival.

Religious excitement, stadiums full of men, signs and wonders joined with laughing and other strange phenomena—none of these, as I have attempted to show, constitute real revival. Sometimes unusual phenomena have been present in the midst of real revival, as we observed, but these are never the *essence* of true revival. They constitute neither proof for nor against the revival.

But if this is true, then why are these present movements *not* revival? My most basic answer relates to the message of the gospel itself, as noted at the end of chapter fifteen. True revivals have always been characterized by an uncommon eagerness to hear the Word of God and an overwhelming sense of the holiness of God and sin. At the center of such revival has always been the person and work of Christ, especially as seen in the cross. Furthermore, true revival always spills over into the lost world and produces an impact that is widely recognized by friend and foe alike. If what we are seeing today is revival then it is surely the strangest revival in church history for it is a revival without the gospel, a revival without the cross, and a revival without the social and spiritual fruit that revivals have always produced. For these reasons I am confident that my analysis, though very different from many in our time, is fundamentally sound.

8. *Can I experience personal revival even if God is not pleased to send a great revival to multitudes?*

The answer to this question is more complicated than at first meets the eye. In one sense, we can be revived at any time. Striking illustrations of this fact exist throughout church history. A.W. Tozer listed ten steps to personal revival. Others have suggested other ways to experience the fresh empowering and cleansing work of the Spirit. All of this can be helpful but it can also discount the simple fact that God deals with each believer according to His own time and manner.

There is no reason whatsoever for any believer to remain in any sin or to live a life of frustration and spiritual deadness. At the same time, setting up formulas that are followed in order to "get the blessing of God" sets one up for massive failure and profound frustration. (I know something of this personally, as I tried many of the personal revival techniques *before* realizing that sanctification is always progressive and thus never complete on this side of heaven!)

The believer should always confess sin, seek wholeheartedly after God, pray for the empowering of the Holy Spirit, and implicitly trust

Christ every day. If you have backslidden in your heart, confess the sin the Spirit reveals to you and resume going forward. And, do not put demands upon God as to how He ought to bless or use your life.

Sometimes major revivals have been sparked by God's work within the life of one single person. It is always right to ask God to revive us day by day. J. Edwin Orr, the grand historian of revival in our time, wrote a marvelous hymn which in part says:

> O Holy Spirit, revival comes from Thee;
>   Send a revival—start the work in me.
> Thy Word declares Thou wilt supply our need;
>   For blessings now, O Lord, I humbly plead.

9. But isn't it dangerous to define revival by what happened in the past?

Again the answer is yes and no. The past can help us understand that there are major elements, and minor elements, in any great move of God. Judging revival from history alone, or by observations and human experience, is ultimately not the best test. A fresh outpouring of the Spirit of God would be just that—fresh. Yet any movement of God must be judged by the Word of God, since it is here alone that God reveals His mind to us. That is why I have continued to insist on judging a movement of the Spirit by its doctrinal and ethical fruit, not by the excitement or joy it produces. Exciting testimonies are not the test. The great reports of healings and long protracted meetings are not the test either.

On the other end of the spectrum we should not fear "excitement" either. If God were to move mightily across our present scene I would expect there to be some unusual happenings. I have no doubt that people would fall down under the weight of their own sin and the deeply felt realization of God's holiness. I personally long to see sinners struck down by the terrors of the wrath to come. (I pray for this when I preach.) At the same time I believe it to be the better part of wisdom to tell those who might fall to get up and "hear the

Word." There is no proof that God is at work in the falling down. The proof can only be seen in a life changed by God's Word. Any movement that centers upon human emotion as an end in itself and denies or distorts important biblical doctrines will only unite people in a way that prepares them for apostasy and confusion. Remember, if people are to be changed, the truth will first enter through the vestibule of their minds and then powerfully move into the sanctuary of their emotions and change their wills. When this pattern is altered by revivalism, the dangers are numerous.

10. What kind of human leaders has God used to influence the church when He is pleased to send real revival?

In every period of history God has given gifts to the church in the form of servants who are a great blessing to that age. Some periods seem to have a good number of such people while others have only a few. Horatius Bonar, the famous Scots minister of the nineteenth century, wrote a small tract titled *True Revivals & the Men God Uses*. In this tract Bonar listed nine characteristics of the kinds of leaders God has used in seasons of revival. Bonar asks the question this way: "What weapons did they employ?"

1. They were in earnest about the great work of the ministry on which they had entered.
2. They were bent upon success.
3. They were men of faith.
4. They were men of labour.
5. They were men of patience.
6. They were men of boldness and determination.
7. They were men of prayer.
8. They were men whose doctrines were of the most decided kind, both as respects law and gospel.
9. They were men of solemn deportment and deep spirituality of soul.[1]

11. What practical things can I do for real revival in my church?

First, make sure that you are right with God yourself. Get a firm understanding of the gospel message and make absolutely sure that you have truly trusted Christ alone to be your righteousness. Many who have made professions have never stopped to ask themselves what they really did when they "became a Christian." Your assurance must not be grounded solely in a past experience but rather in a present trusting of Christ alone.

Second, recognize openly and honestly the need for, and the real possibility of, authentic revival.

Third, find several others who will join you in intercession for revival. Encourage your church to make this type of prayer a regular feature of their ministry. Join prayer groups in your area and encourage those in such existing groups to give more attention to the gospel and to the theology of revival.

Fourth, listen to tapes; read books; distribute sound tracts and booklets on this subject; and read serious histories, biographies, and other accounts of past moves of God's Spirit.

Fifth, make doctrinal reformation a matter of personal and corporate concern as you pray for revival. Urge as many people as possible to consider making doctrinal matters a high priority in church planning and programming.

Sixth, encourage pastors and other church leaders to attend seminars and conferences that encourage sound thinking about revival and prayer.

Annotated Bibliography and Endnotes

Annotated Bibliography

It is helpful for all who pray for revival and have a keen inter-est in the subject to read and think more widely about this sub-ject. I have prepared this list of volumes for this purpose. This is not an exhaustive list, nor is it one that includes only those titles that I personally agree with on every point. I have listed these titles because of their general value for those who wish to pursue the subject further. I have also chosen books that are either still in print or fairly accessible. Countless out-of-print volumes are worth their weight in gold and may cost you the price of gold. The serious student may wish to search for them.

Alexander, Archibald. *The Log College*. Edinburgh, Scotland: Banner of Truth, 1968 reprint of 1851 edition. The "log college" was the name contemptuously given to the ministerial college that was the forerunner of Princeton Seminary. Includes biographical sketches of William Tennent and students greatly used in revival ministry during the First Great Awakening.

Anderson, Neil T. and Elmer L. Towns. *Rivers of Revival*. Ventura, CA: Regal, 1997. One of most recent products of the theology of revivalism, this book is both interesting and distressing. If you want to compare two modern popularly written books on revival with opposite perspectives, compare this title with *When God Moves*.

Armstrong, John H., ed. *The Coming Evangelical Crisis: Current Challenges to the Authority of Scripture and the Gospel*. Chicago: Moody Press, 1996. This recent volume includes essays by a number of evangelical leaders who are all concerned that evan-gelicalism faces a crisis. This crisis has come because of the ravaging effects of revivalism.

_____. *The Compromised Church*, Wheaton, IL: Crossway, 1998. This is a companion volume to the one listed above and addresses how the crisis can be seen in the doctrine and life of the church. Unless we recover a sound view of the church we will compound revivalistic solutions.

_____. *Five Great Evangelists: Preachers of Real Revival*. Fearn, Ross-shire, Scotland: Christian Focus Publications, 1997. A biographical introduction to five of the most wonderfully used evangelists in the history of Christianity. Each was a preacher who knew the presence and blessing of real revival.

Blackaby, Henry T. and Claude V. King. *Experiencing God: Knowing and Doing the Will of God*. Nashville: Baptist Sunday School Board, 1992. A very popular small-group guide that is useful but flawed by revivalistic theology.

Blackaby, Henry T. *Fresh Encounter*. Nashville: Broadman & Holman Publishers, 1996. A study of revival principles that is flawed by revivalistic theology.

Bright, Bill. *The Coming Revival: America's Call to Fast, Pray, and "Seek God's Face."* Orlando, FL: New Life Publications, 1995. This book is one of leading examples of revivalism and its bizarre claims regarding modern revival.

Bryant, David. *The Hope At Hand: National and World Revival for the Twenty-First Century*. Grand Rapids: Baker, 1995. Bryant, best known for his leadership in the "Concerts of Prayer" movement, is an engaging proponent of revival prayer. The weakness is that he is not sufficiently careful theologically to escape several of the pitfalls of revivalism.

_____. *Stand in the Gap: How to Prepare for the Coming World Revival*. Ventura, CA: Regal Books, 1997. The book's cover proclaims the view that "an awesome move of God is unfolding across our nation and across the planet. . . ." Useful, but still needs to be balanced by older, theologically careful books.

Buchanan, James. *The Office and Work of the Holy Spirit*. Edinburgh, Scotland: Banner of Truth, 1966 reprint of 1843 edition. Includes a clear and rich section on revival with information that's rarely found today.

Duewel, Wesley. *Revival Fire*. Grand Rapids: Zondervan, 1995. Though I do not share in Duewel's Wesleyan theology, this an excellent book in many ways.

Edwards, Brian H. *Revival! A People Saturated with God.* Darlington, County Durham, England: Evangelical Press, 1990. This is one of the four or five best general titles on the subject that the average reader should procure. Filled with accounts and stories as well as wise pastoral counsel.

Ellsworth, Roger. *Come Down, Lord!* Edinburgh, Scotland: Banner of Truth, 1988. A very good little book (56 pages) which introduces the subject in a solidly biblical way.

Evans, Eifion. *Fire in the Thatch: The True Nature of Religious Revival.* Bryntirion, Bridgend, Wales: Evangelical Press of Wales, 1996. Evans is one of the most helpful historians of revival writing today. His special interest is his own country of Wales, "the land of awakenings."

Fawcett, Arthur. *The Cambuslang Revival: The Scottish Evangelical Revival of the Eighteenth Century.* Edinburgh, Scotland: Banner of Truth, 1971. An exciting story well told.

Finney, Charles G. *Finney's Systematic Theology.* Minneapolis: Bethany House Publishers, 1994 reprint of 1878 edition. This definitive edition of Finney will demonstrate to the discerning and careful reader just how far he drifted from any semblance of orthodoxy.

_____. *The Memoirs of Charles G. Finney: An Annotated Critical Edition* (Garth M. Rosell & Richard A.G. Dupuis, eds.). Grand Rapids: Zondervan, 1989. This full edition is extremely important for serious scholars. It shows Finney as he really was, not as public-relations people have sought to make him.

_____. *Revivals of Religion.* Grand Rapids: Fleming H. Revell, n.d. This is the famous manual that promotes the steps one should take to *guarantee* revival.

Fish, Henry C. *Handbook of Revivals.* Harrisonburg, VA: Gano Books, 1988 reprint of 1874 edition. A useful and immensely practical book.

Goen, C.G., ed. *The Works of Jonathan Edwards,* Volume 4: "The Great Awakening." New Haven, Connecticut: Yale University Press, 1972. This is the academic and richly annotated edition of Edwards's several important works on revival. For less money and without annotations, get the Banner of Truth editions.

Hanegraaff, Hank. *Counterfeit Revival: Looking for God in All the Wrong Places.* Dallas: Word, 1997. An exposé of the various "counterfeit" movements of revival that have swept America in the last ten years or so. Hanegraaff shows that these movements have gone far beyond older Pentecostalism and are dangerous. He is particularly critical of both the Toronto Blessing and the Brownsville Revival.

Hardman, Keith J. *Seasons of Refreshing: Evangelism and Revivals in America.* Grand Rapids: Baker, 1994. Hardman, who wrote the best biography available on Charles G. Finney, is a good historian. He traces the development of mass evangelism in America in this book.

Hulse, Erroll. *Give Him No Rest: A Call to Prayer for Revival.* Darlington, County Durham, England: Evangelical Press, 1991. The best in-print book available on how prayer relates to revival and why we ought to "give Him no rest" in our pleas for the fulfillment of His commission and the world-encompassing promises of gospel success.

Lloyd-Jones, D. Martyn. *Revival.* Wheaton, IL: Crossway, 1987. Dr. J.I. Packer calls this the most "powerful [and] profound treatment of revival" seen in our age. It is a must-read for anyone serious about this subject.

Lloyd-Jones, D. Martyn. *The Puritans: Their Origins and Successors.* Edinburgh, Scotland: Banner of Truth, 1987. Includes a number of lectures Lloyd-Jones gave at the Puritan and Westminster Conferences in London between 1959 and 1978. Includes his marvelous lectures: "Revival: A Historical and Theological Survey," "Howell Harris and Revival," and "Jonathan Edwards and the Crucial Importance of Revival." This is church history and practical theology at its very best!

Lloyd-Jones, D. Martyn. *Knowing the Times: Addresses on Various Occasions 1942-1977.* Another Lloyd-Jones treasure. The chapters on "Evangelical Unity: An Appeal" and "What Is an Evangelical?" are of great relevance to North America today.

McDow, Malcolm, and Alvin L. Reid. *Firefall: How God Has Shaped History Through Revivals.* Nashville: Broadman & Holman Publishers, 1997. A very helpful historical overview, though the theological arguments are not carefully thought out and the conclusions, as a result, are affected.

Murray, Iain H. *Revival & Revivalism: The Making and Marring of American Evangelicalism 1750-1858.* Edinburgh, Scotland: Banner of Truth, 1994. If you read only one *serious* book on revival make it this one! This is the most interesting and important book available on the subject of how and why American revivalism arose.

_____. *The Puritan Hope: Revival and the Interpretation of Prophecy.* Edinburgh, Scotland: Banner of Truth, 1971. Even if you do not share all the views outlined in this volume you will not find it easy to put this exciting book down. It wonderfully fueled my own hope for God to revive us.

_____. *D. Martyn Lloyd-Jones: The First Forty Years, 1899-1939*. Edinburgh, Scotland: Banner of Truth, 1982. The first 40 years of the most able preacher in Great Britain in our century. His concern for revival and his understanding of the subject is unparalleled. He experienced several visitations of God upon his first pastorate in Aberavon and reading these accounts will give you a picture of God moving in a church.

_____. *D. Martyn Lloyd-Jones: The Fight of Faith, 1939-1981*. The best presentation of modern British evangelicalism seen through the life of a courageous leader who kept the hope of authentic revival alive for an entire generation. A number of wonderful revival references are included.

_____. *Jonathan Edwards: A New Biography*. Edinburgh, Scotland: Banner of Truth, 1987. The best modern biography of Jonathan Edwards. A must for understanding the man and the ministry behind the theologian of revival. Modern promoters of Edwards' idea of "Concerts of Prayer" should read Murray and grasp the profound God-centeredness of Edwards.

Olford, Stephen F. *Heart-Cry for Revival: Expository Sermons on Revival*. Grand Rapids: Fleming H. Revell, 1962. A good wake-up call to prayer and concern for revival.

Orr, J. Edwin. *The Event of the Century: The 1857-1858 Awakening*. Wheaton, IL: International Awakening Press, 1989. A thorough and useful study by a respected historian of revival.

Packer, J.I. *A Quest for Godliness: The Puritan Vision of the Christian Life*. Wheaton, IL: Crossway, 1990. This collection of essays on the Puritans includes several important chapters on revival that should not be missed. It is a vivid, warm, and immensely useful book.

Phillips, Thomas. *The Welsh Revival: Its Origin & Development*. Edinburgh, Scotland: Banner of Truth, 1989 reprint of 1860 edition. The first comprehensive account of a remarkable revival.

Porter, Ebenezer. *Letters on Revival*. Brooklyn, New York: Linde Publications, 1992. This reprint of an 1832 edition is rich. Porter, a Congregational minister, strongly opposed the rise of Finneyism. His counsel might help us get out of some of the current problems that had their origin in the 1830s.

Prime, Samuel. *The Power of Prayer: The New York Revival of 1858.* Edinburgh, Scotland: Banner of Truth, 1991 reprint of an 1859 edition. A very stimulating firsthand account.

Reid, William. *Authentic Records of Revival.* Wheaton, IL: Richard Owen Roberts Publishers, 1980 reprint of 1860 edition. A good account of the awakening that was ongoing in 1860.

Roberts, Richard Owen. *Revival!* Wheaton, IL: Richard Owen Roberts Publishers, 1982. A most important book by an author who has considered revival for nearly 50 years. The section on hindrances is worth the price of the book.

_____, ed. *Salvation in Full Color: Twenty Sermons by Great Awakening Preachers.* Wheaton, IL: International Awakening Press, 1994. An excellent set of sermons showing the kind of preaching that has been visited with the power of true revival.

_____, ed. *Sanctify the Congregation: A Call to the Solemn Assembly and to Corporate Repentance.* Wheaton, IL: International Awakening Press, 1994. Contains 15 wonderfully doctrinal sermons which were useful in calling the church to repentance and the need for revival in days past.

Smeaton, George. *The Doctrine of the Holy Spirit.* Edinburgh, Scotland: Banner of Truth, 1974 reprint of 1889 edition. Smeaton, a Presbyterian theologian, has given us a sound pneumatology that includes the older view of revival.

Sprague, William B. *Lectures on Revivals.* Edinburgh, Scotland: Banner of Truth, 1959 reprint of 1832 edition. This is a classic. Lloyd-Jones highly regarded it. Sprague was a prominent historian and church leader during the Second Great Awakening.

Thomas, I.D.E. *God's Harvest: The Nature of True Revival.* Bryntirion, Bridgend, Wales: Evangelical Press of Wales, 1997. Though it's only 62 pages in length, this recent reprint is clear, beneficial, and warm.

Thornbury, John F. *God Sent Revival: The Story of Asahel Nettleton and the Second Great Awakening.* Darlington, County Durham, England, 1977. If you wish to see the life of the greatest itinerant evangelist of the old-school approach, read this biography. It is a marvelous and thrilling book.

Tracy, Joseph. *The Great Awakening: A History of the Revival of Religion in the Time of Edwards and Whitefield.* Edinburgh, Scotland: Banner of Truth, 1976 reprint of 1842 edition. Often criticized for coining the phrase "The Great Awakening," this is a profitable book, if for no other reason than that it shows something of the marvelous deeds of the Lord during this time period.

Tyler, Bennet. *New England Revivals*. Wheaton, IL: Richard Owen Roberts Publishers, 1980. These accounts appeared in the *Connecticut Evangelical Magazine* from 1797 until 1802. These are some of the most inspiring records of revival I have ever read. I have read these accounts to church gatherings in order to encourage prayer groups for revival.

Wells, David F. *No Place for Truth: Or, Whatever Happened to Evangelical Theology?* Grand Rapids: Eerdmans, 1993. Wells presents the most penetrating analysis available of the state of modern evangelicalism. A must for serious readers.

Wright, Eric H. *Strange Fire? Assessing the Vineyard Movement and the Toronto Blessing*. Darlington, County Durham, England: Evangelical Press, 1996. Many critiques on this movement have been written, both pro and con. This is the best critical approach I have read. Wright has a sound view of revival and applies it carefully to this much-studied movement.

Many of the books listed above, especially those published in Great Britain, are available from Reformation & Revival Ministries, Inc. A catalog is available. Books and the catalog may be ordered, toll free by phone, or by mail request to:

Reformation & Revival Ministries
P.O. Box 88216
Carol Stream, IL 60188
1-888-276-1044 (United States only)

NOTES

CHAPTER TWO—THE PLACE TO BEGIN

1. Article by F. Carlton Booth, in *Baker's Dictionary of Theology*, Everett F. Harrison, ed. (Grand Rapids: Baker, 1960), p. 460.
2. *National & International Religion Report*, Stephen M. Wilke, publisher, Gerald R. McDermott, "Special Supplement" (December 14, 1992), p. 16.
3. Roberts, Richard Owen. *Revival!* (Wheaton, IL: Richard Owen Roberts, 1991), p. 16.
4. Ibid., p. 18.

CHAPTER THREE—IS REVIVAL BIBLICAL

1. Theodore Cuyler, *How to Be a Pastor* (London: James Nisbet, 1891), p. 87.
2. D. Martyn Lloyd-Jones, *Revival* (Wheaton, IL: Crossway, 1987), p. 306.
3. Wesley Duewel, *Revival Fire* (Grand Rapids: Zondervan, 1995), p. 11.
4. Richard B. Gaffin, Jr., *Perspectives on Pentecost: New Testament Teaching on the Gifts of the Holy Spirit* (Grand Rapids: Baker, 1979), pp. 16-17.
5. Ibid., pp. 19-20.
6. Ibid., p. 22.
7. Donald A. Carson, *The Farewell Discourse and Final Prayer of Jesus* (Grand Rapids: baker, 1980), pp. 50-51.
8. Gaffin, *Perspectives on Pentecost*, p. 28.
9. D. Martyn Lloyd-Jones, *The Puritans: Their Origins and Successors* (Edinburgh: Banner of Truth, 1987), p. 8.
10. Ernest H. Trenchard, "The Book of Acts" in F.F. Bruce., ed., *The International Bible Commentary* (Grand Rapids: Zondervan, 1979), p. 1276.
11. John F. MacArthur, Jr., *The MacArthur New Testament Commentary, Acts 1-12* (Chicago: Moody Press, 1994), p. 118.
12. Frederick Dale Bruner, *A Theology of the Holy Spirit* (Grand Rapids: Eerdmans, 1970), p. 254.
13. Iain H. Murray, "The Necessary Ingredients of a Biblical Revival" in *The Banner of Truth*, January 1979, p. 20.

CHAPTER FOUR—THEOLOGY STILL MATTERS

1. "Actual influence" is a phrase used by the theologians of the Westminster Assembly to distinguish between the once-for-all gift of the Holy Spirit received by every believer at salvation, and the continuing work of the Spirit. Bishop Moule, the excellent Greek exegete of the last century, wrote regarding Ephesians 1:17, "We are not to think of the 'giving' of the Spirit as of an isolated deposit of what, once given, is now locally in possession. The first 'gift' is, as it were, the first point in a series of actions, of which each one may be expressed also as a gift." (Quoted in Murray, *Revival and Revivalism*, p. 19). This is how we best understand Luke 11:13 and our asking for the Holy Spirit even as those who already have the Spirit in us.
2. Iain H. Murray, *Revival and Revivalism: The Making and Marring of American Evangelicalism, 1750-1858* (Edinburgh, Scotland: Banner of Truth, 1994), pp. 19-20.
3. Iain H. Murray, "Revival & Revivalism" (a series of four taped messages given January, 1996, in Wheaton, Illinois). Available through Reformation & Revival Ministries, P.O. Box 88216, Carol Stream, IL 60188.

297

A good measure of my thinking was strengthened by these lectures and thus Murray's influence is behind much of the latter part of this chapter, as will be seen by those who hear the tapes and read Murray's numerous helpful works on revival.

CHAPTER FIVE—GOD AT WORK: THE MARKS OF TRUE REVIVAL

1. D. Martyn Lloyd-Jones, *Revival!* (Wheaton, IL: Crossway, 1987), p. 101.
2. Gilbert Egerton, *Flame of God: Distinctives of Revival* (Belfast, Northern Ireland: Ambassador Productions, 1987), p. 57.
3. *Westminster Confession of Faith*, Chapter 27, Article 3.
4. Quoted by Arthur Wallis, *Revival: The Rain from Heaven* (Old Tappan, NJ: Revell, 1979), pp.16-17.
5. Quoted in Wallis, p.17.
6. Reported by Egerton, p. 57.
7. Henry C. Fish, *Handbook of Revivals* (Harrisonburg, VA: Gano Books, 1988 reprint), pp. 200-01.
8. Brian H. Edwards, *Revival! A People Saturated with God* (Darlington, County Durham, England: Evangelical Press, 1990), p.103.
9. Ibid., p.104.
10. Duncan Campbell, *God's Answer: Revival Sermons* (Edinburgh: Faith Mission Publications, 1960), p.89.
11. James Burns, *Revivals: Their Laws and Leaders* (Grand Rapids: Baker, 1960),pp. 40-41.
12. Ibid.,pp. 41-42.
13. *Westminster Shorter Catechism*, Question 87.
14. W.E. Allen, *The History of Revivals of Religion* (Belfast, Northern Ireland: Revival Publishing Company, n.d.),p. 4.
15. James Burns, as quoted by Egerton, pp. 41-42.
16. Cal Thomas, "Christian Coalition Has Strayed Too Far from Its True Calling," 1997, Los Angeles Times Syndicate.

CHAPTER SIX—GREAT TRUTHS: EXALTED BY REVIVAL

1. David F. Wells, *The Bleeding of the Evangelical Church* (Edinburgh: Banner of Truth, 1995), pp. 7-8.
2. Ibid., p. 8.
3. Ibid., p. 8.
4. Gerald McDermott, "The Eighteenth Century Awakening: A Reminder for American Evangelicals in the 1990s," published as a special supplement in *National & International Religion Report* (Roanoke, VA: December 14, 1992), p. 2.
5. Wells, p. 11.
6. Brian H. Edwards, *Revival! A People Saturated with God* (Darlington, County Durham, England: Evangelical Press, 1990), p. 108.
7. Quoted in Edwards, p. 109.
8. Quoted in Edwards, p. 109.
9. Quoted in Edwards, p. 109.
10. Eifion Evans, *Fire in the Thatch* (Bryntirion, Bridgend, Wales: Evangelical Press of Wales, 1996), pp. 35-36.
11. D. Martyn Lloyd-Jones, *Revival* (Wheaton, IL: Crossway, 1987), pp. 55-56.
12. *The Heidelberg Catechism*, Question No. 60.
13. Lloyd-Jones, p. 56.
14. Evans, p. 36.
15. Ibid.
16. Lloyd-Jones, p. 57.
17. Quoted in Eric Hayden, *Spurgeon on Revival* (Grand Rapids: Zondervan, 1962), pp. 17-18. From a sermon preached in 1861.

CHAPTER SEVEN—REVIVALS: THEIR RISE, PROGRESS, AND DECLINE

1. Brian H. Edwards, *Revival! A People Saturated With God* (Darlington, County Durham, England: Evangelical Press, 1990), p. 30.
2. Iain H. Murray, "The Necessary Ingredients of a Biblical Revival" in *The Banner of Truth* (January, 1979), p. 25.

3. Ibid., p. 25.
4. Samuel Davies, *Sermons of the Rev. Samuel Davies* (Morgan, Pennsylvania: Soli Deo Gloria Publishers, 1995 reprint, 3 volumes), 3:624.
5. Quoted in Iain H. Murray, *Revival & Revivalism: The Making and Marring of American Evangelicalism 1750-1858* (Edinburgh: Banner of Truth, 1994), p. 30.
6. Gordon J. Keddie, *The Lord is His Name: Studies in Amos* (Welwyn, England: Evangelical Press, 1986), p. 133.
7. Ibid., p. 132.
8. I.D.E. Thomas, *God's Harvest: The Nature of True Revival* (Bryntirion, Bridgend, Wales: Gwasg Bryntirion Press, 1997), p. 16.
9. Brian H. Edwards, p. 229.
10. Ibid. Quoted by Brian Edwards from his book, *From Death Unto Life*, p. 229.
11. Ibid., p. 229.
12. Iain H. Murray, *D. Martyn Lloyd-Jones: The First Forty Years, 1899-1939* (Edinburgh: Banner of Truth, 1982), p. 204.
13. Thomas, p. 18.

CHAPTER EIGHT—PRAYER: THE CATALYST OF REVIVAL

1. Keith J. Hardman, *The Spiritual Awakeners: American Revivalists from Solomon Stoddard to D.L. Moody* (Chicago: Moody Press, 1983), p. 19.
2. Ibid.
3. Quoted by Iain H. Murray, "Prayer and Revival," in *The Banner of Truth*, October 1974 (Issue 133), p. 1.
4. *Westminster Shorter Catechism*, Question 98.
5. *The Heidelberg Catechism*, Question 116
6. Michael A.G. Haykin, *The Dungeon Flamed with Light: The Evangelical Revivals of the Eighteenth Century* (Richmond Hill, Ontario: Canadian Christian Publications, n.d.), p. 40.
7. Ibid., pp. 42-43.
8. Ibid., p. 44.
9. Ibid., pp. 44-45.
10. John Ryland, Jr., "The Prayer Call of 1784" in *The Nature, Evidences, and Advantages of Humility* (Circular Letter of the Northamptonshire Association, 1784), p. 12; noted in Haykin, pp. 45-47.
11. Ibid., p. 48.
12. Ibid., p. 51.
13. J. Edwin Orr, "The Role of Prayer in Spiritual Awakening," a message given in 1976 and recorded by Campus Crusade for Christ (available in both printed form and video from Campus Crusade), p. 2.
14. Ibid., pp. 2-3.
15. Erroll Hulse, *Give Him No Rest: A Call to Prayer for Revival* (Darlington, County Durham, England: Evangelical Press, 1991), p. 89.
16. From a sermon by Horatius Bonar, "True Revivals and the Men God Uses." This sermon, frequently reprinted, is available in tract form through Chapel Library, 2603 West Wright Street, Pensacola, FL, 32505.

CHAPTER NINE—PREACHING: THE FUEL OF REVIVAL

1. I.D.E. Thomas, *God's Harvest: The Nature of True Revival* (Bryntirion, Bridgend, Wales: Gwasg, Bryntirion Press, 1997), p. 34.
2. Erroll Hulse, *Give Him No Rest: A Call to Prayer for Revival* (Darlington, County Durham, England: Evangelical Press, 1991), pp. 38-39.
3. Abbott-Smith, *A Manual Greek Lexicon*, p. 360.
4. Arturo G. Azurdia III, *The Vitality of the Spirit: A Theology of Spirit-Empowered Preaching* (an unpublished thesis presented to Westminster Theological Seminary in California, 1997), p. 97. This extremely valuable work is planned for publication in the near future. You can read the central argument of this thesis in the book *The Compromised Church*, ed. John H. Armstrong (Wheaton, IL: Crossway, 1998).
5. Ibid., p. 99.
6. Ibid., p. 101.
7. Robert Mounce, *New Testament Preaching* (Grand Rapids: Eerdmans, 1960), p. 58.

8. Eifion Evans, *Fire in the Thatch* (Bryntirion, Bridgend, Wales: Evangelical Press of Wales, 1996), p. 29.

9. John H. Armstrong, *Five Great Evangelists* (Inverness, Scotland: Christian Focus Publications, 1997). This introduction to the lives of John Wesley, George Whitefield, Howell Harris, Asahel Nettleton, and Duncan Matheson will give the reader a glimpse into the kind of men (and preaching) that God used during seasons of authentic revival.

10. Quoted in Brian H. Edwards, *Revival! A People Saturated with God* (Darlington, County Durham, England: Evangelical Press, 1990), p. 106.

CHAPTER TEN—SHOWERS OF BLESSING

1. Richard Owen Roberts, *Revival!* (Wheaton, IL: Richard Owen Roberts Publishers, 1982), p. 87. This analogy is developed well by Roberts in an excellent chapter titled "What Are the Dangers of Revival?"

2. The Puritan Papers, "Increasing the Knowledge of God" (1960), p. 18. From a lecture given at the Puritan Reformed Studies Conference, December 20-21, 1960.

3. Ibid., p. 19.

4. Ibid., p. 21.

5. C.C. Goen, ed., *The Works of Jonathan Edwards*, vol. 4 (New Haven: Yale University Press, 1972), pp. 251-52.

6. Ibid., p. 254.

7. Ibid., p. 255.

8. *National & International Religion Report*, "The 18th Century Awakening: A Reminder for American Evangelicals in the 1990s" by Gerald McDermott, vol. 6, no. 26, December 14, 1992, p. 4.

9. Brian H. Edwards, *Revival! A People Saturated with God* (Darlington, County Durham, England: Evangelical Press, 1990), p. 191.

10. Festo Kivengere, *Revolutionary Love* (Eastbourne, East Sussex, England: Kingsway, 1985), pp. 42-43.

11. C.C. Goen, ed. *The Works of Jonathan Edwards*, pp. 256-58.

12. Theodore Cuyler, *How to Be a Pastor* (London: James Nisbet & Co., 1891), p. 92.

CHAPTER ELEVEN—PROBLEMS AND EXCESSES IN REVIVAL

1. C.C. Goen, ed., *The Works of Jonathan Edwards*, vol. 4 (New Haven: Yale University Press, 1972), p. 316. The Edwards work, published in 1742, with the title *Some Thoughts Concerning the Present Revival of Religion in New England*.

2. Bryn Jones, *Covenant* magazine, Summer 1994, published in the United Kingdom.

3. Deborah Kovach Caldwell, staff writer, in the *Dallas Morning News*, Sunday, October 6, 1996, pp. 28Aff.

4. *Charisma*, October, 1995, p. 21.

5. See Eric E. Wright, *Strange Fire: Assessing the Vineyard Movement and the Toronto Blessing* (Darlington, County Durham, England: Evangelical Press, 1996). Wright, a Canadian, has produced a superb full-length treatment with which I am essentially in agreement at every point. His treatment includes a biblical and historical assessment that is balanced and well written. He is particularly adept at showing why "assessing this movement" (and others like it) is not akin to "quenching the Spirit" as many people often insist. See also Michael S. Horton, ed., *Power Religion: The Selling Out of the Evangelical Church?* (Chicago: Moody Press, 1992), in which appears my own essay on the signs and wonders movement, titled "In Search of Spiritual Power" (chapter 3).

6. J.I. Packer, *A Quest for Godliness* (Wheaton, IL: Crossway, 1990), p. 30. Packer contrasts such with rigid intellectualism and argues that the Puritans had the proper balance so desperately needed in our time.

7. R.E. Davies, *I Will Pour Out My Spirit* (Tunbridge, Wells, England: Monarch Publications, 1992), p. 235.

8. Brian H. Edwards, *Revival! A People Saturated with God* (Darlington, County Durham, England: Evangelical Press, 1990), p. 198.

9. Jonathan Edwards quotation cited, without further reference, in Richard Owen Roberts, *Revival!* p. 86.

10. John F. Thornbury, *God Sent Revival: The Story of Asahel Nettleton and the Second Great Awakening* (Darlington, County Durham, England: 1977), pp. 60-61.

11. Cited in Brian H. Edwards, p. 201.

12. Eifion Evans, *Revival Comes to Wales: The Story of the 1859 Revival in Wales* (Bryntirion, Bridgend: Wales: Evangelical Press of Wales, 1982), in which the story of this awakening is told and analyzed very helpfully.

13. C.C. Goen, ed., *The Works of Jonathan Edwards*, pp. 281-82.

14. R.E. Davies, p. 240.
15. Richard Lovelace, *Dynamics of Spiritual Life: An Evangelical Theology of Renewal* (Downers Grove, IL: InterVarsity Press, 1979), p. 245.
16. Richard Owen Roberts, *Revival!* (Wheaton, IL: Richard Owen Roberts Publishers, 1982), p. 89.
17. Ibid., p. 91.
18. C.C. Goen, ed., *The Works of Jonathan Edwards*, p. 414.
19. R.E. Davies, p. 242.
20. C.C. Goen, ed., *The Works of Jonathan Edwards*, p. 244.
21. Lovelace, pp. 257-61.
22. C.C. Goen, ed., *Works of Jonathan Edwards*, pp. 438-39.
23. Ibid., p. 452.

CHAPTER TWELVE—REVIVAL AND REVIVALISM,

1. *Cyclopedia of Biblical, Theological, and Ecclesiastical Literature,* John McClintock and James Strong, eds. (Grand Rapids: Baker, 1981 reprint), vol. 8, p. 1075.
2. Arthur Wallis, *Revival: The Rain from Heaven* (Old Tappan, NJ: Revell, 1979), p. 38.
3. Iain H. Murray, *Revival & Revivalism: The Making and Marring of American Evangelicalism 1750-1858* (Edinburgh: Banner of Truth, 1994), p. xviii. This major theological-historical study is the most important single volume that can be consulted on the shift from *revival* to *revivalism* in American church history.
4. John H. Armstrong, *Five Great Evangelists* (Inverness, Scotland: Christian Focus Publications, 1997). Much of the material included here on Charles G. Finney can be found in full in this earlier book, which is a popular-level introduction to the lives of five men who were wonderfully used as revival preachers and evangelists.
5. Ibid., p. 188.
6. Ibid., p. 189.
7. Ibid., see chapter 4, pages 161-202 for more on the life of Asahel Nettleton.
8. Ibid., p. 191.
9. Ibid.
10. Michael S. Horton, "The Solas of the Reformation," in James M. Boice and Benjamin Sasse, eds., *Here We Stand: A Call from Confessing Evangelicals* (Grand Rapids: Baker, 1996), p. 119.
11. Charles G. Finney, *Revivals of Religion* (Old Tappan, NJ: Revell, 1968 edition), pp. 2-5.
12. Ibid.
13. Bob Pyke, "Charles G. Finney and the Second Great Awakening," in *Reformation & Revival Journal,* vol. 6, no. 1, 1997, p. 41.
14. Ibid., p. 42.
15. Ibid.
16. Ibid., pp. 42-43.
17. Ibid., p. 43.
18. Garth M. Rosell and Richard A.G. Dupuis, eds., *The Memoirs of Charles G. Finney: The Complete Restored Text* (Grand Rapids: Zondervan, 1989), p. 288.
19. Charles G. Finney, *Systematic Theology* (Minneapolis: Bethany House, 1976), pp. 347-48, 350.
20. Ibid., pp. 344-45.
21. Ibid., pp. 206, 209, 217.
22. Ibid., p. 236.
23. Ibid., pp. 320-21.
24. Benjamin B. Warfield, *Perfectionism*, vol. 2 (New York: Oxford University Press, 1931), p. 193.
25. Cited by Iain H. Murray, p. xv.
26. Ibid., p. xviii.
27. Richard Cardwardine, *Transatlantic Revivalism: Popular Evangelicalism in Britain and America, 1790-1865* (Westport, CT: Greenwood Press, 1978), cited in Murray, p. xix.
28. Hank Hanegraaff, *Counterfeit Revival* (Dallas: Word, 1997). This bestselling book adequately exposes the growth of a radical revivalism movement that has spawned errors similar to many seen in the time of Finney. What I fear is that many individuals who profitably read Hanegraaff will not realize that this counterfeit

revivalism which he critiques so well actually arose in the historical context outlined in this chapter. To fight "counterfeit" revivals with revivalism and the theology of revivalism will not provide a full solution, nor will it allow us to return to the older view of revival.

29. Boice and Sasse, cited by Horton, p. 201.

CHAPTER THIRTEEN—REVIVAL: IT'S IN THE AIR!

1. Larry B. Stammer, "God Is Up to Something, and It's Big" *Los Angeles Times*, December 31, 1995, pp. A1, A20. All of the quotations in this section are taken from this same article.
2. Quoted in *Illinois Baptist*, July 20, 1994. The comments were delivered in Billy Graham's keynote address to the North American Conference for Itinerant Evangelists, held June 30–July 1 at the Commonwealth Convention Center, Louisville, Kentucky.
3. David F. Wells, *No Place for Truth: Or Whatever Happened to Evangelical Theology?* (Grand Rapids: Eerdmans, 1993), p. 301.
4. Bill Bright, *The Coming Revival* (Orlando, FL: New Life Publications, 1995), p. 35.
5. Ibid., pp. 82, 89.
6. Ibid., p. 154.
7. Ibid., p. 155.
8. Ibid.
9. Ibid.
10. *International Renewal Ministries Newsline*, "Special Edition," November 1995.
11. Ibid.
12. "Portland Teeters on Revival's Edge; Graham Gives a Push," *Christianity Today*, November 9, 1992. This news report by Ken Sidey is fairly typical of how such events have been reported in the Christian mainstream media in recent years. Sidey writes: ". . . the spiritual logjam appears ready to break. A continuing series of pastoral prayer meetings, capped in late September by a Billy Graham crusade, has brought Portland to what many church leaders there believe is the 'threshold' of revival" (p. 60). Terry Dirks comments, "We'd had enough principles, how-tos, seminars, conferences—when we knew in ourselves we were not what God wanted us to be" (p. 60). This last statement raises a serious question: What do you replace the seminars and how-tos with? More of the same, except this time the emphasis is more on prayer as a kind of technique for getting revival. The faulty thinking is still obvious—pray enough, pray with the right measure of brokenness, get enough people together to do the same with you, impact a large number of pastors for this same effort, unite different groups and churches around the same earnest desire, and you'll have revival. Only occasionally do these proponents say that God *may* send this revival.
13. Joe Aldrich, *Prayer Summits: Seeking God's Agenda for Your Community* (Portland, OR: Multnomah, 1992), back cover.
14. Ibid., pp. 101-02.
15. "Great Awakenings: Americans Are Becoming Fascinated with Prayer and Spirituality. Is It Time to Rejoice?" by Timothy Jones, *Christianity Today*, November 8, 1993, p. 23.
16. Claude V. King and Henry T. Blackaby, *Experiencing God: Knowing and Doing the Will of God* (Nashville: Lifeway, 1990), p. 21. This book is reviewed critically, but fairly, in *Reformation & Revival Journal*, vol. 6, no. 1, 1997, by Robert Dalberg, pp. 161-67. The reader should consult this review for a full survey. Dalberg concludes that the book has the following serious flaws: 1) a deficient understanding of the sufficiency of Scripture; 2) an overconcern with mystical leading; 3) a deficient understanding of sanctification; 4) a false assertion that God always reveals His providence; 5) a deficient understanding of how God is known; 6) imprecise or simply wrong theological statements. Dalberg concludes: "This study was for me a lifeline that was meant for a good purpose, but it is tangled in so many knots that I would have to spend too much time untangling it to make much use of it."
17. David Bryant, *Stand in the Gap: How to Prepare for the Coming World Revival* (Ventura, CA: Regal, 1997).
18. *Christianity Today*, November 8, 1993, pp. 23-24.
19. John H. Armstrong, ed., *The Coming Evangelical Crisis: Current Challenges to the Authority of Scripture and Gospel* (Chicago: Moody Press, 1996), p. 228. My chapter is titled "How Shall We Wage Our Warfare?" It is a critique of the approach adopted by C. Peter Wagner and a large number of charismatics and mainstream evangelicals.
20. *Christianity Today*, p. 24.

21. Ibid.
22. John H. Armstrong, ed., quoted in *The Compromised Church* (Wheaton, IL: Crossway, 1998). See the chapter by Donald S. Whitney titled "Doctrine and Devotion: A Reunion Devoutly to Be Desired." Whitney develops my point very well, showing that evangelical spirituality should be developed out of the treasures of the older proponents of reformation and revival such as Calvin, Luther, Bunyan, Edwards, etc.
23. See Douglas Wilson and David Hagopian, *Beyond Promises* (Moscow, ID: Canon Press, 1996), for the finest biblical and theological critique yet written on this movement. I wrote the foreword to this excellent book because I believe it is both fair and aimed at correcting brethren in a proper Christian spirit. Too many anti-PK books have yet to adopt a correct tone in "dealing gently." It is always easy to "blast" big movements and this generally only drives people to adopt a resistant, defensive posture if we are not careful. All of us, and all movements influenced by any of us, should show a willingness to be corrected in love. *Christianity Today* (February 6, 1995), in a major survey of the PK movement, referred to it as "Manhood's Great Awakening"—an interesting title to say the least!
24. *New Man*, November–December 1995, pp. 20-26. The quotes in this section are all from this article and issue. The reference to the advertisement is on page 47. David Halbrook is a writer and editor for Promise Keepers in Denver, Colorado.
25. This official letter was sent to thousands of men. It should be noted that the wildly popular Washington rally was not the first such gathering by evangelicals at the nation's capital. Since 1980 there have been at least four such massive meetings, the PK one being the largest in attendance. The previous three were organized by charismatic pastors John and Anne Gimenez. In each case, numerous references were made to 2 Chronicles 7:14 and to the promises of revival that would come if only we met the conditions. In the 1996 Washington for Jesus two-day event (April 29-30), leaders claimed that 500,000 people came to witness "an outpouring of the Holy Spirit." Jerry Falwell preached, reminding the attendees of "their heritage," and controversial charismatic television minister Benny Hinn led a healing service on the Mall. See *Charisma* magazine, July 1996, pp. 12-13.
26. *National & International Religion Report*, March 4, 1996.
27. Reported in *The ACCC Challenge*, April 1996.
28. Ibid.
29. *National & International Religion Report*, March 4, 1996.
30. Reported in *The ACCC Challenge*, April 1996.
31. See Moody, July/August 1995 for a report.
32. G.I. Williamson in *New Horizons*, January 1996, p. 20.
33. Ibid. This conclusion is similar to that which Williamson reached regarding PK, though his analysis is a bit more critical than mine.

CHAPTER FOURTEEN—HOW SHALL I RESPOND?

1. Bill Bright, *The Coming Revival* (Orlando FL: New Life Publications, 1995), p. 77.
2. *Westminster Confession of Faith*, Chapter 6, Article 5, and Chapter 13, Article 2.
3. Martin Luther, *Luther's Works*, vol. 31 (Philadelphia: Muhlenberg Press, 1957), p. 297.
4. Martin Luther, cited in *Present Truth*, August 1973, p. 17.
5. Curtis Dickinson, cited in *Present Truth*, August 1973, p. 11.
6. Ibid.
7. Robert Brinsmead, *Present Truth*, August 1973, p. 15.

CHAPTER FIFTEEN—WHAT TO DO UNTIL REVIVAL COMES

1. J.I. Packer, *God in Our Midst* (Ann Arbor, MI: Servant Books, 1987), pp. 26-34.
2. Ibid., pp. 39-40.
3. Martyn Lloyd-Jones, *Revival* (Wheaton, IL: Crossway, 1987), pp. 26-27.
4. Cited by Roland Lamb in *The Challenge of the Reformation for Today* (Carlisle, PA: Puritan Publications, 1968), p. 37.
5. Ibid., p. 38.
6. John Piper, "Lovers of Truth in a Politically Correct World." A paper given in a forum presented at the Baptist General Conference annual meeting in Des Moines, Iowa, July, 1993. This paper has influenced a good number of the paragraphs that follow in this section.

7. David F. Wells, *No Place for Truth: Or Whatever Happened to Evangelical Theology?* (Grand Rapids: Eerdmans), p. 101.
8. John Cionca, *Heart and Mind* (publication of Bethel Theological Seminary, St. Paul, Minnesota, Spring 1993, pp. 8-9).
9. David F. Wells, pp. 11-12.
10. Os Guinness, *The American Hour*, 1992. Cited by John Piper in "Lovers of Truth," p. 2.
11. J. Gresham Machen, *What Is Faith?* (Edinburgh: Banner of Truth, 1991 reprint), p. 34.
12. Ibid., pp. 13-14.
13. An indulgence is "a remission before God of the temporal punishment due to sins whose guilt has already been forgiven, which the faithful Christian who is duly disposed gains under certain prescribed conditions through the action of the church, which, as a minister of redemption, dispenses and applies with authority the treasury of the satisfactions of Christ and the saints" (Paul VI, apostolic constitution, *Indulgentiarum doctrina*, Norm 1), cited in *Catechism of the Catholic Church* (New York: Catholic Book Publishing, 1994), p. 370. According to Roman Catholic theology, sin has a double consequence—eternal and temporal. Mortal sins bring eternal death and hell, while venial sins bring purgatory and temporal consequences which require cleansing. The believer must strive, using "works of mercy and charity" and doing penance to put off "the old man." Indulgences benefit both the living and the dead who are being "purged" in purgatory while awaiting entrance into heaven. During Luther's time the sale of these indulgences, on slips of paper with the church's blessing stated, was used widely to finance the building of St. Peter's and the needs of the papacy in Rome. The infamous Tetzel was the German "salesman" of these indulgences whom Luther openly opposed.
14. Ian R.K. Paisley, *The "Fifty-Nine" Revival* (Belfast, Ireland: Martyr's Memorial Free Presbyterian Church Press, 1981), pp. 7-8.
15. Ibid., p. 8.
16. Ibid., p. 9.
17. Ibid., p. 10.
18. This entire section is based upon the article by Wayne Detzler, "Inerrancy and Revival in Germany," published in *The Journal of the Evangelical Theological Society*, September 1985, pp. 327-33.
19. Thomas J. Nettles, "Better Way: Church Growth Through Revival and Reformation" in Michael Scott Horton, ed., *Power Religion* (Chicago: Moody Press, 1992), p. 166.
20. Ibid., p. 185.
21. N.D. Kloosterman, "Reformation Through Revival," *Mid-America Messenger*, January 1992, p. 2.
22. Lidie H. Edmunds, "My Faith Has Found a Resting Place," 1891.
23. David Kingdon, "Do We Need a Theology for a Day of Small Things?" *The Evangelical Magazine of Wales*, 1994, p. 8.
24. Raymond Ortlund, Jr., *A Passion for God* (Wheaton, IL: Crossway, 1994), p. 267.

APPENDIX 1

1. Jonathan Edwards, *Works* (Edinburgh: Banner of Truth, 1834, 1974 reprint) I:426.
2. Ibid., II:291.
3. J.I. Packer, *A Quest for Godliness* (Wheaton, IL: Crossway, 1990), p. 327.

APPENDIX 2

1. Robert H. Lescelius, "Revival: Fact or Fiction?" (a privately published piece, n.d.), p. 2.
2. John J. Davis, *Christ's Victorious Kingdom: Postmillennialism Reconsidered* (Grand Rapids: Baker, 1986), pp. 12-13.
3. Ibid., pp. 10-11.
4. Quoted in Iain H. Murray, *The Puritan Hope: Revival and the Interpretation of Prophecy* (Edinburgh: Banner of Truth, 1971), cited on pp. xii-xiv.

APPENDIX 3

1. Horatius Bonar, *True Revivals & the Men God Uses*. Reprinted by Chapel Library, 2603 W. Wright Street, Pensacola, FL 32505.